Finding My Voice

Finding My Voice

My Journey to the West Wing and the Path Forward

◆ ◆ ◆ ◆ ◆

Valerie Jarrett

VIKING

VIKING

An imprint of Penguin Random House LLC
penguinrandomhouse.com

Copyright © 2019 Embarcadero LLC

Page 1, top left, top right, middle left, middle right, page 2, top, page 5, bottom right: James Bowman; page 4, bottom left: Barbara Bowman; page 4, bottom right: Ballintine Photographers; page 6, bottom left, page 7, top: © David Katz 2008; pages 8 and 9, page 11, bottom, page 12, top and middle, page 13, top, pages 14 and 15: Pete Souza, Barack Obama Presidential Library; page 10, top left: Christine Otte; page 10, top right and bottom: Amanda Hein Photography; page 13, middle: AP Photo/Evan Vucci; page 13, bottom: Amanda Lucidon; page 16, top: Mandel Ngan/AFP/Getty Images. All other photographs courtesy of the author.

Library of Congress Cataloging-in-Publication Data

Names: Jarrett, Valerie, 1956- author.
Title: Finding my voice : my journey to the West Wing and
the path forward / Valerie Jarrett.
Description: New York City : Viking, an imprint of
Penguin Random House LLC, [2019] |
Identifiers: LCCN 2019002213 (print) | LCCN 2019002615 (ebook) |
ISBN 9780525558149 (ebook) | ISBN 9780525558132 (hbk.)
Subjects: LCSH: Jarrett, Valerie, 1956- | United States--Politics and
government--2009-2017. | Presidents--United States--Staff. | Obama,
Barack--Friends and associates. | Obama, Michelle, 1964---Friends and
associates. | African American lawyers--Biography. |
Politicians--Illinois--Chicago--Biography. | Lawyers--United
States--Biography. | African American women--Biography.
Classification: LCC E907 (ebook) | LCC E907 .J37 2019 (print) |
DDC 973.932092 [B] --dc23
LC record available at https://lccn.loc.gov/2019002213

Printed in the United States of America
1 3 5 7 9 10 8 6 4 2

BOOK DESIGN BY LUCIA BERNARD

Penguin is committed to publishing works of quality and integrity.
In that spirit, we are proud to offer this book to our readers; however,
the story, the experiences, and the words are the author's alone.

*To my darling daughter, Laura, who was the inspiration
that helped me find my voice;*

*to my parents, Barbara and Jim Bowman, who loved me
unconditionally and set high expectations by example;*

*and to my grandmother Pudden, who taught me
the importance of kindness and grace.*

Contents

◆ ◆ ◆

Preface

The summer sun reflecting off Lake Michigan caught my eye as I turned my chair toward the window. I was always drawn to the spectacular panoramic view of Chicago from the floor-to-ceiling window of my office on the seventy-ninth floor of the Sears Tower. Perhaps because I'd spent the first five years of my life living in a desert far away, I never took Lake Michigan for granted. It has always brought me peace and tranquillity. The best part of my daily commute to work was driving downtown, heading north from South Kenwood along the five-mile stretch of the lake's shoreline. I love water. And the sun. In the summer, at our family dinners that my ninety-year-old mom still hosts every Sunday, my cousins say, "There she goes again," when I keep moving my chair so that I'm directly in the sun, chasing its warmth until the day's last rays sink behind our home.

But on this particular afternoon in the summer of 1987, the gorgeous sunshine and vast waters dotted with bobbling white sailboats did nothing to improve my mood. I'd turned my back to the office door, hoping that nobody would catch me crying. "Never cry at work" was one of my many cardinal rules. And yet here I was.

Who was I in that moment? Well, most important, I was a mom. From the moment twenty months earlier when the doctor announced, "It's a girl!" and placed her perfect little brown body on my chest, Laura, named after both my grandmother and my husband's, had become the center of my universe. I'd had no idea I was capable of such unconditional love.

I had also essentially been a single mom since seven months after Laura's birth. My husband chose to move to Michigan to complete his medical residency, leaving our marriage dangling by a thread.

I was also a daughter—the only child of two parents who loved each other and me unconditionally and showed me by their example, and our family legacy, the value of commitment, hard work, and excellence.

And I was a lawyer. The first in my family. My position as an associate at a high-powered corporate law firm had made my parents so proud, and I was the envy of many.

Ten years earlier I had ambitiously created a plan for my life based on a need for order and direction. I had this notion that by sheer force of will I could drive my life in a rigid linear path, and that it was somehow a sign of strength if I had the self-control to never waver from my intended course.

Law school, work, marriage, baby, bliss. I'd pursued my plan with the single-mindedness of purpose that I'd had since I was a child. I thought it would deliver happiness. And from a distance it might have looked like the perfect life. But as my plans were crumbling around me, I was now sure of just one thing: I was miserable.

My own mother had been a professional working mom, well before it was common to do so—a passionate educator who managed to pour her energies into raising me and taking care of my dad while also establishing a world-class child development research institute. And she always seemed so competent and fully prepared for the everyday challenges— so adept at what I now recognize was a mighty juggle. I'd never questioned that I myself would someday be a happily married, successful working mom.

I am a morning person, so normally I'm unable to stay awake past 10 p.m. But after my husband, Bobby, moved away, I found myself wide awake at midnight, 1 a.m., 2 a.m. I was twenty-nine years old and ter-rified to be alone. I found myself popping into Laura's bedroom mul-tiple times a night to make sure she was OK. Being singularly responsible for my precious baby was unexpected, overwhelming, and not a part of my plan.

So on that gorgeous summer day, the reality slowly crept in that my marriage bore no resemblance to the perfect one of my parents. They had each been the other's best friend and, other than an occasional business trip, they never chose to spend a night apart.

Alma Brown, Laura's sitter, a tall black woman twenty years my se-nior whose face showed wrinkles from both laughter and hardship, walked in my front door at 8 a.m. sharp every morning, radiating the casual confidence that comes from decades of caregiving. I'd exit the apartment quickly and then linger outside the door waiting for Laura to stop crying, which, no doubt because of Mrs. Brown's expert and loving touch, took only a minute. But my heartache from our separation stayed with me from the minute I closed that door until I opened it again in the evening. I awoke every morning (feeling like it had been only min-utes since I patted Laura to sleep the night before) with the sole goal of getting myself home as soon as I could. My workday had become a strict exercise in efficiency. Social meals, phone calls with my friends, and even occasional watercooler conversations had all been abandoned.

The ache made it hard to focus. Walking into my office, I'd find my unfilled time sheets from the day before on the top of my large to-do pile. Lawyers bill their clients by time, each day parsed into six-minute increments and recorded on a time sheet to be tallied up by the billing department. That's how the firm made money. But instead of carefully logging my hours, I'd sit there each morning sipping my third cup of coffee (I always gulped down two before leaving home) and wondering what it was I'd done the previous day. With neither head nor heart in the work, I always ended up tallying myself short. After nine hours at my desk, I often produced only four billable hours. And the work I had done was mediocre. I was not good at my job. The soft voice inside me kept telling me that I needed to change my life, but it's hard to listen to your voice if you don't trust it.

Over the span of the next thirty years, my career took what many would think was a zigzag, not a trajectory upward. Some might call it a step down to go into city government, but I did it, as a staff lawyer, and then rose to be a cabinet member for a mayor. I would be a CEO and a board chair to several organizations and always looked for ways to advocate for equality and civic engagement. Those experiences each prepared me to spend eight years in President Obama's White House, where I was the longest-serving senior advisor to any president in history. All while I raised Laura as a single mom, marveling at how she found her own confident voice, had the courage to also change careers in pursuit of her passion, and had the good sense to marry a man who reminds me of my dad.

People assume I always knew where I was going and the path I would take, but the truth is, for a long time, I knew neither.

What follows is the story of how I found my voice and learned to trust it—a voice that went from barely audible, even to me, to one I hope has been a catalyst for change, and has been a source of strength and empowerment for others. My journey has been exhilarating, challenging, and yes, at times, very painful, but what an adventure!

Finding My Voice

Chapter 1

The Gift of Freedom

My earliest memories are of my childhood in Iran. Like everyone, I've no doubt blurred my actual childhood memories with stories recounted by my parents and my own vivid imagination, but my recollection of my first five years is that they were perfect. I was born in Shiraz, a city over four thousand years old, known for its beautiful gardens and for being the home of artists, scholars, and poets during the height of the Persian Empire.

My mother recently reminded me that it actually snowed in the winter, but all I can remember is blue skies and warm, bright sunshine. The gated community where we lived was a compound for the families of the thirty or so doctors who worked at the hospital, many of whom came from all over the world. We lived in a comfortable two-bedroom bungalow surrounded by trees and flower beds. There was a park with tennis courts and a huge swimming pool. Every year in December, we'd cut down a Christmas tree from a large patch of nearby woods. We even had a small zoo on the compound, with mountain sheep, goats, a bear, and a jackal which was allowed to roam free around the compound and was known to take toys and hide them from time to time.

I felt I had all I could possibly want or need in that special place. Even at the age of three or four, I was allowed to explore as I chose, always under the watchful eye of Saroya, my nanny and our family's housekeeper and cook. Saroya was small, barely five feet tall, gentle, and kind. She had a son of her own, whom she left with her mother during the day while at work. We were always joined on these walks by our Belgian shepherd, Dovuum, whom I nicknamed Doddy. One time I fell down in the street. A passerby saw me crying and approached me to see if I was OK, only to have Doddy snarl and keep him at bay. Someone ran to find Saroya and she came, whisked me up in her arms, and took me home, with Doddy following dutifully behind. They were my protectors.

The pool was my favorite place of all. My mother taught me to swim before I could walk, and I loved diving and splashing about in the deep end for hours and hours. My parents had a good friend, Tom, whose real name was Thelma. She headed the Iran-America Society and her husband, Dale, was an engineer with Point Four, an American foreign assistance program. Tom did all sorts of activities with me, like taking me to a local preschool. She encouraged me to practice English with the young Iranian students who were trying to learn the language. But I would speak only in Farsi—an early sign of my long-standing desire to be like everyone else. It was in the pool, though, that Tom and I had the most fun. She'd put me on her shoulders, then she would climb on Dale's shoulders, and Dale would slowly walk down into the deep end until we were all well submerged, then I would pop up to the surface, laughing and coughing from swallowing water. Once Doddy, always my bodyguard, spotted our circus act and tried to rescue me by diving in the water. Chaos ensued, as dogs were strictly forbidden in the pool.

Outside the compound, my parents and I often explored the city and the surrounding countryside. My best friend was Roshan Firouz, an American-Iranian girl about my age. Her parents, Narsi and Louise, were my parents' best friends, and we were inseperable, running around together at one of the two Firouz farms, Big Lou and Little Lou, both named after Louise and their relative sizes. Roshan was scrappy and forever coaxing me into mischievous adventures. They had a huge donkey, Laura, and we'd climb up on her and ride her around and play endless games of make-believe, with all the different farm animals as the characters in our stories.

My parents and I traveled all over, but one of our favorite day trips was to the ancient Persian city of Persepolis, where I'd climb up and down the old stone stairs, run circles around the columns, and hide among the monuments. Either we'd pack a picnic lunch for the day or my parents would take me to a hotel nearby for a treat. An afternoon entertaining myself among the ruins, topped off by a delicious dinner prepared by Saroya back home, made for a day I still treasure.

Saroya did all our shopping and made all our meals. While kids my age in America were eating hot dogs, Oreos, and peanut-butter-and-jelly sandwiches, I was devouring her lamb, rice pilaf, and the cool cucumbers and yogurt of *mast-o-khiar*. She cooked with saffron, cumin, and dried barberry, spices we'd buy when she took me to Vakil Bazaar in the old city. I loved to smell all the fragrant and colorful spices heaped in copper pots and burlap sacks. When I am traveling the world as an adult, particularly when visiting different bazaars and markets throughout the Middle East, the familiar smells always take me back to those early years and make me smile.

To this day I still love all Persian food (except eggplant), but my favorite dish is any kind of rice. No meal in my home is complete without a serving of rice. After we moved back to America, it took me until high school to develop a taste for a good hot dog at a baseball game, and it was only a few years ago that my daughter convinced me to try peanut butter. Not bad.

Iran may have been a magical place for me, as the child of a Western doctor, but that certainly didn't mean Iran was a magical place for everyone. Mohammad Reza Shah, the last shah of Iran, had pursued many modernizing reforms, among them the improvements to the health care system that had built the hospital that brought us there. But he was simultaneously a brutal dictator who established the SAVAK, the secret police force that terrorized dissidents and disappeared people at will.

I'm often asked why I was born in Iran. My father once said I should tell people, "Because that's where my mother was at the time of my birth." But that answer never seems to satisfy anyone, particularly border guards and customs officials. The truth about why we were in Iran is somewhat complicated, but what it boils down to is really quite simple: we were there because my father was black, and he needed a job.

I arrived in this world just as America's civil rights movement was gaining momentum. The rights and opportunities for which black people were marching and fighting in the United States, my parents and I were privileged to enjoy in Iran. While many black families were often confined to redlined slums, we had a lovely house in a cosmopolitan neighborhood. While black people in America were marching for the right to enjoy public pools and parks, our neighborhood had lush green spaces where I could run and play and a big blue swimming pool, where people stared only when my dog jumped in the pool with me. While black students in the United States had just begun to be bused into hostile white neighborhoods to integrate the schools, I attended an excellent school with loving teachers, filled with kids from all over the world.

The freedom of mind that I had always known, and that had taken my father thirty-odd years to achieve, was the same freedom that brave little children my own age had risked their lives to attain—children like Ruby Bridges, who at age six in 1960 was the first black child to desegregate the all-white William Frantz Elementary School in New Orleans. I met Ruby Bridges fifty-one years later when President Obama invited her to the White House to view the famous Norman Rockwell painting of her walking to school, hair perfectly combed and wearing a starched white dress, escorted by large armed guards. I told Ruby in the Oval Office that I was in awe of her courage and bravery at such a young age, and that she had fought for a freedom that I took for granted.

M y father, Jim Bowman, had always wanted to be a doctor. He grew up in Washington, DC, in the 1930s and 1940s. In DC in that era, his life experiences were determined by the color of his skin, including where he could attend school. Living in DC, however, meant he was relatively fortunate. The son of a prominent dentist in the city's small black middle class, he was able to attend Dunbar High School, the premier high school in Washington, and perhaps the country, for black Americans at the time. As oppressive and unjust as segregation was, it did mean that black scholars with PhDs from Harvard and other Ivy League schools often had no choice but to teach at the high school level, at schools like Dunbar. So at a time when few black children had access to quality schools, my father's education was first-rate—and the lessons stuck. His grammar was impeccable, and he corrected mine throughout my life, even when it made me sound ridiculous. I used to ring the doorbell when we visited my grandmother, and when she said, "Who is it?" I wasn't allowed to say, "It's me." I had to say, "It is I." All that was missing was "*Hark!*"

Graduating at the top of his class at the age of sixteen, my father went on to Howard University for undergraduate and medical school, the famous historically black university in DC and his own father's alma mater. Had my dad chosen a different career, he might have found more doors opened to him, but as the civil rights movement began making inroads across the color line, medicine would prove to be one of Jim Crow's most tenacious holdouts. Which is unsurprising, given the intimate nature of doctor/patient relationships and the pervasive racist myths about black people and disease that kept us from sharing swimming pools, let alone hospitals, with white people. Desegregation in health care didn't begin in earnest until the passage in 1965 of Medicare and Medicaid, programs that threatened to strip federal funding from any hospital that engaged in racial discrimination.

When my dad graduated from medical school in 1947, he joined DC's Freedmen's Hospital for a one-year residency. During that year his mother, only thirty-eight years old, died in Freedmen's from hypertension while he was on duty. In a quiet moment of openness, he once shared with me how helpless and guilty he felt that he could not save her. From Freedmen's he was offered a huge opportunity: a residency at Chicago's prestigious St. Luke's Hospital. He was the hospital's first, and only, black resident. After attending only all-black schools, he was thrilled to break the color barrier, but even then the door opened only partway. He wasn't allowed to live with his white colleagues in the residents' quarters adjacent to the hospital. He had to find room and board on the south side of town where blacks were allowed to live, five miles away from the hospital, and travel by bus or streetcar—a very long and tiring commute after a thirty-six-hour shift. He was also instructed to enter the hospital through the back door. This he refused to do. He showed up on his first day and walked through the front door like all the white doctors. Word of his act of defiance spread quickly through the black staff. The next morning many of them were waiting out front when he arrived, and they all walked in together. Nobody objected.

Chicago was like that. It had a patchy attitude toward segregation. Some freedoms were allowed, some weren't. Marshall Field's, the famous department store, was a classic example. Black people could shop at Marshall Field's, but they couldn't work there. It was a checkered landscape that my mother's family had learned to navigate. Through education that led to financial stability, they became one of the most politically connected black families of the time, carving out a measure of status and access unavailable to most black Chicagoans. They, and others in the black middle class, built their own businesses and social network, but they were second-class citizens nonetheless, and their relative degree of freedom existed in a very narrow lane.

For my mother, Barbara, there was no equivalent to Dunbar High School; in Chicago, all-black schools offered second-rate educations. Fortunately, her father, Robert Rochon Taylor, was a leading figure in

Chicago business and civic circles, even outside the black community. He came to prominence through the city's real estate, banking, and insurance industries, which led to his appointment as the first black chairman of the Chicago Housing Authority in 1941. Thanks to his prominence, he was able to obtain special permission for my mother and her older sister Lauranita to leave their all-black neighborhood, and travel to the then white neighborhood of South Englewood to go to its all-white elementary and high schools. That put her on a path to attend the Northfield School for Girls, an elite prep school in Massachusetts, which in turn opened the door for her to enroll at the small, predominantly white, women's college, Sarah Lawrence, in the Bronx, New York.

During trips home from college—and after my dad flubbed a blind date with her sister—my mom and dad started dating and soon fell in love. After my dad proposed and my mom accepted, they knew they first had to get past her father, who had strong opinions on priorities for his family. And so, in a story that he would retell many times over the years, with embellishment added over time, no doubt, my dad came up with an ingenious strategy to get his way. Over a game of bridge one evening with my mom's parents, my dad took an extra long time to study his hand, and then, when he finally played his card, he casually tossed in, "By the way, Barbara and I are getting married."

It was classic Jimmy Bowman: deliciously provocative with perfect comic timing. But this was no joking matter. A bit flabbergasted, my grandfather finally replied, "But, you know, Barbara has to finish college first."

"That's good," my dad said, "because I can't afford to pay her tuition."

And so my parents were married on June 17, 1950, two weeks after Mom graduated from Sarah Lawrence.

My dad finished his residency that same year, but despite his sterling credentials, he still enjoyed limited job prospects. In most major cities, even the segregated ones, Jim Crow hospitals that served black patients were often white-owned and refused to hire black doctors and nurses. With few options to choose from, my father accepted the position of chair of pathology at Chicago's Provident Hospital. Established in 1891, it was the first black-owned-and-operated hospital in the United States and, as such, one of the only places that would hire him.

While at Howard my father had joined the Army ROTC, graduating as a second lieutenant, and as the Korean War escalated in 1953, the army called him up and stationed him at an army hospital in Colorado, where he and my mom lived for two years. Upon being honorably discharged in 1955, he told my mother he didn't want to return to Provident or, as he put it, "anything that smacked of segregation." He applied to the United States Public Health Service, which offered him a job in Liberia. But the ambassador to Liberia, who was a friend of my parents, told them, "Do not, under any circumstances, come here." It simply wasn't safe. Then, when it seemed like Provident would be the only viable option, a white colleague of my father's was offered a job as the chair of pathology at the Nemazee Hospital, a newly constructed facility just staffing up in Shiraz, Iran. He declined the position but passed along the contact information to my dad.

Iran, which is a little less than seven thousand miles from the South Side of Chicago, had certainly never been on my parents' radar. But after many lengthy discussions, my parents decided that it would be the adventure of a lifetime, a chance for them to be alone together away from all that was familiar, including the racism and discrimination they'd endured their entire lives. So my father applied, and received an offer.

When my parents announced to family and close friends that my dad was considering the job, nobody was shocked since many knew they wanted to go abroad, but my grandparents wanted to keep the family close and this was too far away. However, my parents had made up their minds. And so he accepted the job, and off they went.

The day my parents boarded the plane for Iran, a country on the other side of the world, they didn't speak a word of the language, knew not a soul, or anything about the nation, its government, its culture or customs beyond what they learned from the Encyclopedia Britannica—nothing. All they knew about this strange and exotic place was that it was willing to give a black doctor an opportunity far better than any available to him in the country where he was born.

Which is how, on November 14, 1956, after a "very challenging labor" and a "risky high-forceps delivery"—as my mother frequently described it during my youth, much to my embarrassment—I entered this world, the second baby born at Nemazee Hospital. I was always relieved that they'd practiced on one other baby first.

H ad I merely spent those first five years of my life in Iran, that would have been adventure enough for a lifetime. But from there my father's career really took off. Trained as a pathologist, at Nemazee he became interested in genetics, and in particular in favism, a genetic blood disorder that produces an allergic reaction to fava beans. It's caused by an enzyme deficiency and, being hereditary, is common among certain ethnic groups in Iran. What followed was his lifelong study of inherited blood diseases throughout the Middle East, Africa, Mexico, and America. His work in common enzyme deficiencies later proved important to the larger field of inherited diseases and minority health.

Starting in Iran, and parts of many summers of my youth in the years to come, we traveled the world collecting blood samples for genetic testing. We went to remote deserts, dense cities, rural villages, isolated rainforest jungles—the constant blur of new places, people, customs, and food all seemed perfectly normal to me. My parents left me with babysitters every now and then, but mostly I was by their side, perfectly content to label blood vials and give out Band-Aids for hours anywhere from Nigeria's jungles to rural communities in Mexico. My mom likes to tell a story that happened when I was nine years old and we were in Ghana. She'd given me a little money to spend on the trip. She looked out her hotel window to see me squatting with the street vendors selling tourist trinkets. Having learned in Iran, I could stay in that position with the best of them. And bargain, too. I returned an hour later, happily carting an armload of souvenirs that I'd secured with my excellent negotiating skills—skills that would later serve me well in the political worlds of Chicago and Washington, DC.

We went everywhere and did everything. While I was still in diapers, we drove nearly four thousand miles from London to Shiraz, flying only over the English Channel. In Russia my father made me try caviar, which I loved, and took me to Lenin's tomb, which I absolutely did not. In Egypt I delighted in riding camels past the Sphinx and the Great Pyramid, and in India I was mesmerized by snake charmers and water buffalo under the towering spires of the Taj Mahal. In Uganda our plane touched down in the middle of a military coup after curfew, and my parents had to convince armed soldiers to wave us through numerous checkpoints to reach our hotel. In the villages of the Yucatán, I brushed my teeth with soft drinks and ate peppers so hot they seemed to set my mouth on fire, which I tried to wash down with a big swig of Coca-Cola, something you should never, never do.

One story, which became an oft-repeated tale about my dad, took place in Mexico City. We awoke in the middle of the night to find our hotel swaying like a ship at sea. I felt slightly nauseous from the motion and asked my mom what was happening. "An earthquake!" she shouted, a rare time I remember her ever raising her voice. My mother grabbed my hand and we ran for the stairs to the lobby, calling back to my father to hurry up. "I'm right behind you," he said. It was madness, people running down the stairs into the lobby in their underwear, screaming in fear. My mother and I waited in the lobby a good twenty minutes and only then, right after management had given the all clear, did my father appear, having taken the time to neatly dress in his robe, pajamas, and slippers, casually emerging without an ounce of concern. I think he might have even taken the time to shave. The next morning the parking lot was empty. All of the tourists had decided to abandon their plans and evacuate. My parents simply laughed. A mere earthquake, even one that left electrical wires dangling in the streets, would not intimidate them.

I always knew my father as confident, fearless, and cheerful—a glass-half-full type of person. But before living in Iran, that natural exuberance had always been dimmed by the brutal realities of Jim Crow's limitations on what he would be permitted to achieve, the constant blatant and subtle reminders that he was considered "less than" because he was black—a belief that he had internalized, as so many marginalized people do, even though it wasn't true. But after his experience in Iran, and certainly by the time we started to travel the world for his research, he had emerged from the cloud of his own limitations. He felt liberated. Outside of the United States, and in his own mind, he was no longer defined by the color of his skin. He was no longer a "colored" doctor. He was simply a doctor, a respected chief pathologist, a published academic.

His self-confidence had grown along with his reputation. He'd experienced success based on merit and hard work, just as my mother had years earlier by the time she graduated from college, and thanks to both of them I grew up believing that was possible. It's much easier to be what you see. My parents were my role models, and they gave me the early impression that my potential in life was limited only by my willingness to work hard and be resilient, combined with a good bit of luck. My mom and dad had taken me across the color line and around the world, showing me what was possible, so that I could dare to imagine any kind of life I wanted.

It was only years later that I truly understood how lucky I was.

I had been given that freedom as a gift, from birth. So even after moving to Chicago, where the laws and social customs still tried to curtail opportunities for black people, in my mind I was already free—and no one could take that away from me.

The segregation in the United States that my parents had left behind in 1955 was still alive and well when we arrived in 1961. Still, they were homesick. My mother's father had died when I was only six months old, and we'd missed the funeral. My mother was very close with her family, and she wanted me to know them. They always knew we'd leave Iran eventually. It just so happened that I was the one who hastened their decision along.

Iran had massive inequalities of wealth and a rigid caste system. Those who were wealthy were *very* wealthy and lived very well. Those who were poor lived in unspeakable conditions. I can vividly remember seeing people with severe disabilities begging on the streets, shunned by society and with no means of support and no place to go. Those in the lowest caste who were lucky enough to have jobs often worked as servants, and it was socially acceptable to abuse and beat them.

Saroya was a member of that class. Twenty-eight years old, she had only a sixth-grade education. I loved her dearly, but as I neared age five, I showed a sign that I had begun to internalize the mores of Iran's caste system as my own. My mother walked into the house one afternoon to see me giving Saroya a swift kick, as hard as I could, probably because she'd told me I couldn't do what I wanted to do, though I don't remember exactly why. Horrified, my mother immediately swooped in, gave my rear end a rare swat, and said firmly, *"No, Lally!"* That's the nickname I gave myself at a young age when I could not pronounce Valerie.

Now it was Soroya's turn to be horrified. She turned to my mother and said, "Why did you do that?"

"Because she kicked you!"

"No, no," Saroya said, "it's fine."

"No," my mother replied, "it's not fine."

Saroya then went on to explain that she thought it was OK for us to kick her and beat her whenever we liked. She knew that was her place. She was grateful that we let her work in our home, and she was scared we would think that she thought she was above her station.

My parents had never adopted Iran's social norms as their own, and they'd always treated everyone with respect, no matter their standing. Having grown up under Jim Crow in America, for them to see their daughter behaving the way I had was totally unacceptable. That night, as we sat down to dinner, my mother turned to my father and said, "I think it's time for us to head home."

· *Chapter 2* ·

Inheritance

H*ey, you! Hey, Red! Turn around!"*
I recognized the voice of the girl yelling behind me instantly. It wasn't hard. I heard it all the time, since bullying me was her favorite after-school activity. She kept on yelling, but I didn't turn around. Instead, I kept walking, trying to ignore her and the familiar queasiness growing in my stomach. I lived only four blocks from school but had learned from past failed attempts that I couldn't outrun her. So I braced myself, knowing what was coming. Then it came: a hard shove from behind. I tumbled forward and went down on the pavement with a thud.

Welcome to Beulah Shoesmith Elementary: South Kenwood, Chicago, 1962.

Shoesmith was a rough experience for me. Predominantly black student body, overcrowded, struggling teachers. Mostly good kids, but more than a few tough kids as well. I was a fair-skinned, freckle-faced, red-haired five-year-old placed into a second-grade class with kids nearly two years older than me. I spoke with a British accent, and none of my classmates had ever heard of Iran. I didn't understand the slang the kids used, and I didn't know much about the customs, or the culture. All of which no doubt made me a likely target for bullying.

Splayed out on the sidewalk in front of school, books scattered, I was slowly pulling myself to my feet, fully prepared to be knocked down again, when I heard another voice.

"*Leave her alone!*"

It was my younger cousin, Lauren, coming to my rescue. Again.

Lauren was seven months younger and ten pounds lighter than I, but she had a well-deserved reputation as a mighty tough fighter. Maybe because she was the youngest of three kids, she had learned how to protect herself—and, thankfully, me. The bully backed away while Lauren helped me gather my books. It was humiliating to rely on my younger cousin for protection, but I was relieved to escape with nothing more than a couple of bruises on my knees and my ego.

The transition from Iran had not been easy. Our path home to America had taken a yearlong detour through London, where my father was awarded a fellowship in genetics at the Galton Laboratory of University College London. After living a carefree life in a world full of sunshine, bright colors, and best friends, I was dropped abruptly in the middle of a strange, mostly gray and chilly place known as Muswell Hill, a quiet, stodgy, middle-class neighborhood in London. I'd left behind Saroya's warmth and indulgence for the cold indifference of our new housekeeper, Mrs. Baldwin, who was not unkind but made it clear that I was an unwelcome bother.

Living in London was, for me, the beginning of a retreat into shyness that would last well into adulthood. London was not an "adventure" like our other travels. It was supposed to be home, but to me, my "home" was Shiraz. Facing this strange new world, I pulled back into a shell. The first few months of school, I was too embarrassed to raise my hand in class to ask to go to the bathroom, preferring to sit in wet bloomers rather than draw attention to myself—a problem that was solved only when my mother made good on her threat to spank me if it happened again. My fear of her discipline turned out to be greater than my fear of speaking up in class.

A year later, the move to America was also hard for me and my dad. Discrimination in the medical profession had scarcely improved, and despite enthusiastic recommendations from many white colleagues, most major hospitals still refused to open their doors to a black doctor, even one as qualified and experienced as my dad. But he kept knocking on doors and, through some combination of perseverance, talent, charm, and just plain luck, while delivering a paper on his research at a genetics conference in Mexico, my father managed to meet and impress the dean of the University of Chicago's medical center, who invited him to become the school's only black faculty member. The South Side of Chicago, where my mother had grown up and was so familiar to her, was also home to many in my large extended family, home to everyone but me—and that left me at the mercy of the bullies at Beulah Shoesmith Elementary.

Being different was uncomfortable for me. I just wanted to fit in and be like everyone else. All my family and new classmates said "tomato" while I said "to-mah-to." So I dropped the British accent in less than a week. Despite knowing French and Farsi, I refused to speak any language but English. My mother was proud to have mastered a new language. She often spoke Farsi when we were in public and she didn't want people to understand what she was saying. But when people turned to stare, I would plead with her to stop.

Another characteristic that I tried to change was my hair. Nearly everyone in my family had long, thick hair, some curly, some straight—historically referred to by some in the black community as "good hair"—everyone but me. As soon as my grandmother (Pudden, we all called her) thought I was old enough, she told my mother I had outgrown the hot comb used to temporarily iron out the coarseness of my hair, and she took me to the salon where they straightened my hair with chemicals. I still remember smiling with pride as I looked at myself in the mirror and saw my nearly shoulder-length hair bounce when I turned my head from side to side. My look then conformed to what I had envied in others, and to what society told us all was "pretty." It was not until several years later during the Black Is Beautiful movement that the definition of pretty began to evolve. But even today, many within the black community still struggle to embrace a broad and in-clusive definition of our beauty.

One characteristic that I could not change was my skin color—a factor that would prove confusing throughout my childhood. I had a brown-skinned friend who used to say everyone in my family was "light, bright, and damn near white"—an overstatement to be sure, but her tone left me wondering: Was that supposed to be a good thing or a bad thing? When we left Iran, my parents had told me that, in addition to worrying about the cultural differences there, they wanted us to return home so I could grow up with a better understanding of my identity as a black person, which would have been hard to do in Shiraz since we were the only blacks from America who lived there. Yet one of the many reasons I was bullied by the black girls at Shoesmith was because of my fair skin. *If this is supposed to be my community*, I wondered, *why am I treated poorly?*

As I grew up, I came to understand that slavery had produced a caste system that left deep scars, separating blacks based on color. Those with a darker complexion often faced worse treatment than those with lighter skin. And nearly a hundred years later, growing up in Chicago, the vestiges of the harsh color line and the discrimination it produced trig-gered both resentment and envy within the black community. It also meant that those who had the ability to situationally or even perma-nently "pass" for white had a choice to make.

One of my early memories is getting all dressed up to go to see the fabulous Christmas decorations at Marshall Field's with Pudden. We stopped for a delicious chicken-salad lunch at the magnificent Walnut Room, the department store's famous restaurant. Although I was obliv-ious to it at the time, I was later told blacks were not welcome there. But Pudden—fair-skinned with dead-straight hair—and I blended right into the all-white room; no one was rude or treated us poorly. Other than the black servers who gave us knowing glances, no one there knew we were black. When I was young we never discussed it, but being there was a privilege only those as fair as Pudden and I could pull off—and our presence there was a confounding decision I wrestled to understand as I grew older. Pudden did not live as a white woman, as some fair-skin blacks in her generation chose to do, but she wasn't interested in drawing unnecessary attention to her race. She never once made me think she wasn't proud to be black. In fact, her social circle, other than some of her husband's business associates, was almost entirely black. Yet she also never explicitly acknowledged the comforts of life she chose to enjoy as a result of her complexion. That day in Marshall Field's, I imagine she simply wanted to give her granddaughter a special experience, but looking back, I wonder if she felt more conflicted than I knew about how she navigated her decision to go where others could not.

Pudden and my mom both told me stories of their family trips to Tuskegee, Alabama, to visit my great-grandfather. They would drive from Chicago and spend the night in friends' homes along the way. But one time they passed through a southern town, where they knew nobody, and there were no hotels that allowed "negroes" to stay. So my grandmother, the fairest in their family, checked in to a "whites only" motel, leaving everyone else in the car. Then, when the clerk was not looking, my darker-skin grandfather and their two daughters sneaked into their room. They described it to me as a convenience, but it was also a privilege.

My first memory of encountering racism is from the age of ten, when my parents sent me to an all-girls sleep-away camp in Michigan. I was the only black girl there, and on the very last day of camp, as I was packing up my clothes, this one girl with whom I'd become good friends started talking to me about what a fun time we'd had, and then out of nowhere she suddenly blindsided me by blurting out, "You know, I thought you were a nigger when I first met you. I'm really sorry."

I froze. My face turned bright red. Did I want to lash out in outrage? Nope. All I wanted to do was get out of there as fast as I could. In my overactive imagination, I pictured myself saying, "Oh, but I *am*!" only to have her beat me up the way the black girls had done five years before. So I didn't tell her the truth. I just mumbled something like "Oh, that's too bad." Then I finished packing and was anxious to leave. I never mentioned it to my parents or to anyone else. I was too ashamed.

Fifty years later, I'm still embarrassed that I let her insult me that way without confronting her and telling the truth. But in the moment, it felt simpler to go along rather than give voice to my outrage. For most people of color there are circumstances where putting up with those random acts of racism is easier because of the fear that the consequences of speaking out will be even worse. Whether it's at school, at the office, or in the criminal justice system, being outspoken about racism always risks a backlash. That fact, coupled with my natural shyness, meant that my default response to racially tinged situations was to keep quiet.

The following summer I went back to that same camp, only this time my cousin Lauren, who is brown-skinned, came with me. With Lauren by my side, there could be no sidestepping the fact of our race, and, sure enough, one day some girl called her a nigger. I knew that I had to defend her, because when we were younger, she always stood up for me, but I was paralyzed by the thought. Luckily, before I could even think of how to respond, a friend of ours, a big, burly white girl, stepped between us and the bully and pushed her off. "Don't you ever say that to her again," she said, threatening the other girl.

Thank God, I thought, grateful that she'd stuck up for us.

Since I was so painfully shy and scared to speak up for myself, or for others, it would be a years-long struggle for me to find my voice, but I drew strength from my parents, and also from stories about the struggles and accomplishments of so many other members of my family.

My family's story, or at least one chapter of it, began in the port city of Wilmington, North Carolina. My great-great-great-grandfather, Angus Taylor, was white. He owned my great-great-great-grandmother, an enslaved woman whose name I do not know. In 1823 she had a son by him, Henry, who was freed at the end of the Civil War and would go on to live and work as a carpenter in Wilmington.

Henry's son, Robert Robinson Taylor, was born in 1868 in humble beginnings, but because Henry believed that the path to a better life depended on a good education, he encouraged Robert to study hard and look beyond Wilmington for opportunities. Robert did so well that he crashed through a racial barrier and became the first black student to attend the Massachusetts Institute of Technology in Boston. The tuition, a fortune at the time, was paid out of the $5,000 his father had saved from his carpenter's wages.

After graduating in 1892, Robert Robinson Taylor went on to become America's first accredited black architect, hired by Booker T. Washington to design many of the buildings on the campus of the famous Tuskegee Institute in Alabama. His first building, Science Hall, was built entirely by students under his direction, all the way down to the manufacturing of the bricks.

Several years thereafter, Washington and Taylor began to work with Julius Rosenwald, the president of Sears, Roebuck & Co., who had pledged part of his department-store fortune to help finance more than five thousand schools for black children across the South, many of which were designed by my great-grandfather.

Taylor's son, my grandfather, Robert Rochon Taylor, didn't start out in life quite as diligent. Raised in Tuskegee, he was sent to Howard Academy, the renowned boarding school affiliated with Howard University, only to be expelled for what has been described to me only as "youthful impropriety." To teach him a lesson, his father made him work for three years at a sawmill he'd designed in Opelika, Alabama. The lesson apparently worked, because from there my grandfather went on to graduate from the University of Illinois with a degree in business administration. By then he shared his father's keen appreciation for the value of a good education.

By 1929 my grandfather had joined the family profession, partnering with Julius Rosenwald in planning, building, and eventually managing a massive apartment complex between Forty-sixth Street and Forty-seventh, along Michigan Avenue, in a black neighborhood known as Bronzeville on the South Side of Chicago. Its official name was the Michigan Boulevard Garden Apartments, but everyone called it the Rosenwald Building. With over four hundred beautiful yet affordable units, it soon became a coveted address for black Chicagoans, from Pullman porters and postal workers to doctors and lawyers. It had its share of celebrity residents as well: musicians like Nat "King" Cole and Quincy Jones, the poet Gwendolyn Brooks, and heavyweight boxing champion Joe Louis.

As the manager of the Rosenwald Building, my grandfather raised his two daughters there along with his wife, the matriarch of our clan, Laura Dorothy Vaughn Jennings, my grandmother Pudden. Short for "pudding," it was a nickname bestowed on her by my father because, he said, she was so sweet. Pudden was born in Berkeley, California. After her father died when she was five, her mother moved the family briefly to Louisville, Kentucky, to live with her late husband's mother. They did not get along, so she finally settled in Chicago. Pudden's mother raised her and her two siblings, Mormon and Ulsa Alone, on her own, working as a clerk at the Chicago Board of Education and taking in fine sewing and needlepoint at night.

At that time, racially restrictive covenants confined black Chicagoans to neighborhoods like Bronzeville, where the Rosenwald Building was located. But in 1948 the legality of those covenants was struck down by the Supreme Court, and slowly black families began moving out. In 1957, after my grandfather died, Pudden decided to move out of the Rosenwald Building and buy an apartment building with her daughter, my aunt Lauranita Dugas, and Aunt Lauranita's husband, Uncle Lester. It was at 5000 South Woodlawn, just two miles away from the Rosenwald Building in the neighborhood of South Kenwood. At the time, Aunt Lauranita and Uncle Lester had two and a half children—Gail, Jeffrey, and Lauren on the way.

The building had two units on the first floor that they leased out and two units on the second floor, secured by a locked door at the bottom of the stairs, so Pudden and the Dugases usually left the door open between their two apartments.

South Kenwood was, at the time, a largely white neighborhood surrounded by Lake Michigan on one side and low-income black communities on all others. As more black families began to move in, white families started to move out. The process sped up exponentially during the unrest of the civil rights era, as unscrupulous real estate brokers known as blockbusters started canvassing the neighborhood, exploiting white homeowners' fears of racial turnover and convincing them to sell their houses at below-market rates so the blockbusters could then flip them to black families at inflated prices using predatory financing. When that happened, property values fell, and businesses moved out. The same process was playing out in the adjoining area of Hyde Park, home to the University of Chicago. White flight became so prevalent that, at one point, the university considered moving out of the city and into the suburbs. It decided to stay, perhaps in part because the city acquired large tracts of land that buffered the campus as part of urban renewal initiatives and gave them to the university. The land grab (which is what it really was) helped stabilize the neighborhood, but it caused a rift between the university and many of the displaced residents and community leaders that has taken decades to bridge.

The university and a coalition of progressive homeowners and politicians wanted to see Hyde Park–South Kenwood become an inclusive and racially integrated community. (Leon Despres, the alderman representing the ward, was so liberal that when muggers shot him twice in the leg, he didn't press charges because he blamed the criminals' actions on the larger societal factors that had shaped them.) This was in stark contrast to most of Chicago, where racism and discrimination was still prevalent.

Fortunately for us, my father's new job included assistance in financing a spacious apartment in Madison Park, a gorgeous two-block enclave in South Kenwood just a block and a half from Pudden and the

Dugas family. Then, five years later, my parents were able to afford their dream house three blocks from Madison Park on Greenwood Avenue, a wide and leafy street of landmarked single-family homes, many dating back to the 1800s. Ours was the smallest house on the block, but I loved it, especially the circular staircase in the front, whose banister my cousins and I took turns sliding down, and the large backyard, where my parents have hosted countless occasions.

South Kenwood was also home to several members of my mother's large and welcoming clan. Pudden's Woodlawn home was always the hub of activity. If any of our parents were running late from work, or if we were sick during a school day, she was always right there, sitting in her favorite chair next to the window in her "little front room" visible from the street.

The same day we moved into our home on Greenwood, one of my cousins, Ann Cook, moved into an apartment a block away with her four children. The Dibbles, Ann's brother Gene and his wife, Jeanette, and their five kids, lived across the park from our old apartment on Madison Park. Our cousin Bill Feaman, his wife, Nancy, and their four kids were three blocks away. And Jewel Lafontant, who was a cousin of a cousin, lived with her son, my lifelong friend John Rogers, at the corner of our block. Jewel was the first black deputy solicitor general under President Richard Nixon—she was our family's one Republican and our block on Greenwood, where the Obamas now also have a home today, bears Jewel's name on an honorary street sign. In all, sixteen cousins lived within the radius of just a few blocks, including four girls who were all my age.

I grew up in an era when parents didn't believe in programming much of their children's time. After my chores on a weekend morning, my parents would open the door and say, "Find your cousins." And I would. Our parents also did not believe in much pampering either. If I returned home in tears after an argument with a cousin or friend, my parents would say, "Go back and work it out. You'll be fine." "You'll be fine" was an expression I heard again and again as I grew older.

We'd all meet up and make a day of picking blackberries in a neighbor's yard, riding our bikes along the lakefront, making up games, and building elaborate blanket forts with the folding TV tables and chairs in my grandmother's little front room. Most of us loved to play tennis, and Aunt Ann and my dad would often take us to play in Lake Meadows or Dolton, Illinois. In Iran I had been an only child, so entering into this close society of so many children was a wholly new experience for me. Being alone was natural, even comfortable for me. I never felt lonely. I simply developed a rich fantasy world as a way of entertaining myself, always perfectly happy to wander around alone or play with the dogs, chickens, or donkeys on the compound. Now, suddenly, I was rarely alone, and after the initial shock of all the new faces, I began to appreciate that I had the best of all worlds: built in playmates when I wanted them, yet I still enjoyed the attention and benefits of being an only child.

Our extended family lived as one unit. The parents all parented one another's children, which often worked to the children's advantage. "Forum shopping" is a legal term that refers to the way lawyers seek out the most favorable jurisdiction in which to file a claim in an effort to secure the judgment they want. This was exactly what we kids would do. We would forum shop among the adults. If you wanted sympathy and to be told you were absolutely right no matter what, you went to Aunt Lauranita. If you had a mechanical or electrical problem, Uncle Lester was your guy. If you were sick, my dad was on twenty-four-hour call. If you wanted tough love and the hard truth, you went to my mom. Advice about boys, talk to Aunt Ann. There were adventures to be had with Uncle Gene, who rounded up all the kids and took us to the Indiana Dunes. We never knew if we would return home that night—or days later, as sometimes happened, no doubt to the other parents' delight! Uncle Lester made hamburgers with potato chips on Saturday nights for whoever wanted to come by. The Cook family ate dinner during the week at four thirty. I'd often eat there and then go home for a second dinner with my parents. My grandmother always had a pot of soup and a pan of gingerbread ready in the winter. And on weekends and during the summer, we kids always just slept wherever we were at bedtime. We thought we were getting away with what we wanted by forum shopping, but unbeknownst to us, our parents were always communicating to ensure that important information did not slip through the cracks, and that they never contradicted one another. Well, almost never.

Pudden was the heart of our family. Everybody loved Pudden, and because she traveled often with my parents and me and she and I always bunked together, perhaps that's why I felt a special bond between us. Looking back, my guess is that she made each of her grandchildren feel she loved us the best. She embodied all that I could hope a grandmother is supposed to be. I trusted her completely and could confide anything in her, absolutely anything. Nothing seemed to shock her. She was hip and always wanted to know the latest, whether it was gossip or dance moves. Not long after we moved to Chicago, after an argument with my mother, I announced that I was going to run away from home. "Don't go without your undershirts," my mom replied, which took me by surprise. Why wasn't she trying to stop me? *And why was she helping me pack?* I thought. Then she watched me march out of the house, knowing full well there was only one place I would go. And off I went with my little suitcase, directly to Pudden's house around the corner, because where else would I go? I knew I could count on Pudden to sympathize with my outrage and protect me from her daughter. (Pudden lived by the firm belief that grandparents and grandchildren are bonded by a common enemy.) I stayed for a couple of hours, eating my favorite snack of Ritz crackers and cheddar cheese. Then my mom showed up, took my hand, and, without a word, walked me home. *How did she know where I was?* I wondered.

No matter what happened, Pudden was always on my side, offering steadfast love and support. She encouraged us all to be kind to one another, showing us countless times by her example the meaning of love and forgiveness. When my cousins and I squabbled, she would force us to make up. She believed there should only be room for goodness in our hearts.

And there was plenty of warmth. Literal warmth. Having learned needlepoint, knitting, and sewing from her mother, Pudden taught me the same, and would sit in her little front room, knitting afghans for her children, grandchildren, and great-nieces and great-nephews. She gave them to my generation as gifts when we graduated from high school. That way we could take them off to college with us and still have a way to wrap ourselves up in Pudden's love on cold winter nights. I still have mine (and my former husband's). Even now, a quarter century after her death, whenever I drive by her old home, I look up at the window in her little front room and feel comfort as I imagine that I still see her sitting there.

Pudden's home was more than just a safe and loving place in the present. It was also our link to the past. The walls and side tables were lined with well-preserved black-and-white photographs in ornate, beautiful frames. There were pictures of great-aunts and great-uncles, great-grandfathers and great-grandmothers—our whole family tree going back as far as her memory could trace it. In the living room, Pudden even had a Certificate of Office commemorating the elected tenure of another of my great-great-grandfathers, Victor Rochon. Born in 1843 in St. Martinville, he was one of the first black legislators voted into the Louisiana House of Representatives during Reconstruction. He had given a famous speech in 1890 denouncing Louisiana's Separate Car Act, a state law that would codify segregation in rail cars. He asked the other members of the legislature whether it made sense for their black nannies to be able to accompany their children in all-white train cars, while he, a fellow senator, could not ride in those very same cars. He lost the argument in the state legislature, and in 1896 in a landmark case, *Plessy v. Ferguson*, the Supreme Court upheld the constitutionality of racial segregation.

I used to linger in Pudden's home, looking at the photos, trying to imagine the history my relatives had lived through, from slavery to Reconstruction to the Great Migration, where they made their way north to the oppressive streets of Chicago and endured the Great Depression and two world wars. But in spite of any hardships, education was always, always viewed as the path to success. There were my great-aunt and great-uncle, Helen and Gene Dibble, who'd saved to send their five children to New England prep schools because the quality of education in the high school in Tuskegee, Alabama, was so poor. There was Ella Smith, my great-great-grandmother, who'd attended Oberlin when it was still a seminary, before the Civil War. There was my great-great-aunt, Edna Boutte, who received a degree in pharmacy from the Sorbonne in Paris and another degree in social work from the New School in New York City. All the siblings and cousins of my mother's and father's generation finished college.

Given my family's history, and explicitly from my parents, I always knew the expectations of me were high. From a very early age, as I was told the stories behind all the photos on Pudden's walls, I was taught that achieving your dreams was possible with a good education; a strong moral compass; a loving family; hard, honest work; and a lot of good luck. At times those expectations made me believe I could accomplish whatever I wanted. And at times I felt I could never live up to them.

My mother was not an easy act to follow. At Sarah Lawrence College, she toyed with the idea of an art degree before deciding to study labor law, a degree for which she was required to do fieldwork with the women of the International Ladies' Garment Workers' Union. "The only thing I learned," she would later say, "was how to drink gin out of a paper cup." She went to work at a social services agency in the Bronx, which was a true education. Having been raised in a stable, loving home herself, she was shocked at the way children who fell through the cracks were being neglected and abused. She then took a course in child study, worked in a nursery school, and eventually earned a teaching certificate.

Returning to Chicago after graduation, she married my father and accepted a job as an assistant pre-K teacher at the University of Chicago Laboratory Schools, referred to as the Lab Schools, a nursery-through-twelfth-grade private school affiliated with the University of Chicago. Started in 1896 by the progressive education leader John Dewey, it served as a "laboratory" to test new ideas in the classroom. She was only the second black teacher ever hired by the school. While teaching, my mom finished her master's degree in education at the University of Chicago, beginning what turned out to be a lifelong career in early childhood development. She loved that the discipline combined the intellectual rigor of understanding child psychology with the abundant opportunity to give lots of love and snuggles.

In Iran my mother taught social science at the nursing school while also tackling what was, to her, the most important child development project of all: me. I loved my father dearly, but from my earliest recollections and throughout my childhood, my closest companion, and the person I worshipped above all others was my mother. Tall and naturally pretty, she never wore any makeup save for red lipstick, and generally had little interest in fussing over her appearance.

When it came to my development, my mom set high but attainable benchmarks. According to her, by age three, I could sit still and have a long conversation "like a big girl" in two languages, English and Farsi. (After spending time with new friends from France, I added French to the list.) Thanks to my father's encouragement, I could also read by the same age. I had an even temperament, too, able to tag along on my parents' grand adventures without too much complaint or discomfort. The only challenge was that if I didn't eat regularly, my mood could turn ugly. So my mom always carried chocolate bars in her pocketbook for me to nibble on. (Pudden would always carry peppermint candy.)

While my father was a tireless optimist, my mother's encouragement always came with a reality check firmly attached. "Yes, you can do anything," she seemed to say, "but never underestimate what you're up against." I was more like my father. He always hoped for the best, but my mom always planned for the worst. Nowhere was this more evident than in her attitude toward money. My mom says being raised during the Great Depression made her appreciate the value of every dollar, or perhaps I should say penny. To say "frugal" would be an understatement. Considering visits to the hair salon to be a total waste of money, she has always opted to wear her hair up away from her face in a very practical, traditional bun. Anytime my father or I have tried to treat us to a nice restaurant, she's incapable of enjoying the meal without opening the menu, shaking her head, and saying, "I could make this for a fraction of the cost at home." Her clothes, while simple and elegant, have always been purchased on sale. *Always.* Her constant refrain is "You are simply throwing money away if you pay full price." Even today, at ninety years old, she still drives five miles to Costco every single week to buy what her exhaustive research shows is the cheapest gas in Chicago. Whenever I show her a new dress I've bought, the first question she asks me is, "How much did it cost?"

"Tell me if you like it first," I always say.

"Whether or not I like it depends on how much it cost."

My parents debated issues all of the time, it was the family sport, but the only real argument I remember them having was over the lottery. My father played the lottery every week, which to my mother was a waste of money and time. One week the lottery had a particularly large jackpot, and my parents started arguing about what they would do with their imaginary winnings, if somehow they ever actually won them. For my dad it was a no-brainer: He would buy a luxury condo in the Four Seasons Hotel George V off the Champs-Élysées in Paris. Meanwhile, my mother's "fantasy" about this money revolved largely around how much of it they would have to pay in taxes and save for me to have for a rainy day. She said a Parisian condo would be expensive to maintain and eventually leave them bankrupt like so many other people who win the lottery. This discussion then spiraled into raised voices, both of my parents visibly angry, until my mother, furious that her husband would jeopardize our future with his ludicrous condo idea, finally stormed off upstairs—all over money they didn't win and would never have. I just shook my head at the whole exchange, knowing that before the lights turned off, they'd have worked it out. That was their rule—never go to bed angry—and they never did.

Barbara Bowman was a master planner for every hypothetical disaster possible. In Iran she was always acutely aware of what I ate or drank, knowing how ill the wrong fruit or drink could make me. She meticulously washed and peeled, or boiled, every single item that went into my mouth. She trained me to do it as well. At the age of three, while dining at a fancy restaurant on a trip to the United States, I said just a bit too loudly, "Is it OK to drink the water here?!"

My mother was also fairly cool and reserved. She would always hug and kiss me, especially to say good night, but she was not one to be verbally demonstrative with her affection. She says she believes people overuse the word *love*, throwing it in at the end of every phone conversation, trivializing it. But I suppose I missed that spoken affection, because I say it to my own daughter at the end of every phone conversation and whenever else the spirit moves me. My mother was also always the one to point out a flaw, downside, or risk in attempts to tamp down my "unrealistic" enthusiasm a bit. Her characteristic reply when life did not go my way would be, with a shrug, "You'll be fine." When I was young, I thought that my mom lacked confidence in me. It wasn't until I was much older that I began to appreciate that she was just afraid of disappointment, for me, and for her. She believed in me, but she also felt it was her duty to toughen me up, force realism on me, and protect me against life's heartache by always reminding me just how horribly things can go wrong—as a black woman who'd spent her life growing up in Chicago, and being one of "the only" in elite white institutions, she knew a thing or two about being let down.

The mantra my parents drilled into me was that to be successful I would have to work twice as hard. They never finished the sentence, but I knew what they meant: twice as hard as white people. No matter what grades I received, my parents asked me, "Did you give it your best?" If I complained that I had given it my best but the grade "wasn't fair," they responded, "Life isn't fair. You don't always control what happens to you. You can control how you respond when life doesn't go your way. Be resilient and you'll bounce back."

Working hard, sadly, was not a prerequisite for advancement at South Kenwood's Shoesmith Elementary in the early 1960s. With Chicago's segregated black schools being as overcrowded and underfunded as they were, the bullies waiting for me outside posed a far greater challenge than the schoolwork I would face. The overcrowding forced some of the students to have classes in the hallways, and there were never enough books to go around. By 1963 my parents, who wanted to support the public schools, had reached their breaking point. Shoesmith had a revolving door of teachers who tried and failed to address the conditions in the classroom. My fourth-grade class had thirty-plus kids combined in one room with third graders. I had seven teachers that one school year. It was chaos. That spring, the last of the seven took me and five other kids aside and told us we didn't have to do homework anymore. We were "the smart kids," and apparently the teacher thought she could stop teaching us in order to concentrate on the other children in the classroom, teaching to the norm. I ran home, overjoyed, and told my parents.

"The teacher said we never have to do homework again!"

"Well," my mom said, "I guess that's the end of that."

At the end of the year my parents transferred me to the Lab Schools, where my mother had worked in graduate school. Since I was so young, my parents decided I would repeat the fourth grade, with actual homework this time.

By the end of my third year of high school, my parents had coaxed me to go to the same prep school my mother and four of her Dibble cousins had attended, the Northfield School for Girls, which by that time had merged with the neighboring boys' school, Mount Hermon, to become Northfield Mount Hermon (NMH). I was reluctant to go and stay for two years, wanting to graduate with my classmates in Chicago, but I relented because they told me if I graduated from high school at age sixteen, I would only be allowed to go to a small women's college. That was out of the question, so off I went to NMH's beautiful, sprawling, hilly campus in Massachusetts. My stay was made easier by the fact that my cousins Toni Cook and Rochon Dibble were also there, and Rochon's sister Chyla joined us our second year. Since my cousins and I had grown up inseparable, none of us were ever really homesick.

I will confess that at the Lab Schools there were more than a few classes and semesters where I could skate by doing the minimum necessary to earn good grades so that I could be a typical teenage girl, playing bid whist in the cafeteria before school and talking to boys on the phone. But after a couple of months at NMH, I realized that the work was much more challenging and that I better buckle down and start working harder if I wanted to get into my top choice for college: Stanford University.

As college approached, my father wanted me to go to the University of Chicago, so I could be close to home. My mother wanted me to attend her alma mater, Sarah Lawrence. But I'd had my heart set on Stanford ever since a day at the end of my freshman year, when I was standing in the library at the Lab Schools and this handsome, tall, older guy walked in. Mr. Poole, the librarian, recognized the young man and told me to stick around to meet him. His name was John Hope Franklin Jr. I didn't know him, but I knew his father: John Hope Franklin, our neighbor, a good friend of my grandmother, and the famous historian whose pioneering book, *From Slavery to Freedom: A History of African Americans*, sold millions of copies worldwide and became the text often credited as laying the foundation for the future academic field of African American studies. John Jr., a Lab Schools alum, was back visiting his old stomping grounds on spring break, and Mr. Poole mentioned to me that John was a student at Stanford. "I love Stanford," John said, barely glancing up at me. "You should go there."

That was all he said, and that was all it took: for the remainder of high school, I was determined to go to Stanford.

After I shot down my parents' recommendations, my father, naturally, told me I could do whatever I wanted to do. My mother, of course, told me I could apply but, since Stanford was so competitive, I would need a backup plan in case disappointment struck; she made me apply to eight additional schools varying in competitiveness. Then I talked to my NMH guidance counselor about my first choice. "Don't waste your time," he said. "You won't get in." How could he just dismiss my dream? Was he saying that because I wasn't smart enough? Because I was black? Because I was a woman? After reeling for a moment or two, I decided I would just have to prove him wrong, and I applied anyway (and to all eight backups, to satisfy my mom). I was accepted to all of them. With my acceptance letters in hand, I marched back into his office and laid each letter on his desk, one at a time, saving Stanford's for last.

"I got into nine schools," I said, "including Stanford, thank you."

"Congratulations," he said, barely looking up from his desk. Decades later, I told my mom what the counselor had done. She was appalled but hardly surprised.

Back in Chicago for the summer, for some foolish reason I decided that, after being away at prep school for two years, I was too mature to have my parents take me to college. I was going to go and move in by myself. My mother didn't seem surprised, since nobody had taken her to college either, and acquiesced to my request to go alone.

Of course, that headstrong girl who insisted on going off on her own, who had walked into that counselor's office with such defiant swagger, was still, underneath, shy and often still filled with self-doubt. I had gotten into Stanford, but was it a mistake? Was affirmative action a factor? Did I belong there? I'd never visited Stanford or spent any time in California, and as my departure date approached I became more than a bit nervous.

As I packed up to leave, folding the new afghan Pudden had knitted for me into my suitcase, my mind turned where it often did (and still does) when I'm facing a new challenge and don't know how it will turn out. I thought about all the photos and portraits in my grandmother's home and all that my people who came before me had accomplished. I thought about Victor Rochon and the speech he gave in the Louisiana House of Representatives, about my grandfather and his ambitious work with the Chicago Housing Authority. But mostly I thought about my great-grandfather, Robert Robinson Taylor. How had he, the son of a slave, summoned the courage to leave home and take the long, lonely train ride to what must have seemed like a foreign land to study at MIT? How had he handled the responsibility, knowing that the tuition his father, Henry, had invested in him was such a huge sacrifice? How was he treated by his white classmates, most of whom likely had no prior exposure to black people as peers? Reminding myself that they had been through far more difficult times and not only survived but thrived, I said to myself, "Come on, Valerie. You can do this." And that became my mantra whenever the seeds of self-doubt creep in.

Right before I left, my ever-frugal mother sat me down and said, "Look, I know you're going to want to have fun, and you'll be tempted from time to time to cut class. If you do, this is what it will cost Dad and me." Then she handed me a piece of paper where she had worked out a breakdown of how much tuition they were spending per class—not how much per semester, but how much for each individual class, for every hour and every day.

"It has and will always be a given that we support your education for as long as you want to go," she continued, "but do *not* throw our money away."

I knew I couldn't let them down.

I hugged my parents good-bye.

And off I went, by myself.

· Chapter 3 ·

The Best Laid Plans

I pulled up on Stanford's campus on a beautiful, sunny California afternoon, with two huge yellow suitcases I'd shoved onto a shuttle bus that picked up the other students who were traveling alone at the San Francisco airport. As we wound through the campus to my dorm, my eyes tried to absorb the massive palm trees, the swimming pools and tennis courts, the buildings with red-tiled roofs tucked behind perfectly landscaped yards with tropical flowers. It didn't look like any college I had ever seen. It looked like a country club.

The bus dropped me off at Lagunita Court, a cluster of residential halls, one of which had been renamed from Olivo Magnolia to Ujamaa—the Swahili word that means extended family, because half of its residents were black students. It was a time when the civil rights activism of the 1960s had catalyzed the Black Power movement of the 1970s, and with it a sense of pride took hold. "Black houses" were cropping up at predominantly white colleges and universities across America, not because black students wanted to be separate from white people—after all, the students had chosen to go to those schools instead of historically black colleges. They just wanted to have a close association on those campuses with other black people. I'd applied to live in Ujamaa over my parents' objections. "You don't need to go to Stanford to live in a black house," my mother said. "You grew up in a black house." But my parents' generation, having spent their lives trying to get out of segregated black spaces, didn't understand what their children were going through. High-achieving black kids, many having spent our entire lives feeling somewhat isolated in predominantly white places, were longing for a sense of community and solidarity. Those who grew up in predominantly black communities also felt the black houses eased their transition from home.

At the end of the first day of orientation, the dorm leader gathered the freshmen from all the dorms at Lagunita Court, which included Ujamaa, for a talk. "I want to go through the rules," he said. After two years at NMH, with its many rules and restrictions, I had come prepared with a little notebook and pen. I took it out, ready to write down his instructions. "There are none," he said.

Welcome to Stanford University, 1974.

My first thought was *Heaven!* But lingering somewhere in my subconscious was the knowledge that what he was saying didn't fully apply to me, or any of the other black students in Ujamaa. There are always rules for black people in predominantly white spaces; we had either been explicit warned of that, or we just knew intuitively that there is very little margin for error. I carried the responsibility of an additional set of expectations as well. The fact that generation after generation of my family had overcome enormous obstacles to succeed, and my parents had made sacrifices so I could have the opportunity to be on that campus, was never far from my mind.

My time at Stanford wasn't much different from the years I'd spent at NMH. In fact, most of the courses seemed easier. I worked hard competing against myself to earn good grades because it gave me a sense of accomplishment. I always assumed I would be a doctor just like my dad, but a high school anthropology class piqued my interest, too. I ended up majoring in psychology because I earned my highest grades there—and also because after six weeks of organic chemistry, and a visit to my medical-school boyfriend's anatomy class where he was dissecting a cadaver, I decided premed was out of the question. I found many of my professors to be inspiring, but nothing triggered a true passion for a particular career. Perhaps the fact that my parents provided me with infinite possibilities made it harder for me to zero in; when the sky's the limit, it can be overwhelming.

By my senior year, I still didn't have a clear sense of direction. I suggested to my parents that I take a year off to travel, as some of my classmates planned to do. "And who's paying for that?" my mother scoffed. She told me she was worried if I stopped going to school I'd never go back, and a bachelor's degree was simply not going to open enough doors on its own. "So pick a graduate school," she said.

I signed up for the GMAT, thinking I might go to business school, but then there was a great party the night before the test. I stayed out too late and in the morning thought better of it. Who was I kidding? I wasn't going to business school. I was good at probability and statistics, but back then I didn't have any interest in business. I skipped the test.

Then one weekend I drove up to San Francisco to see my best friend, Gwen. Gwen had been a junior when I was a freshman, and I'd met her the first day I arrived at school, introduced by her boyfriend, whom I knew from the Lab Schools. She'd grown up in Los Angeles, and I'd spent many long weekends and each Thanksgiving holiday with her family. By the time I was grappling with career choices in my senior year, she was in her second year of law school at UC Hastings College of the Law in San Francisco, and she loved it. I was crashing on her couch one weekend, lamenting my lack of direction, and she said, "Try law school. Even if you don't love it, it'll buy you some time, and if you don't end up practicing law, it's still a good degree to have."

Gwen had never led me astray before, so I sat for the LSAT, scored fairly high, and started applying to various law schools. I was accepted at the University of Michigan very early in the process, before I'd even submitted all my applications. At that time, Michigan ranked number two in the country. I couldn't believe I'd gotten in. After the shock wore off, I decided if I was good enough for Michigan Law School, then Michigan Law School was good enough for me.

With my grad school decision made, I decided that it was time for me to stop moving aimlessly through life, that what I needed was a sense of order and direction, a linear path. So one evening I made myself a checklist of the goals I wanted to accomplish in the next ten years. My plan was this:

1. Graduate from Stanford.
2. Graduate from Michigan.
3. Discover my career passion.
4. Fall in love and marry.
5. Have a baby.
6. Be a fulfilled, satisfied, and happy wife and working mom.

I was convinced that if I could just have the discipline and self-control to accomplish items one through five, then I would be able to check off item number six. So I graduated from Stanford, item one, and packed myself off to Ann Arbor to check off item two.

I prepped for law school by reading Scott Turow's terrifying *One L: The Turbulent True Story of a First Year at Harvard Law School*. Turow had been my teaching assistant in a first-year writing course at Stanford and I thought he was terrific, so I believed every story he told. The Socratic method of calling on students in lieu of traditional lecturing gave me the shudders. There were no lawyers in my family, and when I arrived at Michigan, I knew nothing about the law other than what I had read in Scott's book or seen on *Perry Mason*. First semester we were required to take a class called Torts. *What was a tort?*

It was terribly intimidating for someone as shy as me. On day one, both my criminal and property law professors went down the list alphabetically, and thanks to my last name, Bowman, I was called on in both classes. When I heard my name, my cheeks began to burn a deep red, an awful reflex triggered whenever I was forced to speak publicly. The students who always aggressively raised their hands first were called "gunners." I hesitated before answering in both classes, and as I saw hands shoot up all around me, I thought to myself, *How do they know the answers so quickly?* After day one, I wasn't sure there would be a day two.

A high school classmate from the Lab Schools in Chicago was one year ahead of me at Michigan. She laughed with a knowing expression on her face and said, "Don't worry. It'll get better." I wasn't so sure. It was brutal at first, as I struggled to learn this whole new language of the law—*res ipsa loquitur*, the rule against perpetuities, *mens rea*, and the statutes of limitations. But I discovered that I really enjoyed legal writing, the order and logic of framing an argument. I also excelled at it, so much so that in my second and third years I was selected to help teach first-year writing.

When it came time to explore my career options again, I flirted with the idea of going to Washington, DC. I clerked for a DC law firm the summer after my second year, but didn't really enjoy the work (a sign). Then, during my third year, I interviewed with the Securities and Exchange Commission, the Federal Trade Commission, and the few other federal agencies that came to campus to recruit. But DC was definitely a company town. During the summer I spent there, nearly every lunch and dinner conversation I had revolved around one topic, politics, which I thought might get boring quickly.

In the end I realized I was homesick. Including my time at boarding school, I'd been gone for nine years, and I was uneasy about settling permanently away from my family. So I decided to return home to Chicago after I graduated from Michigan in 1981. I became an associate at Pope, Ballard, Shepard & Fowle. The firm's offer was certainly attractive, financially. The starting salary was $30,000 a year, and I couldn't imagine what I was going to do with all that money!

In the early 1980s, women at big firms tried to make our appearance and attitudes conform to that of the men; we wanted to blend in and be taken seriously. It began with our attire. On my first day of work I wore a dark-blue suit with a white silk blouse. (I abandoned the blue silk ribbon that was intended to be tied around my neck; that was simply a bow too far.) When I arrived, I found that Nancy Yaeli, the other woman in my class who began work the same day, had shown up in the exact same outfit. We clicked immediately, laughing about how ridiculous we looked. But we knew we had to play by their rules.

Walking in, I knew I'd be judged not just by my gender but also by my race. Not long after I started, I found out that the only other black associate at the firm had failed the bar exam the year before. Failing wasn't going to be an option for me. I threw myself into my studies to make sure I passed the bar, petrified of what the white lawyers would think not just of me, but of other black lawyers if I failed, too. Thankfully, I passed.

At first, having my own office and an assistant was exciting. But reality seeped in quickly. As much as I tried to gin up some passion for corporate law, the work grew tedious fast, and it was hard pretending I was as devoted to it as the guys in my practice group appeared to be. Filing articles of incorporation, doing due diligence by reviewing volumes of documents for banks before they formed holding companies, and drafting registration statements for the offering of stocks—yuck. And the partner who supervised us was a real stickler for details—not, I discovered, my long suit. I started to venture more into the firm's real estate practice, and that was relatively better.

I thought I had finally found my path, and having checked off items one through three on my Ten-Year Plan, I realized I had left one off, and I made a mental amendment to the list. After husband and baby, I added, mistakenly, "Make partner at Pope, Ballard, Shepard & Fowle." That step, I knew, would simply be a matter of working hard and staying focused. That I was confident I could do. The open question at that point was having a family. In order to have a baby, I needed to marry. In order to marry, I needed to find a husband. And I knew that, for me, finding a husband wouldn't simply be a matter of finding *a* husband. I had to find *the* husband, meaning the one I thought would be the perfect one for me.

In June of 1982, my family and nearly everyone we knew spilled out of the University of Chicago's Rockefeller Chapel into a warm and sunny afternoon. It was the day of my cousin Chyla's wedding. Chyla's dad, my uncle Gene, had spent weeks driving around Chicago with a stack of Xeroxed wedding invitations in his car, handing out additional ones to nearly everyone he knew, so the guests filled every pew in the massive Gothic-style church.

Everyone lingered outside the chapel for a while, enjoying the sun for a moment before heading to the reception four blocks away at the university's International House. I was chatting with several of my cousins, laughing at how Rochon, Chyla's sister and maid of honor, had dropped the ring as she handed it to Chyla during the ceremony. It had hit the marble floor and pinged down the aisle, sending a ripple of gasps and giggles through the whole congregation. As we rehashed the episode, Earl Dickerson—Uncle Earl, as I called him—emerged from the church.

Uncle Earl was the grandson of a slave. At sixteen years old he stowed away on a train to Chicago, where he eventually attended the University of Chicago Law School and married Katherine Mimms, Pudden's best friend. Although my parents were not at all religious, Pudden was, and she believed I would go to hell if I wasn't baptized. So the first time we visited the United States, when I was about seven months old, she snuck away to have me baptized without telling my mom, asking Katherine to be my godmother. Pudden later confessed what she had done, and my mom, always the pragmatist, shrugged. "I don't believe in any of that stuff," she said, "but Lally can't have too many people looking out for her." And indeed, I grew up enjoying great love and affection from both Aunt Katherine and Uncle Earl. But on that day the focus of my attention wasn't Uncle Earl. Rather, it was the very handsome young man escorting him, Bobby Jarrett.

When my parents were growing up, the black middle class in Chicago and DC was small, so small that it seemed everybody knew everybody. No matter where they went, if two people were black and in a certain social stratum, they could find someone they knew in common in two seconds flat. When I started to bring boyfriends home, Pudden would always say, "Well, who is he?" Which meant, "Who are his parents? Who are his grandparents?" She assumed that the tight-knit community she and my grandfather had cultivated for their daughters would continue through my generation, but when she asked those questions my cousins and I always cringed.

Just as many black people had moved out of segregated communities as soon as they were able, my generation rebelled against any limits imposed on our social lives. Although in school my boyfriends had always been black, I had no interest in limiting my choices to those with family connections and backgrounds similar to my own. But Bobby Jarrett was an exception. I'd had a crush on him since I was eight. He was four years older than me and went to Catholic school, so we hadn't socialized much growing up. But our moms grew up in the Rosenwald Building together and our dads were both members of the Boule, a professional fraternity for prominent black men. Bobby and my cousin Jeff had also both been altar boys at church. Whenever my grandmother took me with her to church, I'd watch Bobby saunter down the aisle, pretending to look pious, but with a mischievous twinkle in his eye, and that was enough for me to develop totally unrequited feelings for him. One time in college, I sat in front of him at midnight mass on Christmas Eve, and when I worked up the nerve to turn around and say hello, I saw he was holding hands with the woman sitting next to him. I was heartbroken.

Standing in front of Rockefeller Chapel that day, seeing Bobby Jarrett made me hope that maybe now he would notice me. Uncle Earl walked right over to me with Bobby in tow and greeted me warmly. And Bobby, who'd never given me a second glance before, did the same. My cheeks began to flush! I was so smitten, I swiftly ditched my cousins and joined Uncle Earl and Bobby as they walked to the reception. Uncle Earl, then in his nineties, set the pace, and we strolled along slowly beside him.

I noticed how attentive Bobby was to Uncle Earl as he engaged him in one of his favorite activities: sparring over the news of the day. Bobby held his own, which was no easy task; Uncle Earl had argued and won a case against racially restrictive covenants before the U.S. Supreme Court, a ruling that had paved the way to open up previously segregated neighborhoods, such as South Kenwood, for black residents and homeowners. Uncle Earl was an outstanding lawyer who loved a good debate. And, as I would soon discover, so did Bobby.

After we sauntered to the reception, much to my disappointment, Bobby, Uncle Earl, and I were almost instantly separated in the enormous crowd. Later in the evening Bobby and I bumped into each other in the hallway just as I was about to leave. He casually took my hand, looked me right in the eye, and said, "Do you mind if I call you sometime?"

"Yeah, sure," I said, doing my best to appear nonchalant. "Call me."

Unlike so many of the boys I'd dated, Bobby felt comfortable, like the boy next door. His father, the famed syndicated columnist, Vernon Jarrett, was a larger-than-life figure who began his groundbreaking career in journalism at the black-owned weekly paper the *Chicago Defender* but later became the *Chicago Tribune*'s first black syndicated columnist, known for unsparing views on politics and race. He went on to become an op-ed writer for the *Chicago Sun-Times* and was one of the founders of the National Association of Black Journalists and the NAACP's Afro-Academic, Cultural, Technological and Scientific Olympics. Bobby's mother taught first grade in a poor-performing Chicago public school, where she often dipped into her own pocket to buy her students school supplies and books that they could not afford. Her goal was to make sure every child finished the grade knowing how to read. She and my mom shared a passionate belief in the importance of early education and how disparities in its quality could influence life's trajectory.

In college Bobby apparently liked to party a little too much, and when Vernon Jarrett received his son's poor grades, he pulled up to the Nashville campus of his son's school, Fisk University, in a stretch limousine. "Pack up and get in the car," he said to his son.

"Where are we going?" Bobby asked.

"Home to Chicago. Right now. The party's over."

Bobby straightened up, graduating from Chicago's Roosevelt University and then going on to med school at the University of Illinois. He still liked to party, but his passion for medicine motivated him to be more serious about his studies. We reconnected just as he was starting a surgical residency at Mt. Sinai Hospital on the West Side of Chicago, and I liked the fact that he was a doctor like my dad.

When men say they'll call, they usually mean they'll call sometime before they die, while women assume they mean they'll call within the next day or two. I certainly did, and I'd almost given up on hearing from Bobby when he finally called about a week later to invite me on our first date: dinner at Uncle Earl's home. Not exactly romantic, but I would have said yes to any offer. Bobby and Uncle Earl seemed to pick up their debate from the other day, and it continued late into the night. Watching them going at it reminded me of the spirited conversations around my parents' dinner table. Having spent so much of my life enjoying time with Pudden, I was also attracted to the fact that Bobby could have so much fun with one of her contemporaries.

Even though Bobby's work schedule was brutal—twelve-hour shifts and being on call all night every third night—we started seeing more of each other. Bobby was outgoing, a little irreverent, smart, funny, and always the center of attention in any room he was in. Like my father, Bobby was very well read, and loved to discuss books of all topics, from black history to Greek philosophy. His book collection was rivaled only by his record collection. He had eclectic taste from classical music to jazz, and, other than holing up with a book, Bobby's favorite activity was attending the opera. Although I didn't care for the opera, my parents enjoyed it as well. A man who felt so familiar, who was outgoing, and who enjoyed the simple pleasures of being with family was just what I wanted. Bobby seemed perfect.

As 1982 gave way to 1983, Bobby and I planned to spend our first New Year's Eve together. It was a holiday I usually detested because of the unrealistic hype and the large, impersonal parties. But this year, with Bobby, the occasion finally made sense. Instead of standing around awkwardly at midnight without a date at some big, overblown party, we had an intimate dinner with my cousin Jeff and his wife, Lynn, and two other couples who were close friends. As we laughed and talked over good food and champagne, I thought, *This is how New Year's Eve is supposed to be spent—with people you truly love.*

That night I made it my New Year's resolution that we would be married before the next new year came around. Bobby not only seemed right for me but also fit nicely into my plan of becoming a successful lawyer, falling in love, getting married, and having a baby, all by age thirty.

Two weeks later, after dinner at my parents' home, while I was driving Bobby home down South Lake Shore Drive, without much context or romance, he nonchalantly proposed, and I said yes.

B y the time my dad and I arrived at the church on my wedding day, September 3, 1983, I was very nervous. Unlike Bobby, my shyness and aversion to being the center of any group's attention had not faded through the years. In the church basement, while we waited for the ceremony to begin, one of my bridesmaids, Judi Brown, started reeling off one dirty joke after another, and, as embarrassing as it was (because my dad was right there), it lightened the mood and helped me relax.

After my seven bridesmaids (don't ask) walked down the aisle, just as I was set to follow them, I hesitated for a moment. My dad patted my arm and said, "Just remember, everyone here loves you. Look directly at them as you walk. You'll be fine." And he was right. I still remember the expression on the face of Pudden's good friend, whom we called Mama

Hazel. Her face lit up when I caught her eye, she winked and I began to breathe normally.

Then came the vows. I *always* cry at weddings, even at weddings in movies. But standing there at the altar with Bobby that day, even though I'd been scared I was going to break down and ruin my makeup, I didn't. I didn't shed a single tear, never even felt the urge to fight them back. Nothing.

It was probably some kind of sign or red flag, but I didn't have time to dwell on it, as I was then whisked away to our wedding reception: four hundred people in my parents' backyard; a two-hour receiving line; ninety-degree heat in the long-sleeve satin dress with precious, tiny buttons down the back that my mother had been married in before me, and her sister before her.

In the beginning of our courtship and through most of our engagement, Bobby had been all charm, as we so often surrounded ourselves with friends and family. But as we spent more time alone together, the charm subsided. He was never angry or mean, just aloof, distant. His excuse was that he was always tired, which was plausible given his demanding schedule, so I was never terribly concerned, but clearly it had registered.

We honeymooned in St. Croix, where Bobby's godmother gave us two weeks' use of her home as a wedding present. On our first night, Bobby jumped into the swimming pool without remembering to take out his contact lenses. Out they popped, and we spent the next two days with me driving Bobby around the island looking for an optician who could replace them. Not exactly a seductive start.

Then came the sunset. I love sunsets, always have and still do. Back then I thought there could be nothing more romantic than watching the sun set over the ocean with my one true love. On our third day in St. Croix, when Bobby could see again, we set off for a drive to the west side of the island, arriving just in time to watch the bright-yellow sun drop into the ocean. As we walked along the water's edge, Bobby walked about ten feet out into the water to look down at a school of bright, translucent fish swimming all around. He called out for me to come look, and then, just as the sun melted into the horizon, he shifted places and blocked my view of it. And my only thought was *If I could just move him out of the way* . . .

Again, like my tear-free vows, not a good sign. If only I'd been paying attention during our courtship to who Bobby really was instead of who I hoped he would be. But I was too determined to make my fanciful notion of the perfect marriage come true. After the honeymoon, I threw myself into trying to be the perfect wife, reenacting the daily rituals of the happiest marriage I knew: my parents'.

Although they enjoyed their big circle of family and friends, my parents spent almost all their time together. They didn't even like to be in separate rooms. My mother loved to watch her favorite chefs, Julia Child and Jacques Pepin, on cooking shows. My father did not. Yet he sat in his favorite chair and suffered through countless hours of her shows just to be by her side. And they never went to bed angry. That was a household rule: no one was allowed to go to bed without resolving an argument, sealed with a kiss, no matter how angry you were. It wasn't such a hard rule for my parents to follow, since they never really fought; even today, the argument about the imaginary lottery winnings is the only one I can remember.

And if my parents were my model for a successful marriage, my model for a successful husband was my dad. There was so much to admire about him. I got a kick out of the fact that he always wore bow ties long before they were in fashion, and I was so proud when he would rush to the hospital when someone in our large extended family had any emergency, of which there were many over the years.

My father was very romantic, and demonstratively so. Every Valentine's Day he gave my mom the mushiest card he could find, which he would then read out loud to us. He enjoyed the theater of a dramatic delivery with deep emotion and making everyone laugh, despite my mom's standard less-than-enthusiastic reactions. My mom, who is pretty reserved and pretends to be uncomfortable with overt displays of affection, would always shrug him off, saying, "Oh, Jim. Those cards are such a waste of money." But secretly she loved that *he* loved doing it. Their love was an unselfish love. For a long time I took it for granted that the way my dad treated my mom and me was how all men who professed love would behave. When they didn't, I was not only surprised but very, very disappointed.

After working all day, I would rush home to our duplex on Cornell Avenue and cook dinner, just as my mom had always done. But unlike my dad, who was home like clockwork every night before six, Bobby had an erratic schedule, and he never called to say when he was going to be late. I often gave up waiting for him and ate dinner alone.

On the evenings when he did come home, Bobby began a nightly ritual of gobbling down his home-cooked meal and then heading down to the basement. He would spend the entire evening down there, surrounded by his books and records. He'd put on a headset, lean back on the couch, and either read or close his eyes and listen to music, slowly making his way through a bottle of wine.

We hadn't lived together before the wedding and had only dated for about a year, so I wasn't sure if this behavior was just a temporary result of the stresses of his residency, or if this was actually the man I had married. The longer it persisted, the more upset I became; I felt like his behavior was a rejection of me. Blocking me out to the point of wearing headphones was not passive-aggressive but *aggressive*.

We argued about it, a lot. Or, rather, I argued a lot. Bobby wasn't really a fighter. He preferred to evade.

The harder I pushed, the more he withdrew. The mistake I made in trying to imitate my parents was that I defined myself as an "us," not recognizing that my parents were also each whole as individuals. I expected Bobby to make me whole, rather than being my own person and giving us space to come together.

"You work so much," I'd say. "You're never here, and when you are here, you're not really here. At least not for me."

"I don't know what you mean."

"Come on, Bobby. Drinking wine by yourself all night while I'm upstairs alone? That just doesn't seem normal to me. What's going on?"

"I'm tired. I'm working so hard. I just need to unwind. This is how I unwind."

Yet whenever we went out to a party or someone's home for dinner, Bobby was his normal life-of-the-party self, which only served to confuse me more and make me feel inadequate. "You're fake!" I accused him. "You're not the person you pretend to be with everyone else."

Fighting didn't help, and I tried everything else. I tried giving him his space, in the hope that it was a phase and he'd come around. I'd putter around the house, trying to find little chores to occupy me, like doing laundry or paying the bills, waiting for him to come to me. No luck. I tried planning date nights in the hope of coaxing out his old, gregarious self. That didn't work either.

Then: a last-ditch effort. One of my cousins had given me sexy lingerie during my bridal shower. It was very low cut in the front and plunged down to, shall we say, my lower back in the rear. I slid into it and went downstairs to Bobby's cave. Then I leaned against the door frame seductively, in some ridiculous pose I'd probably seen in a movie, and asked him if he was coming to bed. He looked up at me with a totally blank expression. I might as well have been wearing a burlap sack. I felt humiliated.

And still no luck.

I went back upstairs, watched some TV, read a little, and then finally fell asleep before Bobby came up from his lair.

I used to beat myself up. How could I be the product of such a close, strong marriage, only to find my own faltering after less than six months? But comparing my situation to my parents' only made me feel worse. At the time, I was too absorbed in my own struggles to figure out why Bobby behaved the way he did. Looking back, I think he too married the person who felt comfortable; he knew I was the kind of woman who would make his worried parents think he had settled down. But I also think he thought if he opened up and I really got to know him, I would be disappointed, as his parents too often had been.

Although I worried about my marriage to Bobby constantly, I kept it mostly to myself. Pudden had cautioned me that one should never speak poorly of one's spouse, because though I might forgive his transgressions, those who loved me might not. So other than confiding in Lynn and my bridesmaid Judi, who'd been divorced several years earlier, I stayed quiet.

Then, late one summer night, Bobby didn't come home, and he wasn't scheduled to be on call. In a panic, I called my cousin Jeff, who came right over. I didn't think Bobby was seeing someone else. I thought he was unconscious in a local hospital or someplace worse. When he finally did come home around ten the next morning, Bobby said he'd had too much to drink and, not wanting to drive home, had fallen asleep in his car in a parking lot. He vowed to stop drinking. "I'm going to stay on the straight and narrow," he said, "because I love you dearly."

I wanted to believe him, really I did. My whole life when I had worked twice as hard as others, I had achieved my goals. So despite mounting evidence to the contrary, I believed that I could work harder and fix my marriage through sheer force of will—and by having a baby.

Chapter 4

It's a Girl!

Conventional wisdom says children never improve shaky relationships. I thought I knew better. I was certain that becoming a family would bring us closer and motivate Bobby to honor his pledge. Plus, at age twenty-eight, I was eager to have a child. Time was ticking away, both on my Ten-Year Plan and on my biological clock.

The first month Bobby and I began trying, I became pregnant and I was elated. Two weeks to the day after my period was late, it was Valentine's Day. I squeezed in a doctor's appointment so that she could confirm what I already suspected. That night I gave Bobby a valentine with a note that read, "We're going to go from two to three." He reread the note a couple of times before tearing up with joy.

That night, we shared the news with his parents and mine, which, like everything else during my first month of pregnancy, was a thrill. Bobby was sober and more attentive to me. But he couldn't keep it up. In less than two months, he was back to his erratic, inattentive self.

When I was six months pregnant, we decided to take a vacation to Egypt, a two-week cruise along the Nile River. We figured it was the last time we'd have an adventurous trip for a long while. Bobby had never traveled much, and I was looking forward to sharing with him a familiar and special place. On our first morning, at a hotel outside of Cairo, I woke up at 6 a.m. to find him gone. I looked for him all around the hotel, but he wasn't there. The hotel was across the street from the Great Pyramid and Sphinx of Giza, so I wandered across the street and walked up the steep hill to the enormous ancient monuments, and there he was, watching the sunrise, alone.

"How could you leave me without telling me you were going?" I asked.

"I didn't want to wake you," he shrugged, showing no appreciation for how it might feel to wake up pregnant and alone. For the rest of the trip, it was the same. Despite my pleas, he was always "going off exploring for a few hours" that turned out to be sometimes late into the night, leaving me to worry on the cruise ship, which was really more of a rickety boat, with engine fumes that made me queasy.

Not long after we returned home, I had a serious scare. I started bleeding and it wouldn't stop. My OB-GYN, Dr. Jimmy Jones, a close friend of my parents, prescribed a weekend of bed rest. I spent the next three days in bed feeling a terrible mix of guilt for taking such a strenuous trip, fierce protectiveness, and desperate powerlessness. Every time I went to the bathroom, I hoped the bleeding had stopped and that my baby was OK.

By the morning of day four I had stopped bleeding, and thankfully there were no other frightening episodes for the rest of my pregnancy. But that scare gave me a small preview of the love I was about to feel. Throughout my pregnancy, the only way I avoided morning sickness was by eating five square meals a day, every day. When the scale tipped to one hundred ninety pounds, I refused to look at it anymore. I was *done*. I made it well past full term, and when I was ten days past due, I'd finally had enough.

I packed my bags and went to see Dr. Jones. He suggested we give it "another couple days."

"No, no," I said. "I'll meet you at the hospital. I'm not going home without a baby."

"You really want Pitocin?" he asked, referring to the drug used to induce labor. "It's not very pleasant."

"It can't be any more unpleasant than carrying around eighty extra pounds on my hundred-and-ten-pound frame."

I was admitted to the University of Chicago Medical Center and induced at 11 a.m., whereupon I quickly learned that "not very pleasant" was an astonishing understatement. My labor was excruciating, and it went on and on and on. My mom and Bobby were there, but my dad had left town the day before to honor a commitment at a conference, so he kept calling my mom every half hour to check on my status. As the day went on, my father grew worried enough to call the chairman of the OB-GYN department and ask him to check on me. He did, and promptly told my mother he thought I might need a cesarean.

Nobody told me, because I had made my feelings on the subject clear. Somehow, I'd adopted a ridiculous notion that my femininity was tied to natural childbirth; I hadn't even attended the Lamaze class where C-sections were covered. I was determined to give birth naturally, no matter what. In the late afternoon an anesthesiologist came by to see if I wanted an epidural to blunt some of the pain. Before I could answer, Bobby said, "We aren't having any pain medicine." To which I responded, "*We* are not having a baby. I am." I said yes.

Then, around 10 p.m., a first-year resident came in and told me, without much bedside manner, that the baby's heart rate was going down and she needed my consent to attach an internal monitor to my baby's head, something else I had hoped to avoid. Nothing was going according to plan.

Another three hours went by. Finally the same resident returned, and in a very gentle tone said, "Your baby's in distress. We need to take her."

I felt I was completely losing control of the situation. Just then Dr. Jones appeared. I'd wondered where he had been. Little did I know, he had been taking a nap to rest up for what he knew was going to be an inevitable surgery. By that point, my stubborn desire to stay in control of my own natural labor was colliding with my heartrending concern for my unborn child's well-being.

"Take her," I said. "Where do I sign?"

They did an emergency C-section and at 1:58 a.m. on October 29, 1985, and in the single most extraordinary moment of my life, the doctors laid my newborn, brown-skinned baby on my chest and, as my arms reflexively folded around her, he announced, "It's a girl." I'd wanted a girl desperately, and I was granted my wish—a healthy, beautiful baby girl. Eight pounds, eleven ounces. We named her Laura, after both my grandmother and Bobby's.

It was a glorious celebration. I had twenty-one visitors the first day, and I wound up staying in the hospital for one whole week. (Those were the days!) I loved pushing that call button: "Ginger ale, please," "Please bring me my baby," and "Take her away, please." The Demerol shots they gave me for the pain that first day made me euphoric. At times I could barely focus, though I was attentive enough to catch one error on Laura's birth certificate. Having looked only at me, the administrator had mistakenly written that her race was white—just as my mother's birth certificate had.

At the end of my stay, I pleaded with Dr. Jones for one more day. I was petrified of leaving. Were they really going to give us this tiny human to take home by ourselves, when we had no idea what we were doing? I'd never even changed a diaper before. As Bobby and I struggled to put Laura into her car seat properly, I turned to him and said, "They shouldn't let us have her. This is malpractice."

For the next three months I took care of Laura by myself, with regular assists from my parents and my grandmother. Then, in the last month of my four-month leave, after interviewing one woman who told me Laura had been reincarnated and another who snatched Laura from me and kissed her on the mouth, I hired Alma Brown to be Laura's caregiver. I knew the first time I heard her calm, friendly voice on the phone that she would be perfect. The sleepless days and nights, the constant new discoveries about looking after this tiny creature, the struggle breast-feeding (Would Laura starve if I didn't produce enough milk?), and the sleep deprivation—it was all hard. At least, I thought it was hard. Then, at the end of four and a half months, I went back to work, and that's when I finally learned what the meaning of "hard" really was.

The year before Laura was born I'd switched to a new, more prestigious firm, Sonnenschein, Carlin, Nath & Rosenthal. It had the best real estate practice in the city, and I felt by going there I was taking the next great step in a family tradition started by my famous real estate developer grandfather and my pioneering architect great-grandfather.

But the allure of real estate law quickly evaporated as I was consumed with drafting loan documents for the construction of office buildings, shopping centers, and hotels. *Yawn* (again). I spent endless days negotiating with developers over casualty clauses in insurance and force majeure language. I couldn't believe I had gone through the ordeal of law school for a practice as tedious and boring as this. I found myself much more interested in looking over the architectural designs and the financing structures that made these deals possible rather than drafting the loan documents I was supposed to be working on. Not surprisingly, I was fairly unimpressive at my job.

I had been dreading my first day back at work, and it was agony, mentally and physically. During a long meeting I wanted so badly to excuse myself to pump my breasts, but I was trying to show everyone that all was back to normal. I did my best to ignore the pain and discomfort. Then I looked down and saw the big wet spots of leaking milk on my blouse. Like countless other working mothers, I wondered, *What am I doing? Why did I leave that precious angel at home? To be here? Doing this?*

The 1980s, for all the badass "we can have it all" slogans, were not an easy time to be a woman in the workplace. My firm had a four-month paid maternity leave policy, due in no small part to two female partners with children who had advocated for the change. They also let me take an extra two weeks without pay. By the standards of the era, that was considered very generous; many firms had no set maternity leave beyond sick-day policies. Needless to say, there was no paternity leave at all for men. Only 25 percent of my classmates in law school were women. The number who went on to be associates at major firms was even lower, and the number who made partner, lower still. It was a boys' club, and the other women and I were left to try mightily to fit in, pretending to ourselves, and one another, that we could be just like "one of the guys."

At holiday parties that I attended given by law firms around the city, I swallowed hard and tried to look the other way when women were harassed, and I ducked out early to avoid falling prey myself. When I was pregnant, I tried to pretend that I wasn't. One late night, eight and a half months along and in full beached-whale mode, I was working with several lawyers to close a deal that stretched past one in the morning. I kept excusing myself from the conference room to "go to the Xerox machine" or "go back to my office to pick up some more documents" or "go buy a snack from the vending machine." What I was really doing was going to pee. But why couldn't I just say that? Because I was so busy trying to act like nothing was going on with my body below my head.

As soon as I became a working mother, my focus shifted. No longer just a hardworking lawyer but a superhuman earth mother as well. After working all day and well into the evening, I stayed up to all hours making homemade baby food. It was impossible to keep all of the balls in the air, and I had more than most working moms going in my favor. Very supportive parents nearby. A professional degree. I could afford the highest-quality child care. Yet I was still holding on by my fingertips. I couldn't imagine how much harder it must be for poor and working-class families trying to both provide and be good parents.

The only advantage I didn't have was an equal partner in parenting at home. There were times when Bobby tried to lend a hand, but watching him change a diaper, or warm up a bottle, exasperated me so much that I would just do it myself. I have to admit: I took a certain pleasure in being better than him at taking care of Laura. But of course that was totally self-defeating, as it increased my workload while lessening Bobby's responsibilities, and his confidence. A perverse sense of pride drove me to want to do everything myself.

Meanwhile, back at the office, being "one of the guys" meant pretending that the demands of motherhood simply didn't exist so I could convince everyone that I was as dedicated and undistracted as the men around me. When I had to take Laura to the pediatrician, instead of being up front about it, I'd evasively say I had to be "out of the office for a while." I thought that success meant competing with men on an uneven playing field while continuing to excel in the traditional roles of a wife and mother. I was setting impossibly high standards for myself, and looking back now, it shouldn't have been surprising that I was constantly falling short and disappointed with myself.

Exhausted and aching for my baby, I used to sit at my desk with a file in my hand, saying to myself, "You have to *focus!*" But I couldn't bring myself to speak up. I couldn't bring myself to go to the partners, even those who were women, and point out all the ways the politics of the boys' club were unfair. And my pride would not let me confide in anyone, even to my close friends, most of whom were professional women themselves, and I now suspect they were equally reluctant to confide in me. My silence stemmed mostly from my shame in feeling alone—as though I were the *only* overwhelmed working mother. I told myself that if I was just smarter, more organized, and more efficient, if I just tried harder and slept less, perhaps it all wouldn't be so hard.

As women of my generation fought to gain equity in the workplace, we made an unspoken pact to pretend, even to one another, that we had it all under control. We didn't. We couldn't possibly.

Instead of improving after Laura was born, my marriage only deteriorated further. I hadn't anticipated how little patience I would have for trying to take care of Bobby once I had an actual baby. My entire orientation pivoted away from him and toward Laura. I completely lost interest in working on our marriage. In the evenings I went to my corner of our tiny apartment with Laura, and he went to his, alone. I didn't see myself getting divorced, so I just assumed this was my new depressing status quo. It was the life I had chosen and the life with which I was stuck. Then, on the third Friday of March, only a month after I'd returned to work, Bobby called me with startling news.

A few months earlier, Bobby had been cut from his surgery residency and had applied for the match, where residents and hospitals rank each other and then hopefully are paired up. Bobby had ranked surgical gynecology programs in Chicago, but he hadn't matched anywhere; none of the area hospitals had selected him. My father had offered to find him a place at a Chicago pathology department, but Bobby didn't want to do that. He only wanted surgery. After hearing the news I told him I would rush right home so we could talk. When I arrived, he told me, "The only place I could find a residency in surgery is Pontiac, Michigan." When I said we'd have to discuss it, he confessed that he'd already accepted the position. He said he was afraid he would lose it, but I'm sure he also feared that I would try to talk him out of accepting it.

I was furious. A decision to move out of state so soon after having a child should have been made together. He went to his corner and I to mine, and that was it. Bobby didn't ask me to come with him, and I didn't offer. My moving didn't make practical sense on any level. I made twice as much money as he did. Moving would also mean starting all over, taking the Michigan bar, and finding a new job. Not to mention losing the support structure of my family and Mrs. Brown, upon whom I relied to help me take care of Laura during my ten-hour workdays. I just couldn't believe that Laura and I weren't enough to keep him in Chicago, but I wasn't about to ask him not to go, because I didn't want him to resent me for standing in the way of his professional dreams.

The Michigan residency started in four months, and the closer it came to the time of his departure, the more terrified I was about what it would mean for me and for us. Living alone in Chicago as a single mom certainly was not what I had imagined when I tried to save our marriage by having a child. Then, as we expected, one early July morning, Bobby packed his belongings, kissed Laura good-bye while she slept in her crib, and walked out the front door. I had no idea how I was going to manage a baby by myself or what was in store for me next, because none of this was part of my Ten-Year Plan.

Looking back on those years when I was a young working mom, I wish I hadn't defined success as achieving the mighty juggle with flawless perfection. I wish I had not felt it would make me appear weak or vulnerable to admit to myself, as well as more openly to others, when I was struggling and needed help. I wish I'd known that Laura would have been just fine with baby food from a jar. I wish that I had embraced the thrill of the zig and zag rather than crave straight lines. I wish I had understood that hard work doesn't always prevent failures, and that my failures do not define me. In fact, missteps often teach valuable lessons, and provide the resilience to bounce back stronger.

Chapter 5

The Quiet Voice

B y the time I turned thirty, my marriage was on life support. Bobby had been in Michigan for over a year. It was hard in the beginning, but I slowly began to realize how my life had actually improved with him out of the picture. I was relieved to no longer be juggling his wants and needs with those of my daily life. I started to appreciate how lonely I'd been when he was there-but-not-there, coming home late and hiding behind his headphones and records in the basement. It was a loneliness far more painful than I had ever experienced when I was single.

Once he left, we didn't communicate or see each other much. He was busy, and I was busy—at least that was the excuse we both used to avoid each other. I can count on one hand the number of times he came home during that first year, and I was no more eager to visit him in Michigan. I went only twice. I began to dread our visits.

For my thirtieth birthday, Bobby used his residency schedule as an excuse not to come home. Since I didn't want to go out and leave Laura with a sitter, and as I was in no mood to celebrate, I invited three of my close childhood girlfriends to come over and to spend the evening with me. In lieu of showing up, Bobby had sent an arrangement of bright, primary-color carnations in the shape of a small triangular tree. Stunningly ugly. I plopped it in the middle of the dining room table, and the four of us just sat there, inhaling my favorite cheesecake and downing homemade daiquiris, staring at the floral monstrosity. At first no one wanted to comment, but after a few drinks I couldn't hold back. "What *is* the message he is sending me with flowers that look like that?" Nobody answered, but we all knew. Finally, a little after 8 p.m., I called it. "Just go home," I said. "Party's over. I'm going to bed." They were relieved. So was I.

My daughter once said to me that my marriage was the best mistake I ever made. I know what she meant, but I would put it differently: in my wrong-headed, last ditch attempt to save my marriage, the very best decision I ever made was having my daughter. The moment Laura came into this world, she made me want to be a stronger person. She made me realize I *had* to be a stronger person. I'd been caught up in an immature daydream, and marrying Bobby had only given me a false sense of fulfillment and security. When he left for Michigan, I was a new mom, terrified and miserable, and with him gone I feared life would only get worse. Instead, the opposite happened. Every day without Bobby there, I became more self-assured, more confident. For the first time, I enjoyed being on my own, pouring all my love and attention into this little person who was completely reliant on me. I'd look down at Laura, asleep in my arms, and I'd say to myself, "This little girl is counting on me to take care of her, so I'd better stop waiting on somebody else to take care of me."

Knowing that my daughter was depending on me was enough to propel me out of bed, trudge downtown, and stick it out at work. But I knew I couldn't last at that law firm much longer. All I was doing was helping wealthy clients mitigate risk so they could become even wealthier. It left me feeling empty, without purpose. Being an associate at a high-powered corporate firm, I felt constant, enormous pressure to produce clients, yet I didn't really have any prospects, and I was utterly uninterested in cultivating any. A partner with whom I regularly worked gave me the ultimate backhanded compliment one day. "Valerie," he said, "you'd make a much better partner than you do an associate." I understood what he meant: I wasn't good at my job. But I didn't need him to tell me that. I knew it already. Early on, I thought the sacrifices would be worth it when I became a partner. But by my sixth year out of law school I had realized that the life of the partners didn't seem much better either.

On the seventy-ninth floor of the Sears Tower, I had the world literally at my feet, but I was at my lowest ebb. My career had hit a wall, and my marriage was falling apart. Except for Laura, my Ten-Year Plan felt like a ten-year disaster. I used to close my office door and spend hours lost in my own thoughts, often in tears, staring east out over the calming, peaceful waters of Lake Michigan. I wished they could transport me someplace, anyplace, else. This simply could not be my life. I wanted and expected so much more. But I knew that just looking out over the water wasn't going to take me anywhere. What I didn't realize at the time, and what I would come to understand only with the help of a good friend, was that the path I needed to take was right there in front of me, outside my office window. All I had to do was shift my gaze a few blocks northeast, to city hall.

When Harold Washington was elected Chicago's first black mayor in 1983, it sent a shock wave through the entire city. He was a beloved figure among the black, Latino, and liberal lakefront constituencies. He had a big, roaring laugh, a twinkle in his eye, and a personality so warm and charismatic that even people who didn't want to like him couldn't help but be charmed. He was a captivating speaker, too, always dropping four- and five-syllable words in new and creative ways. Still, no one thought he would actually win. That was true for black voters and white voters, for political insiders and everyday folks as well. Chicago, with its history, we all believed, was not ready for a black mayor. But to everyone's surprise, Washington wound up winning the three-way Democratic primary after the other two candidates—then Mayor Jane Byrne and Richard M. Daley, son of the late Mayor Richard J. Daley—split the white vote.

The racism of Washington's opponents rose to the surface quickly, however, when he faced Republican Bernard Epton in the general election. People circulated pamphlets with pictures of chicken bones and watermelons. The Republican candidate's campaign slogan was "Before it's too late." One of the ugliest moments came when Washington went to stump with Vice President Walter Mondale at a Catholic church in the city's white northwest side. He was met by an angry mob shouting, "Blacks go home!" and the church's door had been defaced with the spray-painted words "Nigger die."

But Chicago turned out to be more Democratic than it was racist, and on April 12, 1983, Washington was elected mayor. Walking the four blocks to my office the next morning, wearing my "Harold for Mayor" button on my jacket, I felt an enormous sense of pride—not just because he was black but also because he was both the underdog and a reformer whose message of inclusion and opportunity for all resonated profoundly with me. But even in the short walk I could see a deep divide in the reactions my button provoked. All the black people nodded and smiled and winked. Some of the white folks did, too, but many just looked away. When I arrived at my law firm, people were more stunned than celebratory. Nobody said a word about it. I lived on the South Side, and nearly everybody else in my office lived to the north, so I used to joke that when we left work, I turned right and they turned left. That statement never felt more true than on that morning.

Once he was in office, however, Harold Washington's energy and enthusiasm for a progressive agenda proved to be contagious. He loved to stop to chat and laugh with anyone and everyone—even the aldermen actively trying to thwart his agenda. He would go on to prove in Chicago, just like black mayors were in Los Angeles, Atlanta, Detroit, and Philadelphia, that black politicians are capable of being leaders for all citizens, regardless of color. Which is why he won reelection by a solid margin four years later, in 1987.

I had volunteered on his campaign, knocking on doors on Election Day to turn out the vote. I was spellbound during his second inaugural speech, which extolled the power of the city's diversity. "Chicago," he said, "has brought together black and white, Asian and Hispanic, male and female, the young, the old, the disabled, gays and lesbians, Muslims, Christians and Jews, business leaders and neighborhood activists, bankers and trade unionists—all have come together to mix and contend, to argue and to reason, to confront our problems and not merely to contain them. We didn't come together out of love for one another. Where that is lacking, that will follow. A civil society, a civilization, a city that works, requires simply that we behave well toward each other." Those words certainly still ring true to me today.

Mayor Washington had big ideals and a grand vision of humanity, a vision that I wouldn't see realized on a much larger scale until twenty-five years later, on election night in 2008, when people of all kinds and all races gathered in Grant Park to celebrate Barack Obama's victory. As President Obama himself has often said, "Had there not been a Mayor Washington, there might not have been a President Obama."

When Washington was first elected, several of Chicago's top black lawyers left private practice to work for his administration. I knew that because I knew all of them. Then, as now, there weren't many black lawyers at large corporate firms in Chicago, and we banded together just like the black kids sitting together in the cafeteria, at the Lab Schools, or in the Ujamaa dorm at Stanford. It was a way to commiserate about our shared dilemmas. It was also a network for younger associates like me to reach out to more experienced lawyers for advice and support.

Elvin Charity was one of those lawyers for me. A graduate of Yale College and Harvard Law, Elvin had already made partner at the firm of Hopkins & Sutter, and he'd taken a two-year leave of absence to serve as chief assistant corporation counsel for real estate in Mayor Washington's first administration. My uncle Lester had introduced me to Elvin and his wife, Roxanne, when they first moved to Chicago in 1981. He had become a close friend, a great mentor, and a brilliant attorney. (Elvin also had an eye for talent: a few years later, in 1989, he hired Harvard Law student Barack Obama as a summer associate.) I desperately needed advice, so I invited Elvin to lunch in the restaurant in the lobby of the Sears Tower. Whispering out of earshot of any collegues from my firm who might have been nearby, I said, "I can't figure out what to do. I'm already on my second law firm, and I can't just keep switching from one to another. That's not going to solve my problem."

"What about joining the Harold Washington administration and practicing law there?" he said.

Elvin's two-year leave from Hopkins & Sutter was winding up, and he was leaving the administration himself. But, he said, it was an exciting time in city hall. Unlike in his first term, Washington now controlled a majority on the city council, and he finally had the power to make some of his progressive initiatives happen. I told Elvin I wasn't sure. It wasn't a path I'd ever considered for myself.

Working in local government would be a major pivot in my Ten-Year Plan. But I drew courage from my dad, whose own circuitous path through Iran and Great Britain to his dream job in Chicago always demonstrated to me the importance of being flexible and willing to pivot.

When I was growing up, and even after I moved back to the city, I didn't know much about how city government worked. I didn't know my alderman's name, let alone the size and scope of the city's budget, or how the garbage got picked up, or the labor contracts and the negotiations that went on to make that happen. What I did know was that if it snowed and the mayor did not make sure it was picked up in all parts of the city, he could lose his election. That is what happened to Mayor Bilandic in 1979 when Chicago had one of its worst snowstorms and the mayor directed the crews to prioritize cleaning the streets on the North Side but not the South Side. The swift reaction was to elect Jane Byrne mayor. I was pretty clueless about everything else. My first and only involvement had come two years earlier when a partner at my firm had nominated me to participate in a Leadership Greater Chicago program, which opened my eyes for the first time to the workings of city government and the broader civic life of our city. The blinders that had kept me focused on one straight career path began to fade away. In the program I had met young leaders from around the city, all engaged in different but seemingly rewarding careers. Elvin insisted. "You should do it," he said. "In city hall you'll go to work every day feeling a part of the common purpose you felt on Election Day. You'll belong to a movement larger and more important than yourself. You'll never regret it, I promise you. Worse comes to worst, you can always go back to a law firm."

And so, against the advice of many, including my parents, who saw a job in city hall as a step down from my corporate one, I decided to explore a move into the public sector. It took a big leap of faith so I began with someone I trusted. I reached out to a childhood friend, Allison Davis, who arranged for me to meet his former partner, Judd Miner. In 1971, the two of them had founded Davis, Miner, Barnhill & Galland—a boutique civil rights law firm with two major claims to fame: it argued a number of important civil rights cases before the U.S. Supreme Court and hired Barack Obama as a young lawyer in 1993. Judd, like Elvin Charity, had left his firm to join the administration as corporation counsel for the city. I interviewed with Judd, and he then passed me on to his deputy, David Narefsky. In August of 1987, David offered me a job working for him in the counsel's office in city hall as the director of collateral land.

It was an awkward, manufactured title, but what it meant was that I had the legal responsibility for managing the redevelopment of large tracts of vacant, city-owned land, specifically around O'Hare International Airport. The mayor wanted it to become a revenue-generating commercial property compatible with the airport. The work was the opposite of sexy. When I described it to my friends, their eyes would glaze over. The pay was less, *much* less, and I traded in my private seventy-ninth-floor office with an unobstructed view of Lake Michigan for a fifth-floor cubicle with a dirty window looking out on an alley. After giving me a ride to city hall on a sticky August morning for my first day of work, my mom said, "After all that college and law school tuition, I can't believe I'm dropping you off at this place."

I didn't care what anyone else thought. From day one, I loved it, and

I knew this was where I belonged. And the timing was perfect. Elvin had been right about the sea change in the city council, which now had a majority of the aldermen supporting the mayor's agenda to make the city fairer and inclusive, including creating city contracts and job opportunities for people of color and women. Under previous administrations, the government's focus had been predominantly on the city's central business district. Mayor Washington wanted to also invest resources in the neighborhoods, and the budget he proposed reflected his priorities: investments in public schools, job-creation and training programs, the park system, and neighborhood infrastructure.

I wasn't the only former corporate lawyer who'd come to work for Mayor Washington and be a part of the change he promised. Judd and his predecessor, Jim Montgomery, who later practiced with Johnnie Cochran, had recruited lawyers from the highest-caliber law firms to bring new skills to help implement the mayor's progressive agenda. I felt an instant kinship not just with the other lawyers but with all the men and women working at city hall. I walked into the office every day giddy with excitement. The people I'd spent years reading about in the newspaper, such as the aldermen and the mayor's top deputies—whenever I passed them in the hall, it felt like a celebrity sighting. The first time I was in a meeting chaired by the mayor's deputy chief of staff, all I could think was: *I can't believe I'm in a meeting with Brenda Gaines!* That was doubly true for Mayor Washington himself. I always took every opportunity I could to hear him speak or just to be in his presence—except for once, and I'll always regret it.

Late in November of 1987, two nights before Thanksgiving, I was leaving work late, around eight o'clock, anxious as always to get home to Laura. I'd been at city hall for just three months at that point. As I walked out of the law department, I could hear Mayor Washington's booming voice coming from his office suite down the hall. It had a cavernous front lobby where receptions were often held, and the mayor was giving a speech to one of the many constituent groups he hosted there several nights a month.

Hearing his voice, I thought, *I should stay and listen.* But then I thought better of it. *I'm so tired, and I miss Laura. I can hear him anytime.* And I left. The very next morning, shortly after 11 a.m., I was working at my desk when one of the assistants ran in and said, "The mayor has collapsed!" Her brother, a policeman stationed on the first floor, had called to tell her that and that emergency responders were trying to resuscitate him. We all rushed out to the lobby of the law department, where a glass door separated us from the hallway right next to the mayor's private office. After several minutes, his door swung open, and there he was, lying on a gurney, his face a deep purple, as the swift-moving EMTs rushed him out of sight. But it was too late. At 1:36 p.m. that afternoon Mayor Washington was pronounced dead of a massive heart attack.

Mayor Washington's tragic death pulled the city apart in profound ways. There was grief and anger, and in the inevitable political power struggle that followed, the city's racist politics crept back into play. After a protracted and divisive city council meeting that lasted until 4 a.m., the aldermen elected fellow Alderman Eugene Sawyer Jr. mayor. Everyone who'd come to city hall to join Mayor Washington was worried that his progressive agenda would erode under Sawyer's old-school politics. The fact that he was a consensus choice made many of us worry about the expectations of the white aldermen who'd supported him. But in the end, Judd Miner, and my primary client, Lucille Dobbins, assistant to the mayor for finance and administration, elected to stay. So I did, too.

During my time at city hall, Lucille became my first professional role model of a powerful, confident black woman. Married to a kind and supportive man, fiercely devoted to her teenage daughter, Lucille was still an indefatigable workaholic. She worked *all the time.* She was tough as nails but took very good care of those she thought deserved her support. I was lucky enough to have her take me under her wing.

Prior to her current position, Lucille had been deputy commissioner in the Department of Planning, where she oversaw the financial planning of the redevelopment of the North and South Loop. Now, from the mayor's office, she handled oversight of all city-financed developments, including my project at O'Hare. With the help of Elvin Charity as outside counsel, Lucille and I began an open process for packaging the land by the airport and putting it out to bid for private developers. Once that project was under way, Lucille began to bring me into other municipal finance and development initiatives outside the original scope of my job.

In large-scale, city-backed real estate developments, financing structures are always extremely complicated, because layers of government subsidies are required in order to make the projects feasible; conventional private financing alone isn't sufficient. So the city steps in—often with state and federal government partners as well—and uses its public resources to achieve various public purposes. It lures private developers with subsidized prices in order to revitalize communities and return property to the tax rolls, or offers manufacturers financial incentives to modernize old buildings, to expand and keep jobs in the city. Lucille and I also tackled complex workouts for several publicly funded projects such as the Chicago Theatre on State Street, a landmark theater in the heart of downtown.

The legal work I specialized in before coming to city hall is known as "papering a deal." After a client makes a business deal with the help of its in-house legal team, outside counsel is brought in and is given the term sheet, which counsel then translates into a legal document. Their job is to scour the details for any possible risks the client could face, from earthquakes to bankruptcy. It's complicated and tedious but necessary. The work I did for the city was similar in form, but not in substance. Yes, I was still papering deals—for less money and in a worse office—but the projects themselves were meaningful to me. I cared about the mission of helping to revitalize the city, and the chance to work with incredibly talented public servants gave me a purpose and satisfaction I'd never felt before.

On every deal we always asked the same question: Will the citizens of Chicago be better off if we do this? Every time we used taxpayer dollars to acquire or finance the redevelopment of a property, we reminded ourselves that the funds came from the public's pocket, so the investment better be worth it. And, importantly, Lucille valued more than just my legal opinions. Now that I was in-house counsel for the city, with no time sheets for me to fill out, or bills for her to pay for my time, she made sure that I was included in the whole process, from the initial policy discussions before a deal was structured all the way through the ribbon cutting of a finished project. She knew I cared as much about the policy as I did about the law. That enabled me to make a dramatic leap professionally and personally.

Too often we can tread water for so long in our misery that it becomes the new normal. As a young woman, and even after I was married, when I was unhappy, I hesitated to speak up. I avoided risks and rocking the boat. I felt like I was leading someone else's life, deferring to the chorus of voices around me rather than heeding the quiet one deep within. I had clung to "my" plan, which, as it turned out, had really been my way of satisfying everyone else. But when Bobby and I separated and my corporate career bottomed out, "my" plan completely fell apart, forcing me to reflect on where I was in my life and whether the future I'd fantasized about made sense any longer. My unhappiness motivated my pivot, but it was also a choice. I learned not only how to trust my own voice and act on what it was telling me, but also how to use my voice to advocate for change and progress for the city that I loved.

A few years later, on one project in particular, the city's effort to lure a major airline to open a five-hundred-person reservation center in the city, I went toe to toe with the commissioner who was the point person on the deal. He was ready to concede to whatever the airline wanted. I was determined to lock in all the terms of the deal up front, as corporations have a checkered history of taking subsidies from cities and then not making good on their promises. So I pulled an all-nighter with the senior partner from the law firm representing the airline. Only after a grueling marathon negotiation was I comfortable that the city's interests were protected, including a long-term commitment to create jobs. I went over the commissioner's head and sealed a better deal for the city.

One reason I had originally picked commercial law over litigation was because litigation would have required me to stand on my feet and speak in front of an audience. It was also because I don't like there being winners and losers. However, when "winning" wasn't about personal advancement, but rather about being a force for public good, I found the confidence to give voice to my opinions and ideas. My clients were now really the citizens of Chicago, and I was emboldened to push back on their behalf when I disagreed with policy makers inside government or folks on the outside trying to take advantage. I started to make trouble. I started to make waves.

My dad put it best when he saw my transformation: "What happened to my shrinking violet?" he said, clearly proud of how far I'd come.

"She's gone," I said, with a confident smile.

U nderstanding the strength of my voice also meant learning to modulate it. I had noticed that when Lucille pushed hard, it made men uncomfortable. It isn't fair that men are given latitude to lose their tempers without repercussion while women are not, but if women waited for every double standard to disappear before moving forward, we'd still be waiting on the right to vote. So I learned to employ my mother's technique of being firm and clear without ever raising my voice. It's a strategy that I use to this day in both my professional and personal lives.

Lucille, shall we say, used a different tack. As the champion of the city, she prided herself on being tough, because her cause was just. "I am the steward for the taxpayers of Chicago," she would say, "and if people are not stepping up as high as they should, well, then we will make them." She held everyone accountable, no matter how wealthy or powerful. I watched the powerful wither in the face of her criticism, and I was aways comfortable being the good cop and she the bad one, roles we often played in meetings.

Toward me, however, Lucille never used a sharp word. She set high expectations, and I was determined to meet them. I never wanted to disappoint her, not because I feared her but because she invested in, taught, and protected me and in return I wanted her approval. Still, keeping pace with her was grueling. Laura would cry and beg me to come home at night in time to tuck her in, and I felt horrible every time I couldn't make it, which began to be too often.

No job, no matter how gratifying, was more important than Laura, but I had been hesitant to broach the subject of leaving work "early," by which I mean "at a normal, reasonable time." I knew the stigma applied to working moms who "weren't fully committed," a nebulous standard often applied arbitrarily to hold women back. But one day I worked up the courage to raise the issue of my work hours with Lucille. Casually, during our regular morning meeting, I said, "I need to figure out how to make it home before Laura's bedtime, but of course I'll work from home as long as is necessary afterward." *Gulp.* I thought she might lay into me. Instead she smiled, no doubt remembering her own challenges as a working mom when her daughter was younger, and said, "Well, your home is on my way home. How about if we move our offices to your home when we need to work late?"

So we did. I even began cooking dinner for Lucille and myself and sometimes for Elvin, who was our outside counsel. I would tuck Laura in bed, and then we'd work late together. It was unorthodox, but she understood my circumstances and was willing to work around my schedule as a single mom. She knew that I would be the most productive if I were able to fulfill my responsibilities to Laura—which was a valuable lesson for me when I became a manager myself.

To be honest, I've lost count of the ways Lucille mentored and helped me. Without her it's unlikely my career would have taken the sharp trajectory upward that it did. One day after David Narefsky announced he was leaving city government, Lucille and I were working with Elvin in a conference room at his firm. Lucille, out of nowhere, said to me, "Your boss should report to you." She was referring to my immediate supervisor—who was between David and me.

"That's ridiculous," I said.

"No, what's ridiculous is you thinking a promotion is going to just fall in your lap without you pushing for it," she said. "You should go tell Judd"—that is, my boss's boss's boss—"that I am your client, and I am telling you that you've earned it."

Elvin piped up that I certainly deserved a promotion, but he doubted Judd would leapfrog me over my boss. I agreed. I couldn't imagine asking for a promotion, let alone two. I naively assumed that when Judd thought I deserved it, he would promote me. It never occurred to me to ask, and I was content where I was. Despite my protests, over the next several weeks Lucille raised the issue every single day. All the strong-arming she usually employed against the people on the opposite side of the negotiating table she now brought to bear on me, so much so that I began to dread seeing her. Her tone became increasingly irritable, and I could sense that she was growing disappointed in my lack of motivation and courage. "What's the worst that could happen?" she argued. "He tells you no and you stay where you are."

Finally, I relented and worked up the nerve to make an appointment to see Judd. I walked into his office and sat down. Too nervous for any small talk, I launched right in.

"So," I said, "I think I've earned a promotion."

Judd didn't respond, so I just kept talking, reading from the little crib sheet in my trembling hands where I'd written down all the reasons why I had earned it. Judd listened silently as I rattled on for what felt like an hour but was probably only a few minutes. At the end of my speech, he nodded and said, "All right."

I was shocked he'd said yes so quickly. Giddy from my adrenaline high, I immediately followed up by asking if I could move into a vacancy in the three-office suite where he was, rather than one of the deputy offices buried in the bowels of the building. Judd, laughing at my nerve, said no. I pointed out that having a woman of color prominently located next to him would show his commitment to diversity. That didn't do it, either. Finally I said, "How about I just move in until you figure out who else you want in the office?" He hesitated for a moment, and I jumped right in with "Thanks, Judd!" I flew out of his office.

I could not wait to tell Lucille! She just smiled. Looking back years later, it seemed a little too easy—and why wasn't Judd surprised? I am now sure Lucille must have already made her feelings clear to Judd before I asked. She wasn't just my mentor, but my advocate as well.

After my promotion, I pushed my colleague Susan Kurland to go ask Judd for a promotion, too. I wanted to do for Susan what Lucille had done for me. Susan had begun in the contracts division but was also overqualified for her current position because of her years in private practice. And of course, it would be more fun for me if she were running the other side of the commercial division of the office.

"Go," I told her. "And ask for yours."

"No, no. I can't," she said.

That sounded familiar.

"If I did it, you can, too."

Judd knew Susan and I were best buddies, so he was probably expecting her, too, and thankfully he said yes to Susan, and she took over supervision of the aviation and contracts practices.

I always share this story with working women, because, just like Susan and me, they all too often shy away from asking for promotions or raises. They don't listen to the quiet voice inside telling them that they have earned it. But I say, "Go for it, because you never know." Even if the answer is no, and it often may be, so what? Ask why, work to improve, wait six months, and ask again. If I hadn't asked for it, I might still be in my cubicle in city hall. And if I hadn't learned to trust my voice at work, I might not have found the courage to speak up for myself at home, either.

Bobby actually managed to make it home for my thirty-first birthday, but by that point we had drifted even further apart, absorbed by our separate lives. We had a deep conversation that night, the kind I'd longed to have had years earlier, about the fears of rejection that kept him so aloof, but I knew it was too late to save our marriage. I had enough self-preservation in me to know that trying to hold on would squeeze the life out of me. *He* was no longer my life. I had my own. Still, I made him a proposition.

"We could go back to square one, start dating again, and this time really try to communicate"—the sage advice given to me by my twice-married Uncle Bill the week before my wedding that I had not followed. "We'd see what happens. But I can't just pick up where we are now."

"I don't want to date you," he said. "You're my wife."

"Well, then, that's it," I said, frankly relieved.

He walked toward the door. Laura, now two, was asleep. This time he didn't stop in her room and kiss her good-bye. Instead, he hurried out quickly so that neither of us would have to face the emotion brimming in the other. As he started for the door, I impulsively said, "Could you leave your key?" I didn't want to endure a second parting in our long-overdue but painful breakup. He didn't say a word. He took the key off the ring, put it down on the table, and walked out. When the door closed, all I really felt was relief as I stared at the key.

The news came as a surprise to my parents, for I had taken my grandmother's dictum, "Never speak poorly about your husband," to the extreme.

"Why didn't you tell me how bad this was years ago?" my mother asked.

"I thought if I ever forgave him, you might not," I answered dutifully.

"Pudden's rule didn't apply to *me*," she said. "I had no idea you were so miserable. You should have left long ago." (She later confessed to me that the night before my wedding, she and my father had hoped I would call it off.)

I was relieved to have their support, but not surprisingly, not everyone in my family felt the same way. I took Pudden for a walk around her block to break the news, and instead of her support I received a rare, strong rebuke. "You made your bed. You have to sleep in it." It was the only time I remember Pudden being openly critical of me in my life. Pudden had been friends with Bobby's great-aunt in the Rosenwald Building. There was a lot of history there. I knew, in her day, you stayed married regardless of whether you were happy. "He's not so bad," she said of Bobby, as though that should have been good enough for me. Judi had told me when I was really ready to divorce, I would not care what anyone thought. She was right. I did not. But I loved Pudden dearly, and her initial reaction stung. "I'm sorry, Pudden." My mind was made up. Seeing my expression, Pudden's tone softened, and she reassured me that even though she disagreed with my decision, it was mine to make. If she felt disappointment in me, she certainly never showed it. But I was disappointed in myself. From Northfield Mount Hermon to Stanford to Michigan Law School to my promotion in the corporation counsel's office, whenever I applied myself, I'd always been able to achieve what I wanted. Effort led to success. But no matter how hard I tried with Bobby, I couldn't make it work. We divorced the following year, in the summer of 1988.

It took me quite a while to realize that my failed marriage didn't make *me* a failure. Accomplished women are often asked, "Can you have it all?" If you think having it all means having everything you want all of the time, and doing it all yourself, the answer is no. But, with luck, life has many chapters, and each stage has unavoidable trade-offs. If we take each chapter in turn and embrace it fully, our decisions and their consequences, the joy and the pain, then, yes, when we reflect back over the arc of our lives, they were whole, complete lives. But I didn't know that at the time, and by expecting that I could be a perfect wife, a perfect mother, and have a perfect career, I set myself up for disappointment. Staying up until two in the morning making baby food from scratch, while trying to be a successful associate at a high-pressure corporate law firm, I only wound up disappointing myself and others. I had created an expectation of myself no human could meet.

One Saturday, I was trying to unlock the garage door while juggling grocery bags, purse, and two-year-old Laura. The door kept closing on me. A man walked up and pleasantly asked if I needed a hand. "No," I snapped. Clearly I did need a hand, but his offer made me feel pitiful and needy. I became so angry I even teared up. Over a guy offering to open a door? He'd hit a nerve in my core sense of competence. Managing every task myself was tied to my definition of independence, yet I also yearned for a husband to take care of me.

The last time I saw Bobby was in 1992, when Laura was seven. Bobby had moved back to Chicago in 1988 after completing his residency in Michigan, but by then he'd found someone new. By the time we were officially divorced, she was pregnant, and soon afterward they were married. He lived only two miles from Laura and me, and yet we never saw him. Neither of us reached out to the other. In an effort to shelter Laura from disappointment, I didn't pressure him to make plans that I knew he would cancel.

One Christmas he made a plan to see her, but when the day arrived, Bobby never called. Not that day or ever again. And neither Laura nor I brought him up again until almost a year later, in November of 1993, when he suddenly and unexpectedly died. My mother received the news from her sister, who had heard from a mutual family friend. She tracked me down in city hall while I was in a meeting with senior staff in the mayor's office. As I rushed home to tell Laura, I wondered how to break the news. I had so many feelings of guilt. I'd often fantasized that Bobby would disappear; I'd never wanted him dead, or physically injured, just to somehow magically vanish from my life. Now that it had come true, I felt awful. But my real anxiety came from trying to figure out how I was going to tell Laura, who was now eight, because I knew there was no good way. I thought perhaps she would mourn the final loss of any chance of reconciliation. She cried, but that was it.

Three years later, my cousin Ann Marchant, whose biological father had also abandoned her at an early age, told Laura that she hoped Laura didn't blame herself for our divorce. "Why would I do that?" Laura replied, puzzled by the question. Ann and I smiled.

Laura had tremendous confidence and self-esteem for a girl who'd grown up without a father, and though I take my fair share of the credit, my dad had a lot to do with that. After Bobby left, my dad told me, "I will step in and be the father, and I will never disappoint her." And he never did. He drove her to and from school nearly every single day, even after she could drive herself, always arriving an hour before school let out in order to be one of the first two or three cars in the pickup line, so that she'd see him the second she came out of those school doors and she'd never wonder if he was coming.

Looking back, I know that part of the reason I married Bobby was that I thought I could make him into my father if I just tried hard enough. Attentive and adoring, my dad set a high bar, often in stark contrast to the other men around me. I loved my father, but during my childhood we'd rarely spent much time on our own together; my mom was always there, too. In 1977, the summer before my senior year at Stanford, while I was studying overseas at its campus at Cliveden in England, Dad said to me, "I want to be the first man to show you Paris." So we met there when he was coming back from a meeting in Nigeria.

I offered to make the hotel reservations, and, hearing my mother's frugal voice in my head, I opted for a two-star hotel. After meeting at the airport, my dad and I pulled up to the place I'd booked, and I could tell by his expression that he wasn't thrilled with the accommodations. It didn't get any better once we were inside. The lobby had a strange odor. The beds in our room were so close together that I had to crawl over his bed to reach mine, and the bathroom was down the hall.

The next morning, over breakfast, he said gently, "This is fine, Lally, but let's see if we can find a hotel closer to the places I want to show you." He chose Le Meurice, opposite the Tuileries Gardens, one of the nicest hotels I had ever been in. We walked all over the city, stopping at the Louvre to see the *Mona Lisa* and shopping in chic boutiques. One night we went to the famous nightclub the Lido, and on our last evening, my dad took me to Maxim's, the restaurant featured in *Gigi*, one of my favorite movies.

Paris with my dad was nothing short of grand, and so was the cost. When the trip was over and the bills started to come in, my mom made a rare long-distance call to me in England to say, "I feel sorry for the next guy who takes you to Paris." I think that was always my dad's intention. I'll never forget the Lido or Maxim's or the *Mona Lisa*, but far more indelible was my father's delight in our time together. After my divorce, I had two realizations. The first was that I couldn't make anybody change. The second was that I deserved a man as good as my father—which may be why I'm still single.

· *Chapter 6* ·

Change from the Ground Up

In the early nineties, anytime you drove from the South Side into downtown Chicago on the massive fourteen-lane Dan Ryan Expressway, to your right you were exposed to the largest and one of the most notorious public housing developments in the country, the Robert Taylor Homes, named after my grandfather.

The Robert Taylor Homes comprised twenty-eight identical, sixteen-story high-rises spanning a campus nearly two miles long along State Street from Thirty-ninth to Fifty-fourth. Their sheer size and condition made them a high-profile symbol of a problem that existed nationwide. Crime-ridden and dilapidated, the Taylor Homes simply warehoused people who were poor without offering any of the services or resources necessary to help the residents move up the rungs of the ladder to the middle class. With no federal, state, or local funding for day care, education, economic development, job training, or counseling, its residents were totally isolated. The Robert Taylor Homes were built in the hopes of providing a better option than the tenements from which many of the residents came, but as a result of flawed policies at the federal level, over time the residents of these buildings became uniformly low income. And because of deliberate local policies of racial segregation, they were predominantly black.

The plight of public housing in Chicago and in other cities across the country was a failure on many levels. It was a failure of urban planners to understand what makes communities thrive and grow. It was our failure as a nation to confront the issues of racial segregation and poverty that we had created. But, at its core, it was a failure of the government to serve the needs of all of its constituents.

In 1948 the Supreme Court determined that racially restrictive covenants were unconstitutional. When that happened, there was a jubilant sense of liberation and freedom in the black community. Gradually, those who could afford to move out of segregated neighborhoods like Bronzeville did. Left behind were neighborhoods that quickly became populated with only low-income residents, which lost both government resources and private investments in the process. Businesses closed, roads deteriorated, schools lost students and funding, and more—all because residents didn't have the political power to demand better. Even the Rosenwald Building, the grand apartments my grandfather had helped build and manage, began to fall into disrepair. There was no comprehensive housing policy providing reinvestment for the low-income black neighborhoods that had been neglected, or for helping to stabilize the white neighborhoods going through racial transition as black families moved in and white families moved out.

As chairman of the Chicago Housing Authority, my grandfather had championed plans that he believed would do exactly that. He viewed it as the government's responsibility to provide quality transitional public housing that architecturally blended into the urban fabric, indistinguishable from market-rate housing. He believed public housing should serve as a way station for those working their way up, and it should also be a place where people could access the services they needed to become self-sufficient, like job training, health clinics, and childcare assistance. In 1950, after decades spent fighting unsuccessfully to create healthy mixed-income and racially diverse communities, when the city council refused to approve a plan to build public housing in any white neighborhoods, my grandfather resigned his position as chairman of the Chicago Housing Authority. Seven years later, while still fighting to secure the financing to turn the Rosenwald into co-op apartments so that it could be restored, he died suddenly of a heart attack. After his death, the city moved forward with its ill-conceived plans for "urban renewal," breaking ground on massive public housing developments. Then, in 1962, in what can only be described as a very cruel irony, five years after my grandfather's death, Mayor Richard J. Daley "honored" him by naming the largest housing development in the world after him. My whole family attended the dedication ceremony, and the adults had mixed emotions. The crowd was led by Mayor Daley through the brand-new buildings and thought they were cause to celebrate. But I overheard my mother and my grandmother murmuring to each other: "This isn't what he would have wanted." Which confused me at the time. The mayor of Chicago kept mentioning my grandfather and the accomplishment of creating the largest public housing development in the world. Why were they concerned?

As I grew older, my mother helped me understand that the Robert Taylor Homes were the epitome of all my grandfather had stood against. Isolated concentrations of very poor people warehoused with no support services, in buildings that literally stood out like sore thumbs in Chicago's landscape.

Anytime we drove by the Robert Taylor Homes, which was often, as they loomed high in the sky just a mile from our home, she would remind me that my grandfather's vision was to create communities with people of all incomes and races living together in safe, habitable homes. As a youngster, watching the nightly news with Pudden in her little front room, every time my grandfather's name flashed on the screen, it was accompanied by a story about violent crimes in the public housing complex. On the ten o'clock news, nothing good was ever reported out of the Robert Taylor Homes. Nothing. *Ever*. I would look over at Pudden, wanting to change the channel to protect her from the pain. She would just close her eyes and shake her head as the name of a person she loved was associated again and again with tragedy.

As my career in city government moved forward, the failure of the Robert Taylor Homes loomed as large in my mind as the towers did on the horizon, and I grew determined to help fulfill my grandfather's vision.

B y the summer of 1991, I was still working in city hall, but I had a very different job. The phone at my desk rang steadily, and I usually didn't even need to answer in order to know who it was. One afternoon I picked up, and, of course, it was the security guard down the hall. "Valerie," he said, "Mrs. Adams is at the front desk. Could you come out to help her?"

My office was only a few feet from the front desk, so I popped right over, as I always did. I didn't know who Mrs. Adams was or what had brought her to city hall, but I did know there would be steam coming out of her ears, and that whatever her problem was, it would be mine to try to solve.

By that time I'd been working in government for almost four years, mostly behind the scenes in the corporation counsel's office, helping to structure and negotiate development deals as a lawyer for the city. Now all that had changed. My career in public service had become a daily exercise in serving the actual public, dealing directly with constituents and addressing their needs as the mayor's deputy chief of staff. I could not have imagined myself in that position two years earlier, when Mayor Richard M. Daley swept into office, replacing Eugene Sawyer, who'd been appointed mayor in the wake of Harold Washington's tragic death.

Daley's election was particularly traumatic for those of us who had come to city hall under Mayor Washington. I was still bruised from the racially polarizing campaign when Washington and Daley had run against each other six years earlier, and it was crushing to think Daley would now be our boss. And, as with any new political administration, we knew Mayor Daley was going to bring in his own team. Nervous about who the new players would be, and in what direction Daley would lead the city, we all did some major soul-searching about whether to remain in government (if we were even given the choice). The new mayor's father, Richard J. Daley, had been mayor of Chicago for more than twenty years and was known for governing the city through the Eleventh Ward machine, operated under a patronage system that left most black Chicagoans feeling powerless. The big question: Would the son follow in his father's footsteps or continue the progressive agenda of Mayor Washington?

The city's corporation counsel, Judd Miner, who had hired me, tendered his resignation immediately. Lucille Dobbins, my primary client, mentor, and friend, didn't believe Mayor Daley would ever be true to Mayor Washington's vision. She left after the transition to start her own firm and hoped I would join her. But I loved my job and decided I was willing to give Daley a chance. It was years before Lucille forgave me for staying. "You'll be compromised," she warned me.

The pressure to leave was intense. Lucille wasn't the only one who thought I was a sellout for staying in city hall. But Mayor Daley embraced Mayor Washington's relentless "fairness" and continued his legacy in several ways. Nearly every Saturday, Daley visited a different ward in the city to meet members of the community and listen to their concerns, including those who had voted against him and were predominantly black. Daley was brushed off in many places and downright booed in others, but he kept on showing up. It was a tribute to his character and resilience that he didn't hold the negative reaction against his detractors, but instead understood that it was a sign that he had yet to earn their trust, and he was determined to do it. And he did. Mayor Daley won the support of the majority of the black wards when he ran for a second term.

It wasn't just Mayor Daley's willingness to engage with his opponents that helped knit the city together, he also continued the progressive agenda started by Mayor Washington, including minority- and women-owned business set-asides on contracts and efforts to diversify the city workforce. Mayor Daley loved his father but understood that he was governing in a very different time. I think that's why he worked so hard to showcase a new image of the city when he hosted the 1996 Democratic National Convention. He was determined to wash away the image of the police in his father's city brutalizing antiwar protesters during the convention of 1968.

Over the course of his first two years in office, Mayor Daley was certainly not perfect, but he earned my respect. He also terrified me. I mostly saw him on television, being gruff and impatient with the reporters, and I never had any direct interactions with him.

Then, one day in June of 1991, my beeper went off while I was in Marshall Field's. There was an underground tunnel from City Hall to the massive department store, so I often went there during lunch for a change of scenery and a little shopping. Recognizing the number as the mayor's office, I raced to the nearest pay phone. Why would the mayor be paging *me*?

His assistant, Mary Ellen, answered the phone. She had previously been an assistant in the law department, and we knew each other well.

"Mayor Daley wants to see you."

"Why?"

"Honey, I don't know. Where are you?"

"I'm in Marshall Field's."

"Run!"

I did just that, but by the time I arrived at the mayor's office, he was in a meeting. "Sit tight," Mary Ellen said. "I'll let you know when he's free."

"Sit tight?"

"I'll call you when he's ready," she said, looking at me with genuine pity.

I spent an agonizing two days sitting by the phone before Mary Ellen summoned me again.

When I walked into his office, the mayor was reading a document.

"So you're Valerie Jarrett?" he said, looking up from his desk.

"Yes," I mumbled.

"Good. I wanted to meet the person who's been writing all these memos to me."

I had actually met Mayor Daley once, four years earlier, when he was still the state's attorney. We had been seated together at the dinner after the wedding of my childhood friend, John Rogers. When I saw my table assignment, I asked John why he'd seated me with Daley instead of my family and friends. He just chuckled and said, "One day he'll be mayor of Chicago. Be nice." I must not have made much of an impression, because the mayor clearly didn't remember me.

My colleague Susan Kurland and I were responsible for drafting detailed cover memos summarizing the documents prepared by the corporation counsel and sent to the mayor for his signature. But we never thought that the mayor was actually reading our memos. Turned out, he was, and he was impressed. After a bit of small talk and some questions about my family and my personal life, he asked, "Would you like to be my deputy chief of staff?"

I stared at him in disbelief, and he stared back, waiting for an answer. I mumbled that I'd like to think about it. He smiled and said, "Take a couple of days." Then, without a good-bye, he began reading some document. I bolted for the door. After speaking with my boss, Kelly Welsh, I learned that the mayor had been doing more than reading my memos. His senior staff had been watching me go toe to toe with department heads on policy matters, and they and Kelly had recommended me for the job. I was flabbergasted.

I wasn't sure what to do. I defined myself professionally as a lawyer and I knew I was good at my job in the counsel's office, but after four years the work was no longer very challenging. It was all well within my comfort zone, and I was becoming restless for a new challenge, but it would mean a different identity from a practicing attorney. After thinking it over and consulting my parents, I decided I could always return to practice law, so I took the leap, and I've never looked back.

In very short order, I knew the job was tailor made for me. From day one I was included in the morning's senior staff meeting. It was a meeting that everyone in city hall knew about, but it took place behind a cloak of secrecy; nothing leaked out of that room, ever. All the important decisions were made there and then were communicated on a need-to-know basis. I was now at the center of it all. From that insider's position, I also had one of the most public-facing roles in the mayor's office. One of my responsibilities was to help ordinary citizens solve their problems with local government, work many people would have found frustrating, but which I really enjoyed.

The sheer volume of angry people who arrived at Chicago's city hall was considerable. They just showed up on our doorstep—every single day—and they were always at their wit's end. People are usually pretty upset before they pick up the phone to call a government agency to complain, so just imagine how irate someone needs to be to take time off work to do it in person.

When Chicago residents showed up, so frustrated by the government that they had no recourse other than to try to see the mayor, it was my job to figure out what the problem was and how we could help. It might be a business owner who had spent months working with the licensing department to start a new business, only to find out that his location was actually zoned for housing, which required him to then find a new site for his business. Or it might be a property owner who'd received an exorbitant water bill and couldn't get a response from the water department as to why. We received complaints about abandoned buildings, underperforming schools, poor road maintenance, trees that needed trimming, garbage, rodents, you name it.

The principal quality that my job required was an unwavering air of calm, no matter how heated the conversation became. Both of my parents were good listeners; they always took a rational, intellectual approach to finding solutions while also having empathy for the person with the problem, and I tried to follow their model. Some people just wanted to vent, and I would simply listen, respectfully, even if I had no magic solution to pull out of my hat. The constituents with whom I spoke might not walk away completely satisfied, but it was on me to try to help and to do so in a way that made them feel respected and heard. Very often they were justifiably upset, and I used the therapeutic and analytical skills I'd learned studying psychology and practicing law to make them know that we cared and wanted to help them. Then I would always do my best to actually solve their problems, and, I hoped, send them on their way happier than when they arrived.

It was in this role that I welcomed Mrs. Adams to city hall on that hot summer day. She started off by informing me that she'd had to pay for a babysitter so that she could come down to city hall, and sure enough, there was the steam coming out of her ears. I took a deep breath, lowered my voice in hopes that she would do the same, and said, "How can I help?"

Mrs. Adams told me that there was an old, dilapidated, abandoned building adjacent to her home. It had not been boarded up by the owner, and some drug dealers had set up shop inside. There was constant traffic of drug users in and out. There were needles on her front lawn, and her children were no longer safe playing out in front of their home. She had repeatedly called the city's nonemergency assistance number to report the criminal activity, but nobody ever followed up. By this point her eyes were filling with tears and her voice had begun to shake. I put my arm around her and led her out of the busy reception area and into my office.

While she collected herself, I called the district commander for her neighborhood and asked him to have the building checked out. I also called the Building Department and asked that the building be boarded up securely that day and that its ownership status be checked to see if the building was eligible for demolition. I apologized to Mrs. Adams and assured her that, as a mom myself, I understood how she must feel. I then sent her on her way, feeling empowered that she had forced us to take her totally legitimate concerns seriously. And finally, I added her complaint to the list of items I would follow up on in the coming days to make sure it was resolved to her satisfaction.

What I enjoyed most about dealing with constituents directly was that I could see the tangible, positive impact that the government could have on their lives every single day, no matter how minor. I could go home each night knowing I'd made a difference, however small. I would have preferred to stay in the job longer, but fate had other ideas in store for me.

As I responded to Mrs. Adams and so many other Chicagoans who were unhappy about how the city was delivering services, I started brainstorming with David Mosena, the mayor's new chief of staff, about how we could reorganize government agencies to make them more consumer friendly and efficient. David and I were promoted at the same time. He had previously been commissioner of planning and one of my clients. Together we came up with the idea of combining a number of departments, including planning and economic development, as well as parts of transportation and housing, into one new consolidated department. All too often in city government, agencies contradicted one another, which frustrated constituents who fell victim to turf battles and conflicting policies. That led to wasted time and money. The Economic Development Department, responsible for attracting and retaining businesses, didn't communicate with the Planning Department, which controls zoning. Or neighborhood redevelopment groups working with the Planning Department didn't have the reality check or the resources to make their plans viable, so they would wind up sitting on a shelf. Our goal was to provide a holistic approach to help businesses, community groups, residents, and aldermen work constructively with a coordinated government.

In October 1991, David and I presented the mayor with our idea for this new department, the Department of Planning and Development. We included a budget, an organizational chart, and the candidate we recommended to head it up. The mayor nodded approvingly as he examined our proposal, made some tweaks, and then essentially signed off on the entire proposal for the department. The only recommendation to which he didn't react positively was our choice for commissioner, which disappointed us both. We had spent a great deal of time on the selection process, we both knew the candidate well, and we thought he was perfect for the job. Then, the next day, a colleague said to me, "You do know the reason why the mayor didn't sign off on your recommendation, right?"

"Why?"

"He wants you to do it."

My first thought was: *Shoot, I should have given the department a bigger budget.*

My second thought was that I didn't want to leave the job I already had. Deputy chief of staff was a perfect job. I had a lot of authority and little responsibility for day-to-day management. Plus, I had been there for only four months. I had barely unpacked my boxes.

Unsure what to do, I scheduled breakfast with a very wise lawyer and family friend, Earl Neal, who'd represented the city of Chicago, and was a valued advisor to every mayor since Mayor Daley's father. I told him about my predicament, and he said without hesitation to take the job, explaining that a staff role, where I advised, is very different from line management responsibility, and that I would never establish my own reputation until I ran my own shop.

"What about the fact that I just started in my present position?" I asked.

"Opportunity rarely knocks at the opportune moment," he said.

I agonized for several days but ultimately said yes. I became Chicago's first commissioner of the Department of Planning and Development and I spent the next four years presiding over, as *The New York Times* later described it, "a rancorous but largely successful makeover of the city's landscape."

"Rancorous" would turn out to be quite the understatement.

Among the many issues I faced in my new position, the legacy of problems caused by redlining and residential segregation was a top priority for me. The neighborhoods torn apart by white flight needed to be revitalized, and Chicago's public housing was in a dire state. By early 1991, there was a growing consensus at the local and federal governments that the dilapidated large-scale public housing developments were a failure. While I was still deputy chief of staff, Vince Lane, the chairman of the Chicago Housing Authority, approached me to help him develop a comprehensive public housing redevelopment policy. Recognizing that large portions were badly deteriorated and beyond repair, he wanted to create a strategy that would include demolishing all the city's large-scale housing developments and replacing them with mixed-income communities. He knew my family connection to the Robert Taylor Homes and I assured Vince I was very willing to help him. We began the planning then, and I continued to tackle this challenge when I became commissioner of the Department of Planning and Development. Forty-one years earlier my grandfather had resigned from the Chicago Housing Authority over the city's refusal to build integrated public housing that would knit the city together and help low-income people pull themselves up. Now, as the head of my newly minted department, I was in a position to fulfill the dream that my grandfather never could.

But first, I had to figure out what on earth I was doing, because I was practically starting from zero. I was a thirty-four-year-old lawyer who'd suddenly gone from comanaging a staff of forty to overseeing more than two hundred people merged from several different departments with different missions and objectives, many who had never worked together before. For the first time I regretted sleeping through the GMAT my senior year of college. If I'd taken it instead of staying up and partying the night before, I could have earned a joint graduate degree in law and business, and then I might have had a clue how to manage this new office. Instead I was left to make up my own rules based on what I'd learned from being managed by others.

My first rule was to listen. I had observed managers over the years who thought they knew all of the answers and ignored the advice from everyone on their teams. Since my team knew I had no formal training in urban planning, there was no point in pretending. So I started all my senior staff meetings by asking them to brief me on what they were doing, so I could learn as much as I could.

Rule number two was to be responsive. I knew from the complaints I heard in the mayor's office that far too many citizens felt ignored by city government. For the first three months I returned every phone call I received the same day. I plowed through all of my mail, often taking files home and reading late at night after I'd tucked Laura into bed. I was so proud that I was taking care of all the incoming communication myself, but it slowly began to sink in that I had not affirmatively moved my own agenda forward. I was so busy reacting to everyone else, I had nothing to show that reflected my own priorities. Rule number two needed some help.

Elvin Charity, once again, came to the rescue. He said, "You need a chief of staff to keep the trains running, and I have the perfect person." He then introduced me to Beth White, describing her as "a gem." From our first interview, I knew Elvin was right. She exuded quiet confidence, and her gentle Southern accent disguised a will of steel. She wrestled my mail and stack of messages away from me, prioritized my day, helped me manage my team (without her own agenda), and enabled me to make timely decisions, even working long hours after I went home to see Laura. Find and hire the right people, then, would be rule number three.

Beth's presence gave me the space I needed to think through how to implement the mayor's agenda, as well as develop my own. Rule number four was to have a proactive agenda. Not to simply react.

It was a challenging time not just for me, but for the city as well. Chicago's manufacturing base was shrinking rapidly as companies looked for expansive "green grass" suburban locations where they could spread out, free from the environmental concerns that came with old multistory manufacturing sites in the city. At the same time, the nineties were the start of the comeback of America's cities, which had been blighted in the seventies and eighties by disinvestment that led to soaring crime rates and fiscal crisis. Chicago was on the cutting edge of that national trend. It had a broad employment base, not dependent on any one industry, and as a result of the efforts that began under Mayor Washington that continued into the nineties, Chicago enjoyed a bustling central business district with theater, restaurants, hotels, and a night scene for young adults. During my four years as commissioner, the population began growing as people started to appreciate the benefits of living in a thriving city, especially the short commute. We had an ambitious commitment to attract investment that would spur revitalization and create new jobs.

One day early in my new position, Mayor Daley called me into his office and said one word: "Trees." I looked at him and waited for the rest of the sentence. "Trees," he said again. "We're going to plant trees everywhere." I was trying desperately to keep manufacturing from leaving the city, and he was talking about trees? Good grief.

It took a while, but I began to see that he was right. What Mayor Daley knew was that for neighborhoods where no one had invested in beautification in recent memory, trees were a transformational symbol of positive change. He planted a whole lot of trees, all over the city, and they helped bring back neighborhood pride and spurred investment. For as long as I could remember there had been a stark contrast between the landscaping on North Lake Shore Drive versus South Lake Shore Drive. Mayor Daley changed that, and those of us who lived on the South Side noticed. We appreciated not only the appearance but also the symbolism—we mattered, too.

Mayor Daley also made less-visible improvements, including rehabilitating the city's hundred-year-old water and sewer system, an initiative whose wisdom I appreciated when Flint, Michigan, experienced a contaminated water crisis at the end of my time in the White House. The state of Michigan and the city had deferred maintenance on Flint's water system for so long that it became a serious public-health crisis, while Mayor Daley understood the importance of upgrading Chicago's water system when nobody else was paying any attention.

One of my primary goals was to start making municipal investments in neighborhoods that had long been ignored by government and business, to reverse their historical decline. A relationship I built with a West Side community organizer who led his neighborhood's revitalization planning process had helped me think through the organization of my new department, and find the right strategy to support redevelopment. The original concept behind our new department was that by bringing together various agencies, all with different functions, we could holistically target a neighborhood with a vast arsenal of tools in our tool kit. To do this, we created a new program called the Strategic Neighborhood Action Program (SNAP), which I considered the gold standard of the new department's mission. It shaped the way I view the role of government at all levels to this day. Instead of providing funding in traditional silos, my department planned with community leaders and then we targeted resources from various departments, including Housing for demolition, rehabilitation, and new construction; Transportation for resurfacing of streets; Parks to beautify open spaces; and Economic Development to attract businesses. SNAP allowed us to comprehensively address the needs identified by neighborhoods, as well as to attract private investment.

First, where should we direct this arsenal of tools? We put out a request for proposals that required strong local support from both elected officials and community organizations, as well as assets that made redevelopment attractive. Initially we selected three neighborhoods to pioneer our approach. The first, not surprisingly, was on the near West Side since it was the model, but the one closer to home was in the North Kenwood–Oakland neighborhood, just blocks from where I grew up.

When we moved from Madison Park in 1968, our new home sat between Forty-ninth and Fiftieth streets on Greenwood Avenue, a short two-block walk to Forty-seventh Street, the dividing line between the neighborhoods of North and South Kenwood. Growing up, I was never allowed to cross Forty-seventh Street. As a young girl, the rule confused me. I was given a wide range to roam if the direction was south, but not to the north. It was unsafe, was all I was told. As I grew older, the invisible barrier troubled me. How could one street be the difference between safe and unsafe?

What I understood by the time I became the commissioner was that my grandmother had been prescient when, upon leaving Bronzeville, she chose the area adjacent to the University of Chicago in South Kenwood. While our neighborhood had safely integrated and stabilized thanks to the progressive political forces at work there, North Kenwood, not having those resources, had cratered due to white flight. Banks wouldn't lend. Investment dried up. Businesses moved out. Properties decayed. The once-thriving area became another struggling, low-income black neighborhood, yet another casualty of America's refusal to deal with issues of class and race in a constructive, sustainable way.

By the 1990s, in contrast to the manicured affluence of South Kenwood and Hyde Park, North Kenwood had become a neighborhood of blighted buildings, pockmarked streets, and empty, overgrown, garbage-strewn lots. Seventy percent of the land in North Kenwood was vacant, and half of that vacant land was owned by the city. Many of the buildings were abandoned, but much of the architecture was gorgeous, and the community was right by Lake Michigan, a short fifteen-minute drive from downtown.

Removing these invisible barriers that were stifling equitable investment and opportunity north of Forty-Seventh Street, and all throughout the city, became my cause.

I believed that North Kenwood had tremendous potential, and the community leaders had many constructive ideas about how to bring it back, but great ideas do not materialize without the leadership necessary to turn them into reality. So began the arduous process of crafting a plan with local leaders and residents that would be embraced by the whole community. The local alderman, Toni Preckwinkle—also my alderman, then years later chairman of the Cook County Board, and, as of this writing, a leading candidate for mayor of Chicago—was and is one of the most effective leaders I've ever met. She ran an open and transparent planning process, and she tried to bring together divergent perspectives and drive toward consensus, lifting up committed residents to help lead the effort. Her partner was Shirley Newsome, appointed by Mayor Daley to the unpaid chair of the North Kenwood Oakland Conservation Community Council. Her day job was as an administrative assistant to a federal judge. Shirley spent countless hours in the evenings at community meetings and fielded calls from her neighbors until late into each night. She was well respected by her neighbors and strong enough to manage conflicting, passionate views.

Still, change is hard, even with the most effective leaders on board. But when it happens, it makes public service feel so worthwhile. It is impossible to undertake public projects of any magnitude without encountering serious disagreement, frustration, resistance, and always fear. Years of experience have taught me that the key to successfully navigating those challenges is to stay committed to true north—not perfection, but simply the greater good—and never turn from its coordinates. The hardest part, even harder than being the object of everyone's rage, is staying on course while recognizing some may inevitably and unfairly suffer in the process.

My deputy, Kelly King, worked closely with Alderman Preckwinkle and Shirley to craft the redevelopment strategy, including creating an extensive preservation plan for the many historically significant nineteenth-century mansions still standing (although barely) in the neighborhood. We also didn't want to displace the people who already lived there, so we financed affordable and public housing that would have disappeared if development were driven completely by market forces. We created toolboxes with federal tax credits and free city-owned land for housing and commercial development with a low-income component and capped sales prices while still giving developers a reasonable return on their investment. We couldn't save every house the local preservation advocates wanted to protect, and we couldn't give the developers the profit margins they had originally demanded, but everyone received just enough to build a broad consensus supporting the plan.

Still, despite the buy-in from the community leadership and major community organizations, the public meeting where we presented the plan was an unmitigated nightmare. It was held in the local park district community center, with a couple hundred people packed into its largest room. There were contentious questions and even hollering, but not by people who actually lived in the community. Organized rabble-rousers and outsiders had come to disrupt the proceedings and stir up fears about gentrification, a legitimate concern but that night, used as a trigger word designed to provoke animosity and resistance to change. The actual residents who lived there had come looking for answers to their questions and to have a conversation. Many of them were legitimately afraid of change. The low-income residents were worried about displacement. Both white and black low- and moderate-income homeowners were highly skeptical about spreading public housing units throughout the community. And everyone wondered if the city would really follow through on its commitments. And even if we did, would the plan actually work?

It was my first experience coming under strong attack by the very community I was trying to help, and at the time it shook me up. I naively used to think people would automatically trust me and my motives. After all, I'd left a high-paying job in the private sector to dedicate myself to being a public servant. But as my parents often said, "Life isn't fair." They also added, "Who told you public service was easy?" A painful lesson, but one that helped me endure more viscious attacks in the White House.

As commissioner of the Department of Planning and Development, it was unavoidable that I would anger residents, developers, community groups, and elected officials across the board. I learned that many of those I was trying to serve had been severely disappointed in the past by my predecessors. "I'm from the government and here to help you" are fighting words to a lot of folks. Trust takes time. Trust takes effort. Trust takes building a record of delivering on promises, and it's a two-way street. Some officials were promoting their own self-interest, and I was simply in the way. A member of the Chicago City Council once explained to me that with elected officials there are no permanent friends and no permanent enemies, only permanent interests, and that I should stop taking criticism so personally. It took time, but I learned to do just that: absorb the pain, a skill that would come in handy many times over the years.

Eventually we were able to bring most of the North Kenwood community on board, the redevelopment plan moved forward, and I learned several valuable strategies for making progress in the public sector. The first is that the community, including the elected officials, must feel that they have been heard and that their concerns are taken seriously. The second is that everyone has to feel a win, not 100 percent of what they want, but a tangible victory for themselves, or if they are in elected office, for them to deliver to their constituency. Third, everyone has to leave the table at least a little bit unhappy, for that's compromise. That there was a give and take and the process was fair. In other words, you rarely hit home runs. You're more likely to get base hits, yet over time they add up.

The success of the North Kenwood–Oakland redevelopment was far from my doing alone. It took dedicated local leadership and strong citizen participation. It also took twenty-five years. When I drive through the neighborhood today, I see new mixed-income housing, architecturally significant buildings that have been restored, great parks, successful charter schools, and a resurgence of new and relocated businesses—including my favorite neighborhood restaurant, the Original Pancake House, which relocated there from South Kenwood. A true sign of progress. Most of the land that was vacant that had been owned by the city has been developed. It's a neighborhood where anyone would choose to live, and I never give a second thought to crossing Forty-seventh Street anymore. That invisible barrier is gone.

Once I found my bearings in the Department of Planning and Development, my only regret was that my grandfather Robert Taylor hadn't lived to see what I was doing. A man before his time, he had a passion for strong and vibrant communities for people of all incomes. He knew that healthy neighborhoods were, are, and always will be the cornerstone of a great city. Creating jobs is vital, but without affordable housing, good schools, paved streets, safe parks, and places to shop, people can't live and raise their families with grace.

Vince Lane and I joined forces with Daniel Levin. Daniel was the chairman of a private real estate development and management company, The Habitat Company, and the receiver for the Chicago Housing Authority, responsible for all its family development. That included the demolition and redevelopment of Chicago's many public housing developments—including the Robert Taylor Homes. It was my chance to both right a historic wrong and do right by my grandfather's legacy.

What made such a massive effort possible was a program from President Clinton's Department of Housing and Urban Development known as HOPE VI, or the Plan for Transformation. HOPE VI gave municipalities the resources needed to tear down these large projects and replace them with humane mixed-income housing. We worked with the local communities to plan the redevelopment of these huge tracts of land and to address the creation of new mixed-income housing that would include homes for residents being displaced.

Focusing on areas we thought had potential for market-rate developments, we started with the Cabrini-Green Homes, a study in the stark contrasts of the city. These high-rises, where so many residents suffered under every epidemic from gun violence to unemployment to drug addiction, were only a short walk from Michigan Avenue's Magnificent Mile in the heart of Chicago's affluent Gold Coast. In rapid succession we also identified other good candidates for demolition, including the Henry Horner Homes near the United Center, a sports arena and big economic engine, and the Lakefront Properties, high-rise public housing buildings in North Kenwood–Oakland, with spectacular views of Lake Michigan. Our goal was to spur the development of healthy communities with low-density public housing woven into the fabric of the neighborhood, indistinguishable from the market-rate housing, improving the schools and parks, and attracting other new amenities. Under the *Gautreaux* consent decree we were required to achieve economic integration—and ultimately racial integration.

Even though these projects were in horrendous condition, they were still people's homes, and we were asking the residents to move. Some couldn't get out fast enough. But there were many who just didn't want to leave no matter the deplorable condition of the buildings. People often resist change, even change that promises to be for the better. Many residents of Chicago's public housing had long suffered from institutional racism at the hands of the government responsible for supporting them. After generations of mismanagement and bad policy, their skepticism and fear were entirely understandable. We had to convince them to trust us, and the process was both challenging and controversial for everyone involved. But, some days by sheer force of will, we kept the process moving ahead.

Cabrini-Green was torn down and replaced by low-rise mixed-income housing that included a school, a new park, and a large commercial development. In the case of the Henry Horner Homes, we reduced the overall number of units by more than half and integrated the area's low-income tenants with new residents who were working- and middle-class. The Lakefront Properties were literally imploded in less than five seconds, and the new housing continues to be built according to Shirley Newsome's Conservation Plan.

For all of these new developments and several more, we set up screening criteria for occupants, just as my grandfather had done in the Rosenwald Building and the Chicago Housing Authority: those who didn't meet the criteria were not offered the right to return. This involved lengthy negotiations, often among competing lawyers representing the residents, but we were determined not to re-create horizontally what we had torn down vertically, a place where law-abiding residents were plagued by gangs and violence. We also had criteria for how the new units should be maintained. Because the city's Housing Authority had historically shown itself to be incompetent and corrupt, taking bribes for repairs or not making them at all, the consent decree also required the new housing to be managed by private companies.

By my fourth year as commissioner, we still had not begun the redevelopment of the Robert Taylor Homes, but the planning was well under way and it was becoming clear that it was time for me to move on. David Mosena, the mayor's chief of staff, had been my protector through the formation and early days of the Department of Planning and Development, but he had left to become commissioner of the Department of Aviation. I'd angered more than a few of the city's major developers over the years—remember, everyone has to leave the table a little bit unhappy—and without David to have my back, my job was growing increasingly unpleasant. It was turning into politics, not public service, which wasn't why I'd gone to city hall eight years before.

I thought about my options: going back to private law practice, maybe teaching. Then a good friend, Marilyn Katz, suggested I move across the table and go to work for The Habitat Company. She thought it could be a good match, especially since Habitat had been tasked with so many new responsibilities with these large redevelopments coming on line. It would have the best of both worlds. I would work in the private sector but continue my public service by redeveloping Chicago communities and improving the lives of residents of public housing. In return, Habitat would benefit from having someone with my experience in law, planning, and the political process as the company embarked on these large, complex public projects. Since I already knew and respected Daniel Levin, I thought it was worth exploring. Marilyn reached out to Dan, and a few weeks later, after several conversations, he called to offer me the job of executive vice president. I was thrilled by the prospect of continuing to do the work I cared so much about, and receiving a private-sector salary just as Laura's Lab Schools tuition was escalating seemed like a great deal to me. I resigned as commissioner on October 3, 1995—incidentally the day of the verdict in the O. J. Simpson trial—and left city hall to start the next chapter in my life.

O ver the years that followed, the plans we'd set in motion at the De-partment of Planning and Development began to come to fruition.

One day in 2007, after I'd become CEO of The Habitat Company, and not long before I began traveling nonstop for the Obama presiden-tial campaign, I received a call from Terry Peterson, the CEO of the Chicago Housing Authority. He called me because the last building of the Robert Taylor Homes was slated for demolition and he had a question.

"Has Laura ever been to Robert Taylor Homes?" he asked.

"No," I said, "she hasn't."

"We're about to tear down the last building. I want you to bring her in for a tour so she can see it. And there's somebody I want you and Laura to meet."

So on a cold winter day, I took Laura and her best friend, Maude, to visit the last high-rise at the Robert Taylor Homes. Maude, who was working on a master's degree in urban planning at the University of Pennsylvania, was curious to have a closer look at the Robert Taylor Homes, about which she had studied in school. We walked into the lobby and saw the elevators were broken, so we climbed the dank, dark, and narrow stairwell. The strong stench of urine lingered in the air even though the building was largely vacant by then. When we reached the second floor, Laura and Maude didn't say a word as we walked around the barren gallery-style corridors, exposed on the outside with iconic, penitentiary-like wire mesh covering the open space. There was an eerie silence as I looked down at an empty playground, trying to imagine what life had been like for the children who had lived there.

Terry knocked on the door of an apartment, and an elderly woman answered. She introduced herself as Mrs. Jamie Jefferson. Walking into her apartment, I felt like Dorothy landing in Oz, going from black and white to Technicolor. It was immaculate. The walls and the floors, the furniture and the decor—everything was fresh, clean, and bright.

Hung on her living room wall were photographs of her ten children, nine girls and one boy, all of whom had been raised in the Robert Taylor Homes and had gone on to college. Mrs. Jefferson exuded immense pride for all she had done to protect and nurture her children so they could thrive under the harshest of circumstances. Nearly everyone had moved out, but she did not want to leave.

She'd moved in right at the beginning, when Taylor first opened in 1962. She repeated what we had also heard from Mayor Richard J. Daley at the opening ceremony. She said, "My family viewed the Taylor Homes as a step up from where we were before. I raised my children here. It is my home."

I too wanted Laura and Maude to meet Mrs. Jefferson so they would better understand the stories I had shared with them about the people I'd met there, and how the criminal stereotypes skewed the image of the residents badly. I knew one visit alone could never fully capture the varied lives of the many people who'd made their homes in public housing. But I wanted the girls to see that the history of the community that lived there was, in reality, more complicated than the singularly violent depiction on the ten o'clock news.

The last of the Robert Taylor Homes was demolished on March 8, 2007, but everyone who had lived there with a lease in good standing was guaranteed a new home.

· *Chapter 7* ·

My Best Hire Ever

The idea that black people need to work twice as hard and be twice as good has been repeated to us time and again. We've absorbed it into our bloodstream. It's become second nature. But for a phrase that's become so commonplace, we often leave out an important part: yes, work twice as hard, so that you can be twice as good, but you need to be lucky, too.

Luck plays an enormous role in all our lives. Working twice as hard earned my father his medical degree, but it was luck that he happened to know a man who happened to know about a job offer in Iran, which was the opportunity that began to allow him to flourish. If you're not working hard, you won't be in a position to take advantage of luck when it comes your way, but you still need the luck. And in the summer of 1991, during the brief four-month window while I was busy working twice as hard as Mayor Daley's deputy chief of staff, luck landed on my desk. Plowing through my ever-growing pile of incoming mail, I saw a handwritten note from Susan Sher, by then the city of Chicago's top lawyer and one of my best friends, attached to a résumé. It read, "Very impressive! Bright, mature, interested in public service. Does NOT want to practice law. Please meet with her." Quickly scanning the résumé, it was obvious why Susan had sent it my way: a twenty-six-year-old

Chicago native, cum laude grad of Princeton, Harvard Law alum, and now second-year associate at the law firm of Sidley Austin.

The name at the top was Michelle Robinson.

I called Michelle in for an interview, and when she walked into my office, I was immediately struck not just by her appearance—tall, strikingly beautiful, simply dressed, with her hair pulled back and barely a hint of makeup—but also by her composed demeanor. She had a firm handshake, made direct eye contact, and exuded a confidence that I had rarely seen in anyone so young.

All the other candidates I'd interviewed had tried to impress me by hard-selling their strengths. Michelle let her résumé speak to her credentials and instead told me about her background growing up in a working-class neighborhood on the South Side of Chicago. Her father, a blue-collar worker with the city's water department, prided himself on working hard even as he endured multiple sclerosis. As she described his involvement as a precinct captain in ward politics and his love for this city, it was clear the loss of her father a few months earlier was still fresh and painful. We compared stories about shared experiences, such as the drudgery of law firm life, the gift of being raised by happily married parents, and being instilled with a sense of responsibility to give back. Michelle talked less to impress than to simply inform. We also talked about loss of young people we loved. Her best friend from college had died too young from cancer. My younger cousin, Jackie Cook, had been killed in 1981 by a drunk driver during the summer after her freshman year in college.

About thirty minutes into what was supposed to be a twenty-minute interview, she got down to business. Innocuous questions that any job candidate might ask, such as the responsibilities of the position, turned into a rigorous and thoughtful grilling. "How many staff are you going to have?" "What will the organizational chart be?" "What kinds of projects will be assigned to me, and who will make those assignments?" "What will happen if I disagree with a decision of Mayor Daley?"

Her questions made me uncomfortable. Not because they weren't perfectly legitimate, but because no one had ever asked them before. I was so used to people selling themselves to me that I was both startled and impressed by the ease with which Michelle turned the tables. *What an unusual young person*, I thought. To be able to realize that it was as important for her to want to work with me as it was for me to want her showed a maturity I certainly didn't possess at her age.

After well over an hour had passed, with meetings stacking up, I was running way late, and I am never late. I straight up offered her the job. Which I had no authority to do! I hadn't talked to David Mosena, the chief of staff, or the mayor. But I was so impressed with Michelle Robinson that I blurted out an offer on the spot. I could tell she was perfect for the job. She exuded competence, as well as character and integrity. It was also clear that her moral compass pointed only in one direction: true north. And, I really liked her. Wisely, Michelle said she needed to think about it.

A few days later, I called Michelle to check in and see if she was ready to accept my offer, which by then I had cleared with my bosses. She got right to the point; she had talked it over with her fiancé, and he had some serious reservations.

What?

Thinking she and I had really clicked, I wasn't expecting that wild card. All the other applicants were clamoring for a job in the mayor's office.

"Who the hell is your fiancé?" I blurted out. "And why do we care what he thinks?"

With a disarming laugh, she said, "His name is Barack Obama, and he thinks the mayor's office could be a dangerous place to work. We're a team and make all big life decisions together."

Barack Obama. I'd heard of him. I didn't know him personally, but there weren't many black lawyers in the country who hadn't heard of the first black president of the *Harvard Law Review* in its then 104-year-history. He also had received some local attention as a successful community organizer on Chicago's South Side before he went to law school. Plus his name is not one you forget.

Michelle said that she and Barack, who had just graduated from law school, wanted to know if I'd be willing to have dinner with the two of them to discuss the job. It was an unconventional request, to say the least. But I really wanted to hire her, and if that's what I had to do to win her over, then dinner it was. What a wise decision on my part!

Within the week I was sitting in a booth across from the young couple at a popular restaurant not far from city hall. From my phone conversation with Michelle, I knew that Barack had recently moved back to Chicago to practice as a civil rights lawyer, and he was wary that Mayor Daley might succumb to machine politics. I understood his reservations, since I, too, had questioned whether the mayor would remain committed to Harold Washington's progressive ideals, so I'd come armed with a slew of arguments to convince them this was the right job for Michelle. But instead of launching into hardball questions about, say, the mayor's plans for the city's decaying neighborhoods, or employment resources for the residents, Barack started by simply asking me, "Where are you from?"

"Chicago," I answered.

"Were you born here?"

I took a deep breath, as I always did whenever I was asked this question.

"No, I was born in Iran," I said.

Typically, at this point in any conversation, I'd receive a look of surprise, followed by a series of banal questions that I'd quickly dispatch so the conversation could move on. But that didn't happen here. Barack smiled and leaned in. He genuinely wanted to know more. He asked thoughtful follow-up questions that proved he was really listening, and I found myself slowly opening up and telling him my story. I described how I arrived in the United States at age five, a redheaded, freckled kid who spoke Farsi, French, and English with an accent, dealt with bullying because I was different, and not surprisingly, just like any kid wanting to fit in. And since I still felt uncomfortable talking about my "exotic" beginnings even as an adult, I suppose I still wanted to fit in.

But Barack's unexpectedly open and curious responses put me at ease. He told me about his own international background and his biracial parents—his African father, who'd abandoned him at the beginning of his life, and the several years of his youth spent in Indonesia with his white mother. He talked about his close relationship with his grandparents, a lot like mine with Pudden.

We discussed memories and ideas that I had previously confided only in my parents—how much we both learned from living abroad, and how we had a different attitude toward the privileges so many Americans take for granted, from civil liberties to clean water. Or how, when we meet a person from another country, or with a different background, we always expect to find something in common, language barrier or not. Appreciating the importance of being willing to search for a common ground. And that we had both figured out early on that while the United States is the greatest country on earth, it's not the only one, and we could, and had, both learned much beyond our shores. As a child I wanted only to blend in, but my conversation with Barack made me feel like I was no longer so unique, for we shared such similar experiences.

Although we had just met, we were already finishing each other's sentences while Michelle listened intently, amused at our bonding session. Finally, as we moved into the third hour of dinner, our discussion turned to city hall. The young couple shared my passion for public service but were unsure how best to serve. Keenly aware of the value of their education and life experiences, they wanted to maximize their abilities to make a positive difference. I delicately told Barack that, although I had enormous respect for his work as a community organizer, there is great value in fighting for the powerless from *inside* government and that desire is what drove me to join city government. The paramount concern for both of them was being able to serve the public and stay true to their values. "I will protect you," I said to Michelle. "I will never ask you to do anything you're uncomfortable doing and will stand in the way of anybody who does." I won both of them over, and in the summer of 1991, Michelle joined me in the mayor's office. And in the many years that followed, life has carried the three of us on an extraordinary journey.

On the same day I resigned from the Department of Planning and Development to join The Habitat Company, Mayor Daley appointed me chair of the board of the Chicago Transit Authority. It was a public peace offering for the rocky way my departure was playing out in the press. The mayor assured me that chairing the CTA would be an easy lift. It was not. Public transit is, alongside housing, one of the biggest lightning rods for angry residents, and at my very first briefing the president of the CTA informed me that he was "exploring options for bankruptcy." A few years later, when we reached the point where demonstrators were showing up in front of my home to protest budget cuts, Laura, thirteen at the time, was mortified. I tried to explain to her that I wanted to be the one who made the tough decisions, and they weren't always popular. That's what leadership means. She was still skeptical and remained so for a long time. One time she stood next to me after a community meeting, watching helplessly as some outraged activist yelled at me inches from my face. Still, chairing the CTA board and working on neighborhood redevelopment at Habitat gave me a large platform in which to continue my public service while working in the private sector.

Michelle, just as I knew she would, easily conquered the bureaucracy of city hall and made magic happen. It was no easy feat, but she was relentless, refusing to ever take no for an answer. One day as I strolled past a conference room, I heard her commanding voice through the door. "You are *not* leaving this room until it's solved." I smiled and kept walking, knowing that with whomever she was speaking didn't stand a chance. After a couple of years in city government, she had left for an extraordinary opportunity to start up the Chicago office of Public Allies, a nonprofit dedicated to young-adult leadership under AmeriCorps. And Barack, though he hadn't yet run for office, had been busy putting the building blocks of his future career in place. Despite being the most sought-after young lawyer in the country after leaving Harvard Law School, he'd chosen Davis, Miner, Barnhill & Galland, a small Chicago law firm rooted in civil rights and community development law. He was also lecturing at the University of Chicago Law School and had, in July 1995, just published his first memoir, *Dreams from My Father*.

Starting with our very first dinner, the three of us gradually developed a very close friendship. After they married in 1992, they moved three blocks away from me, and we spent a lot of time at each other's homes. It was, admittedly, an unusual relationship. I was like a big sister to them as a couple, and also separately as individuals. Michelle and I bonded over our deep Chicago roots and raising children while balancing our career responsibilities, while Barack and I bonded over the exotic, far-flung adventures of our childhoods and his interest in politics, and all three of us shared a dedication to, and sense of responsibility for, careers in public service. We nurtured a relationship and learned we could be completely honest with one another and could share our boldest ideas and confide our deepest fears. We could tell one another hard truths and trust that those truths were said with no agenda but love.

My relationship with Barack and Michelle was one of many overlapping connections in a small group that came into its own on the South Side of Chicago during those years. It was a group of friends so close-knit we felt like family. There was my childhood friend John Rogers, who counted my dad as one of the first investors and corporate directors in his business. John had gone to Princeton with Michelle's brother, Craig. Kelly King Dibble, who had married my cousin Andrew, worked with Michelle and me at City Hall, and had twins the same month Malia was born. There was Eric Whitaker, a former student of my dad's, and later a collegue of Michelle's at the University of Chicago Medical Center, and Marty Nesbitt, Barack's best friend. His wife, Anita Blanchard, an OB-GYN, was also a former student of my dad's, a med school classmate of Eric's, and she delivered both Malia and Sasha Obama. Although we all came from different backgrounds, we were part of a generation of black Americans who understood that every step toward success meant we were all breaking new ground. We all wanted to help one another live up to the high expectations we had set for ourselves.

The election of Mayor Harold Washington had empowered black Chicagoans, both individually and collectively. His success proved our voices mattered. As our group became closer, we all realized we felt firmly connected to that phenomenon. Even for those of us who didn't join government, there was still a level of engagement and interest in politics and service. In fact, politics was often the topic of conversation. And as we each found professional success, we also knew we had a responsibility not just to vote and volunteer to knock on doors, but also to actively support candidates in whom we believed.

From the very first time I met Barack, I suspected he might one day be one of those candidates. Not for president, mind you. Not in my wildest dreams did I imagine that. But I do remember thinking it was entirely plausible that he might one day even be mayor of Chicago. So when he dropped by my office to say he was thinking about running for state senate, I wasn't at all surprised. Alice Palmer, our state senator, had decided not to run for reelection, and since it's always easier to run for an open seat than to challenge an incumbent, Barack thought it would be a good way in, and I agreed. Since I had just started working at The Habitat Company and chairing the Chicago Transit Authority, I wasn't too involved in the campaign. All I remember is going to the first organizational meeting of his kitchen cabinet. I was only there as a friend and fund-raiser, but to me, from the very beginning, it seemed like his first campaign would be a slam dunk, and other than a little messiness when Alice Palmer waffled on running, it was.

Four years after being elected to the state senate, Barack decided to run for a different seat, this time challenging Bobby Rush, the popular incumbent who represented (and still represents) the First Congressional District of Illinois in the U.S. House of Representatives. My involvement in that campaign again was strictly as friend and supporter, but I thought—we all thought—that Barack had a good chance to win based on his sheer talent alone. We were wrong.

The first mistake was that we underestimated the power of the incumbency. Bobby Rush was well-known and had been in office since 1993. He was familiar. There were a number of people who had known the congressman from back in the day when he was a militant Black Panther activist, and they liked that he was a fighter. Barack, on the other hand, was a newcomer without deep roots in Chicago.

There was also a generational divide, and a class divide in the district as well. The First District encompasses two distinct communities, the lower-income, predominantly black North Kenwood–Oakland area, and the neighborhood of Hyde Park–South Kenwood, the racially integrated home of the University of Chicago and the lakefront liberals who had backed Harold Washington. We thought Barack had the appeal to reach both of those constituencies, but in the end, he didn't. While Barack did well with the white progressives and the younger, upwardly mobile segments of the black vote, Bobby Rush proved far more popular with the older generation in North Kenwood and Oakland.

It didn't help Barack's standing when, in 1999, he missed an important vote in the state Senate for an anticrime bill. He, Michelle, and their daughters, Malia and Sasha, were in Hawaii for his annual trip to visit his grandmother when Sasha, who was eighteen months old at the time, came down with an earache. Unwilling to leave Michelle—who was also unwilling to be left—with a sick toddler and a four-year-old, he stayed in Hawaii with his family and missed the vote, and the popular Safe Neighborhoods Act fell five votes short of passing. Barack was widely criticized in the press right in the middle of his race for Congress. Three months later, Bobby Rush won the Democratic primary for the seat by a landslide.

The loss was very painful for all of us. In retrospect, Barack recognized the flaws in his campaign, and we learned a lot about what could go wrong even with talent and commitment. Part of the lesson we took from the loss is that if you're relatively unknown and you go after an incumbent with his own political power base firmly in place, you need to line up big supporters known to the voters to vouch for you. It's just like when you're interviewing someone for a job. If the candidate comes with a recommendation from someone you know, you are more likely to hire him. When he ran against Bobby Rush, Barack didn't have that.

Not long after he lost, Barack came by my office at The Habitat Company one day in search of a sounding board for a few ideas about next steps. We sat around my little conference table and he said, "I gotta figure out what to do next." Having lost the race, he was now trying to balance his political ambitions with the demands of supporting his new family. We tossed a few ideas around, and ultimately he decided to stay where he was, serving in Springfield and supplementing his income with teaching and work at his law firm. But what struck me most about the meeting was what didn't happen. We hardly talked about the loss to Bobby Rush at all. I'd expected him to come into my office dejected and depressed, wanting to commiserate and go over what had gone wrong. But he hadn't. He'd already analyzed it, assessed it, and put it behind him, and all that was on his mind was what to do next.

The toll our public lives and professions took on our families was a constant topic of conversation between the Jarrett and Obama families. After Barack joined the Illinois legislature in 1997, Michelle learned firsthand what it meant to raise children married to a man with a very demanding career. They had Malia in 1998 and Sasha in 2001. And while Barack was still a devoted, loving husband and father, as a public servent his hours were long, and he worked from Springfield Monday through Thursday three months in the fall and two weeks in the spring when the legislature was in session. That, of course, placed a higher burden on Michelle to care for their daughters.

In 2002 Michelle was recruited for the position of executive director for community affairs at the University of Chicago Medical Center, a big job with a lot of thorny responsibilities. When the day came for her interview, she didn't have a sitter. Rather than reschedule with Michael Riordan, the president of the medical center, Michelle, not really interested in the job, simply brought Sasha along, and, mercifully, Sasha stayed asleep in her stroller the whole time. Michelle thought that Michael might as well see up front what her life was like. He was both amused and supportive, which piqued Michelle's interest, and helped Mike win her over. He offered her the job, and she accepted. She started out not pretending her life was organized in neatly separated packages, and Michael respected her for it.

We were both in overdrive during those years, trying to fit all the pieces of our lives together and make things work. Exercise was a prime example. There was just never time. When Laura was about ten, I started sneaking to the gym in our building around 5:30 a.m., before she woke up. Michelle was always more ambitious. Her schedule made mine look like a luxury cruise. She would wake up at four in the morning to go to the gym while her mom babysat. Then she'd be back home and dressed by 7 a.m. to get the girls ready for school.

While Michelle was busy being a solo mom part of the time, I was busy being a single mom all of the time.

Without Mrs. Brown and my parents, I don't know how I would have made it. They were the glue that held my life together. As a single mom I felt plenty of guilt when it came to leaving Laura and working long hours. From the time she was two, I took her to my office, to demystify where I was when I wasn't with her. I wanted her always to be able to picture where I was and what I was doing. My parents had done the same with me. I'd often visited my mom's preschool classroom when I was young. After she founded the Erikson Institute, a graduate school in child development, I would walk the mile between school and her office and hang out there after school until she was ready to go home. I also went to my dad's office at the university, only four blocks from the Lab Schools. There I pretended to be a doctor, too, no doubt the origins of my interest in a career in medicine.

When I was young, my mom also had a rule that anytime I called her at work, no matter the reason, I was to be put through. I can still hear the sound of her high heels clicking, growing louder as she approached the phone. Connecting with my mom whenever I wanted, even if only for a minute, was always reassuring. So, I made the same request of all my assistants. Only once did I come out of a meeting to learn that my daughter had phoned.

"How come you didn't put her through?" I asked my assistant.

"You were behind closed doors."

"My rule means no matter where I am. If I'm with Mayor Daley, you let me know."

"Laura said it wasn't important."

"You can't expect a six-year-old to know if it is important," I said.

My strictness came partly from my mother's example. But because it was just the two of us, I also felt a particular urgency in making sure Laura always knew I was there.

All public servants sacrifice, and so do their families, from our men and women in the military to local police, from city council members to the president of the United States to workers at every level. Disappointing loved ones when a crisis occurs is inevitable. On the first day of the Great Chicago Flood of 1992, I had to cancel a trip to Disney World with my cousin Lynn and her two children. The day the city flooded, the entire downtown had to be evacuated. Businesses were forced to close, and no one knew what the short- or long-term consequences would be. Mayor Daley sent out an announcement that no staff member was to leave the city until the damage from the flood was contained. Since I was responsible for outreach to all of the affected businesses, my team and I were crucial to all aspects of damage control and recovery. But try explaining to an excited six-year-old who has been looking forward to the trip why her favorite cousins are going to Disney World and she is stuck at home.

Several days into the crisis, Laura called and said, "Where are you?" At that exact moment, Mayor Daley was about to begin a press conference where I'd be standing beside him. So I quickly said to Laura, "If you want to see me, turn on the television, and I'll look right at you and smile." A year later I managed to carve out time to take Laura to Euro Disney, by far our favorite day of her childhood. There were countless times when I tried to bolster myself with the knowledge that I was working for the greater good. But it's not easy or simple.

As a working single mother, over time, I found that a support system of good friends is crucial. I forged a network of close friends from many circles of my life, and we always came together to assist one another in our careers. That same network was crucial for raising our families as well. Many of my girlfriends who were married with kids faced the same challenges I had, and by the time I left my law firm job I had stopped pretending I had it all under control, and had begun to appreciate the importance of being honest about my challenges so we could commiserate. We learned together how to ask for help and not always put ourselves last.

Kelly and Michelle used to hang out with a group of young moms who had children around the same age as their four children. Since Laura was older than their children—and I had also been Michelle's and Kelly's boss—I was more a big sister and sounding board than a hang-out buddy. But I always made my home a gathering place where children and adults could come over, relax, and eat a good meal.

Susan Sher joined the city as Kelly Welsh's chief deputy in 1989, moving into the office next to mine. We became each other's sounding boards professionally and personally. Our children were at the Lab Schools together, and we bonded over both the stresses and delights of being single moms.

When Barack was away, Michelle often was chopping veggies or stirring something alongside friends in my kitchen, while Laura played with the younger children. Since I grew up watching my parents entertain both family and friends, as well as work colleagues, I appreciated the value of mealtime in solidifying bonds and helping us all recharge our batteries. Even at ninety, my mom continues the tradition of hosting Sunday dinners every week. Dinner doesn't start until four, but people start coming over at two to help cook or just hang out in the kitchen together.

I tried to give Michelle, Kelly, and several of our other friends their age the benefit of learning from my experiences, and during those years we all had a lot of conversations about setting expectations for ourselves and for others. As much as I blamed Bobby for the problems in our marriage, I had failed to communicate clearly and openly with him about what my expectations of him were. I was so busy trying to be this perfectly accommodating wife, assuming all of the household chores, and parental ones, too, after Laura was born, that I suppressed my own needs. I would try to cajole and convince him to shape up, but I waited for too long to put my foot down and say, "No, this is unacceptable, and if you continue to do it, I'll leave." And by the time I finally did, it was too late, anyway.

The advice I gave to all my girlfriends—advice I had not followed myself—was to start out the way you want to end up. I started out trying so hard to be perfect, which I defined as accommodating. My mother used to see me doing that, and she'd say to me, "You know, you're not actually that nice. Stop pretending that you are, because Bobby's going to be lulled into thinking you're a pushover, and eventually you're going to get tired of playing house." And she was right. People often start out relationships acting like this ideal version of what they think the other person wants, but it's not sustainable. At some point you do become yourself, and then what?

I also encouraged my younger friends to follow Michelle's lead and be up front with their prospective bosses about what they needed in order to thrive. I openly shared my horror stories of juggling—and dropping—way too many balls trying to pretend to my colleagues that my only priority was my work.

A little less than two years after Barack's loss to Bobby Rush, our lives in Hyde Park had settled into a nice rhythm. I was working at The Habitat Company and, in addition to serving as chair of the

CTA, I was the first black chairman of the University of Chicago Medical Center and vice chairman of the University of Chicago Board of Trustees, and the first African American and the first woman to chair the Chicago Stock Exchange. I had joined a number of other corporate and not-for-profit boards, including the Museum of Science and Industry, where my old boss David Mosena was the president. I often tell people about my first real summer jobs at sixteen, as clinic coordinator at the Med Center and docent at the museum, jobs that informed my perspective about both institutions decades later as a board member. Michelle was working for Susan Sher (now the general counsel of the University of Chicago Medical Center). And Barack, having bounced back from his loss to Bobby Rush, was commuting back and forth between serving as state senator in Springfield and teaching as a senior lecturer at the University of Chicago Law School. Our lives were full and busy, but the mighty juggle was doable. Then Barack started dropping hints: he was thinking of running for Illinois's open seat in the U.S. Senate.

There were plenty of reasons why he shouldn't do it. Illinois is a microcosm of the United States, with big, urban centers and large swaths of rural areas. While predominately a blue state, it doesn't necessarily vote Democratic. In 1992, when several women were elected to the Senate on the heels of Anita Hill's grilling during Clarence Thomas's Supreme Court nomination hearings—the "Year of the Woman," people called it—a former Cook County official and Illinois state rep, Carol Moseley Braun, had run and won, becoming the first black woman in the Senate and only the second black senator since Reconstruction. But she lost after one term to a white, male Republican. When Barack started talking about running, the jury was out on the appetite for a statewide candidate in Illinois who was a person of color.

Michelle, for her part, was not pleased that he wanted to run again so soon after his recent loss, and I was surprised myself. I thought it was a bad idea because if he lost the race, his political career would likely be over. Michelle was opposed for more personal reasons. It would only take him farther away from home more, and she already felt like she was carrying much more than her fair share of the family responsibilities, so she asked me if I would host a brunch and invite our closest friends over—to talk him out of it.

"*Absolutely,*" I said.

So one Sunday morning, a group of us gathered around my dining room table and I served a spread of bacon and eggs, bread, orange juice, and fruit. I sat at the head of the table. To my immediate left was Michelle, then Barack, John Rogers, Marty Nesbitt, and a few others. As we sat down, I thought we'd staged an effective ambush, that Barack had no idea he and his ambitions were on the agenda for the morning. But, being the intuitive guy he is, as soon as we were gathered around the table, he seemed to sense that we'd all been given marching orders by Michelle, so he preemptively broached the subject. "There's something I want to talk to you all about," he said, and then launched into all of the reasons why he wanted to run for Senate.

He explained why this race would be different from his first run for Congress. This time there was an open seat, and he had the backing of the powerful Illinois Senate president Emil Jones, and he had a better sense of the ground organization needed to run a successful campaign. Having matured as both a candidate and a legislator, he was also the only state senator from Chicago who frequently traveled to downstate Illinois, so people there knew him and he knew what they cared about. True to his curious nature, he was interested in learning about farming and agriculture. "I vote on issues that affect the entire state," he reasoned. "So I need to understand the state."

I spoke up first. "I think it's a terrible idea," I said. I thought it was a long shot that the people on farms in southern Illinois would rally behind anyone from Chicago. "And," I added, "if you have back-to-back losses, that's it for you in politics."

"But I'm not afraid of that," he said. "I'm OK with knowing that if I lose this race, I'll have to find a new career, and if I'm OK with that, why aren't you?"

I didn't have an answer. But the way he posed the question made me think about courage. Courage isn't the absence of fear. Courage is overcoming fear. It's willingness to risk failure, believing in your own resiliency to survive if you come up short. I think Barack's courage was partly temperment, but also from growing up the way he had. Even though he was a black man, the three people who had loved him most before he met Michelle were all white: his mom and his grandparents. And they believed he could actually do whatever he wanted. The cautionary reality checks I'd heard constantly from my mother growing up just weren't a part of his childhood.

Faced with Barack's well-thought-out analysis and ability to persuade, I was running out of objections to his running, but I'd pledged to Michelle that I'd do whatever I could to talk him out of it. So I threw out the biggest remaining obstacle. "But what about money?" I asked. "Senate campaigns are insanely expensive. Where on earth are you going to get that kind of money?"

With a knowing twinkle in his eye, he said, "You're going to chair my finance committee."

By the end of the three-hour brunch, everyone was on board. Even Michelle. But she had one caveat, which she held in reserve until the very end of the conversation.

"OK," she said. "We'll do this. But if you lose, can we say this is over and you'll get a real job?"

"Yes," he committed.

Barack's senate campaign added a completely new dimension to our relationship. I'd volunteered on his earlier campaigns and had always supported him, but this was my first time taking on a central role and we had a big uphill climb ahead of us.

That year's Democratic primary campaign was a grind. Barack was up against six other candidates in what *The New York Times* called an "an expensive and messy race." One of his opponents was a multimillionaire who poured his own money into his campaign right from the beginning, with glitzy commercials saturating TV and radio stations. Another was a well-known statewide official whom everyone expected would have the party establishment behind him. There were so many players already in the field that it was hard for Barack to find a campaign manager or any other seasoned political operatives with track records of successful statewide campaigns. The most experienced person willing to take him on was the political strategist David Axelrod, well-known to many in Chicago as a *Tribune* reporter and as the key strategist for Mayor Daley's campaigns.

I had one primary qualification to be the chair of Barack's finance committee: my relationships with some of Chicago's wealthiest business leaders. But beyond that I didn't have any experience fund-raising in a statewide campaign, and it was slow going at first. Even among my closest friends, I had trouble drumming up support for such a long-shot candidate. One evening, having convinced the chairman of the University of Chicago, Jim Crown, and the university president, Don Randel, to host a fund-raiser, a dicey ask given there were a number of Republicans on the board, I walked in to the event early and saw that only six people had shown up—including me. My heart sank. But when Barack showed up, he appeared unfazed. While I drank two glasses of wine to calm my nerves at the poor showing, he gave the handful of guests his best campaign pitch. Sitting on a coffee table with the small group gathered around, he was the same man who liked going to country fairs and spending time in southern Illinois, just talking and listening. Authentically caring is the most important political skill; people can tell when you are genuinely interested in their lives.

Luckily, the campaign did improve. With lots of practice and plenty of pressure from the candidate, I got better at asking for money, and as Barack's profile grew, my cell phone started to ring constantly as I rushed between meetings, juggling the ridiculous number of obligations I'd taken on to fill my life after Laura departed for college. I said yes to too many board invitations because I was flattered, but realized I was spread too thin, and I began stepping down unless I cared passionately about the mission and could make a unique contribution.

As the campaign finances improved, one source of tension did develop between the candidate and me: punctuality. I am never late. My father and mother are both punctual, but my dad carried it to an extreme. Punctuality to him meant being early. "Bring a book," he always said. The broader lesson he tried to teach me is that it's rude to keep anybody waiting. Their time is as important as yours, and showing up early is a sign of respect.

Barack, on the other hand, was habitually late, in both his social life and his political life. For the host of a political gathering the two biggest fears are: *Are people going to show up?* and *Will the candidate show up?* I thought Barack should arrive early, to put the host at ease. Barack thought he should arrive later, to be efficient with his time. Whenever I suggested we organize his schedule so he could get places early, he responded, "I'll get there as soon as I can."

His tardiness to fund-raisers was irksome, but not enough to do battle with him. But the time he was late to a televised debate? That was nerve-racking. It was the first televised debate among all seven Democratic primary candidates. Michelle and I had arrived at WTTW, the local public television station sponsoring the debate, forty-five minutes early; Michelle is as punctual as I am. Barack had a vote that day in Springfield. Traveling from there brings you into Chicago on the southeast side. The TV studios, meanwhile, were far northwest of the city, and it was pouring rain.

Half an hour before the start time, Michelle and I inquired of a campaign aide about Barack's ETA. All the aide could tell us was that he was "on his way."

Twenty minutes out, Michelle said, "Call the campaign manager."

I stepped to the side and called him on my cell phone. "I'm sitting with Mrs. Obama, waiting for the debate to begin," I said. "She'd like to know where her husband is."

"Barack's on his way," he said.

"That's what I told her ten minutes ago. I can't go back with that."

He put me on hold for what was probably thirty seconds but felt like an hour. I looked over at Michelle sitting with her arms folded.

The campaign manager came back on. "The senator just passed Soldier Field," he said.

That meant he was at least a half hour away!

Knowing Michelle, I couldn't give her "He's on his way" again. Plus, I wanted to have company in my own panicked state. I told her the truth. Then I watched as she calculated the distance in her head and came up with the same answer I had: it would be impossible for him to get there on time.

Five minutes out from the start, Michelle turned to me again and said in a firm, low voice, "I want to know exactly where he is." I went into the hall and called the campaign manager again. He said Barack was approaching the building, which of course could mean anything. I needed to show her movement, so I relayed the message. The studio audience was packed with supporters of all the candidates, chatting with anticipation, while the two of us sat alone, staring straight ahead in our silent panic.

Two minutes out, one of the TV producers approached us. "Mrs. Obama," she said, "it seems like your husband is not going to make it on time. Would you like to go on for him at the top?"

She looked at me, then turned to the producer with an unmistakable expression that said, "No."

One minute out, the music started, and the moderator, Phil Ponce, read from his teleprompter, "Welcome, ladies and gentlemen! We are joined tonight by the seven candidates for the Democratic nomination for the U.S. Senate representing Illinois." The camera slowly panned across the stage: six candidates all seated in a row, and one empty chair. "We'll be back in sixty seconds!"

In those sixty seconds, Barack Obama strode in, said hello to his opponents, sat in his chair, picked up his microphone, and attached it to his lapel, calm, cool, and collected the whole time. When the cameras came back, Barack was looking out at the room with his thousand-megawatt smile. I could have killed him.

If you were to ask Michelle or me what was the worst moment of the campaign, that would have been it. But the candidate himself was oblivious. He missed the mounting stress as the minutes counted down. He wasn't in the room to watch his empty chair as the credits began to roll. When we fussed at him later, he shrugged and said if he had been late, he would have explained he had a good excuse: he was doing his job in Springfield for his constituents. And that was the difference between us: He simply doesn't sweat. We do.

Michelle is the worrier. She believes if you're not prepared, catastrophe lurks, which is why she's always well organized and well prepared and punctual. Barack, on the other hand, assumes it will work out fine, so he feels perfectly comfortable winging it. For the 2008 Democratic National Convention, her speech was done and practiced to perfection a week ahead of time, while he was still editing his on the way to the convention center. They would both say they are pragmatic—Michelle because she prepares for the worst by systematically analyzing the pros and cons of every decision, Barack because the worst just doesn't scare him. With a deep reservoir of resilience, he believes he can always bounce back. I'm somewhere in between. In general I am not as well organized as she is, but I'm also too afraid to wing it, to assume all will go well, as he does. That was a familiar place for me—I was somewhere between my parents, who had a similar dynamic.

Stressful as that campaign was, Barack kept his calm, cool demeanor the whole time. I saw it break down only once. We were near the end of the Senate primary. He was down in the polls, and he was late to meetings, speeches, and fund-raisers, and he wasn't making phone calls to raise money. At some events he appeared lethargic and, worse, indifferent. His once-passionate stump speech was lackluster. The entire campaign staff felt it. The audiences felt it. I felt it. Even the donors I was calling started to ask, "Does he really want to win?" I invited him to lunch at the East Bank Club to talk about the problem.

"I must be in trouble if you've invited me to lunch," he said slightly sheepishly when he arrived.

I explained to him what I and the other staffers had been seeing. "You seem ambivalent," I said.

He paused, perhaps toying with the idea of bluffing his way through our talk, but then he simply admitted it. "I am," he said.

"What's going on? We don't have to do this, you know."

He sat for a moment. Then tears welled up in his eyes.

"If I win," he said, "it's going to pull me even further away from my family. The magnitude of that is finally sinking in."

Seeing his emotion, the big sister in me came out. I always knew how much Michelle missed him when he was in Springfield or off campaigning, but this was the first time I fully appreciated the impact on him. I never saw it as my role with Barack to be the one to pressure him to make one decision or another. Instead I gave him a safe place to express his feelings, being a sounding board to help him reach his own decisions, and that's what I tried to do at lunch that day. I looked at him and said quietly, "You are one of the few politicians I know who truly puts your family first. So if you don't want to do it, let's not do it. But you need to figure it out."

"I know," he said. "I know."

We parted with a hug after lunch, and I didn't bring up the subject again. Without any explicit declaration from him, I started to see his energy and passion returning to his campaigning. I assumed he came to some sort of inner reconciliation that it was the right decision to move forward. It gradually built up, and within a couple of weeks he hit his stride again. When he came back to life, he was all in.

Barack was still the underdog in the primary, but that quickly turned around when the lead candidate, Blair Hull, a former securities trader who had put $29 million of his own money into his campaign, crashed and burned after it was revealed that one of his ex-wives had taken out an order of protection against him because she feared for her safety during their marriage. Coincidentally, Hull's campaign imploded right around the time we finally had enough money to go on TV with commercials and really push our message, and we surged in the polls.

Twice as hard, twice as good, and three times as lucky.

And Barack's luck didn't end there. That summer, John Kerry tapped him to give the keynote speech at the Democratic National Convention, giving a then relatively unknown candidate a chance to make a name for himself on a global stage. In the general election that fall, the campaign of Barack's Republican opponent, Jack Ryan, also imploded when it came out that he had pressured his then wife to go to sex clubs. Ryan denied his ex-wife's allegations, but it was too late. He was forced out of the race, and the conservative firebrand chosen to replace him, Alan Keyes, though annoying in how low he was willing to stoop to win, never stood a chance. Barack won a whopping 70 percent of the votes.

With his win, Barack became a national figure and a rising star in the Democratic Party. But there would be a personal cost he knew all too well: his family. For a time, Barack tried to make the case that Michelle and the girls should move with him to DC. But I was relieved when they decided the family should remain in Chicago. To take them away from their community, to asking Michelle to raise two small children in a town where she didn't know anyone, without the support of her network, was not the right thing to do—not yet, anyway.

Chapter 8

The Power of Each Voice

By the time John Kerry picked Senate candidate Barack Obama to give a keynote address at the 2004 Democratic Convention in July, he had already been tagged as an up-and-coming political superstar. Then he gave the speech.

I was quite nervous before it began. Sitting with Laura in the Obamas' friends-and-family box in Boston's Fleet Center, waiting for him to come onstage, I couldn't breathe. I thought of all the ways it could turn into a disaster. What if his mind went blank? What if the crowd was flat? What if he said "um" too much? Laura had watched him on TV a few days earlier, and she had mentioned the "ums," a comment I passed along to him. I cared so much about the outcome, yet simply had no control.

I needn't have worried. About three minutes into the speech to the packed stadium, I went from anxious to mesmerized. I was inspired; I felt such pride in how he delivered so passionately a message of unity. "We are not a red America or a blue America. We are the United States of America." When he finished, the convention center erupted in jubilance. He had captured the essence of the American dream for a more perfect union. Everyone in our box was crying and hugging one another when he finished. Our emotion was rippling across the stadium, our country, and the world. That was the first time I fully appreciated his extraordinary ability to connect, to make each of us feel he was speaking directly to us, to see ourselves in his story.

At his party afterward, I stood by the door so I could congratulate Barack as soon as he walked in. Once I caught his eye, he came over to where I was standing with Laura, leaned over, and without saying a word gave me a kiss on the cheek. Then he turned at Laura and asked, "I didn't say 'um' too much, did I?" She replied, laughing, that no, he had not.

Two weeks later, Laura and I escaped on our annual trip to Martha's Vineyard. I rented a home with a beautiful view of the ocean in East Chop. The Obamas needed a break from the grueling campaign, and so they joined us for a few days. On our first morning there, Barack went for a morning run alone along the ocean path by our house. When he returned, he announced to Michelle and me with great surprise, "You'll never guess what happened. Somebody recognized me and took my photo!" Michelle and I both laughed, and she said, "It must have been a pretty good speech," a quip Barack and Michelle started using after the speech when people reacted to him so differently than before it. But I also sensed it was a sign that our lives were beginning to change.

Two years later, after Senator Obama had become even more of a national figure, the buzz and energy he'd unleashed had only grown. For the 2006 midterms he was the hottest ticket in the Democratic Party at every candidate's campaign event. The reception of his second book, *The Audacity of Hope*, was nothing short of astounding. My parents had hosted a party at their home for his first book, *Dreams from My Father*. Only about forty people came, and they'd come only because I'd twisted their arms. Eleven years later, in October of 2006, my parents threw a second book party for Barack. It was pouring rain that night, so I'd asked a young friend to ferry guests into the backyard tent under his umbrella. He could not possibly keep up with the tide, and everyone was drenched but buoyant. Feeling the energy in the tent as Barack addressed the crowd, and tearing up when he spoke about his love for Michelle and her sacrifices, I thought to myself, *He's going to run.*

B arack and I had spoken periodically about his running for president, starting with his Senate victory in 2004. They were always very casual conversations, loose in detail and timing, but I could tell that he was restless in the Senate. The behind-the-scenes antics that kept the Senate from making real progress frustrated him; as he used to say, when comparing the Illinois legislature and the U.S. Senate, "More decimal points, same problems." But after just two years in the Senate, I wasn't convinced the timing was right, especially with Hillary Clinton's formidable presence looming.

Then, right after Christmas of 2006, Laura and I went to Anguilla with a few friends and family. One evening as we sat around chatting before dinner, my phone rang. It was Barack, who, as usual, was in Hawaii with his family for the holidays. I stepped outside into the warm evening air to have a private conversation.

"I'm leaning toward doing this," he said.

I knew exactly what "this" was.

He said he knew it would be a long shot. Hillary Clinton had been a senator longer than he, and she not only was a former First Lady but also had been a major policy advisor to President Clinton. Over the years, she and her husband—who had name recognition, to put it mildly— generated enormous support and loyalty within the Democratic Party and its donors. But what Barack had was a vision for an inclusive America, and he was unburdened by political baggage. He was the new darling of the party and clearly on fire.

Perhaps that's why, even though the odds were very much against Barack, when he said he was leaning toward "this," my only reply was "Great. When do we start?"

The wild card was of course Michelle. She wasn't nearly as quick to climb on board as I was, and if she said no, all bets were off. Once we were back from vacation, she called me up to talk it over, the first of several conversations. She was understandably concerned about what the campaign could mean for their family, including the possibility that it might actually put their lives in danger. She also questioned whether this was the right time for any of them, knowing how hard it had been for her so far to shoulder most of the responsibility for raising their daughters. Michelle was hesitant to stand in the way of his dream, knowing he had a special gift and a true drive to serve. She also wanted us all to face the harsh realities of what this decision would mean to him and their family.

"I'm already hanging on by my fingertips, and now he wants to do *this*?" she said. "How's it going to work?"

"It's going to be really hard," I said, "but we'll figure it out."

But—no surprise here—that wasn't good enough for Michelle. She wanted an accurate gauge of how hard this was going to be, with no sugarcoating, so she would be prepared.

In January of the new year, Barack called together a small group of advisors in David Axelrod's office for a meeting with him and Michelle to play out the scenario of a presidential run. Joining us were Steve Hildebrand, considered the political guru of Iowa; David Plouffe, an associate of Axelrod's with lots of presidential campaign experience; Alyssa Mastromonaco, who had managed scheduling for Senator John Kerry's presidential campaign and now worked in Barack's Senate office; Robert Gibbs, also a Kerry veteran and Barack's communications director; and Pete Rouse, chief of staff at Barack's Senate office in Washington, who with a legacy of forty years on the Hill was nicknamed the "101st senator."

It was the first time I'd met David Plouffe, who'd go on to manage Barack's campaign. He was the real no-nonsense presence that day. As Michelle and Barack peppered everyone with questions about the process and strategy, David was candid to the point of blunt. I liked him instantly.

"Can Barack come home on weekends?" Michelle asked.

"No."

"What about Sunday?"

"No."

And so it went.

That meeting, and the ones that followed, were like master classes in Presidential Campaigning 101. There was no doubt in my mind that Barack was going to run. Regardless of the answers to Michelle's questions or the prospect of an uphill battle, he knew this was his moment and was not about to let the chance slip by without even giving it a shot. When I think now about the candidates I've known who've won, they all had one common trait: they each believed that they were the right person for the job and would do whatever it took to earn the voters' confidence. Barack believed in himself. That was for sure, but during the first meeting, I whispered to Hildebrand, "Can he win?" He smiled and said, "Oh, yes." I clung to that comment on the roller coaster of the next twenty-two months.

Planning moved swiftly from there, and on February 10, 2007, several of the Obamas' close friends and family joined seventeen thousand supporters in front of the Illinois statehouse in Springfield on a sunny, subzero day to watch him announce his candidacy for president of the United States of America.

Barack's campaign announcement was televised live in the United States and around the world, and as I stood surrounded by a euphoric crowd as he took the stage with Michelle and the girls, it all felt surreal. Could my friend actually be running for president of the United States? Was America ready to embrace a brand-new version of America's first family? I was confident, even then, that I was witnessing the start of a new chapter in American history—a history that, for me, traced back to a plantation in North Carolina, and the segregated railcars of Louisiana. We knew that as much as he campaigned on jobs, health care, and the war in Iraq, the subject of race would always be there, shaping and informing every move we made.

The advice of Barack's strategists was to demonstrate his viability as a candidate by winning the Iowa caucuses. Resources—both time and cash—needed to be used strategically. The theory was that there would be time to reach out more broadly after the Iowa caucuses, but only if he won them. So for almost seven months, Barack raised money around the country but campaigned almost exclusively in Iowa. In other words, the vast majority of the campaign's resources needed to be deployed in a state that is 90 percent white.

But what about the black community, an obvious critical part of his base? South Carolina's primary, for example, came just sixteen days after Iowa's, hardly enough time, I worried, to galvanize black voters, especially if they felt ignored until then. Many were loyal to the Clintons— President Clinton having been previously dubbed by some "the first black president." Others, particularly in southern states, were afraid for Barack's safety and were not prepared to root for a black man only to put him in harm's way. Some African Americans simply thought the country was not ready for a black president. My parents were among them. After all, with their experience of segregation in Chicago and DC, Barack's attempt at the presidency seemed impossible. I was fielding a deluge of angry calls from black leaders, but given the campaign's Iowa strategy, there wasn't much I could do other than reinforce our position and beg for patience.

By August of 2007, Barack's poll numbers had dropped low enough with voters of all colors that it was time to worry. The Obamas and I were together again on Martha's Vineyard, and on their last day there, Barack received an email from Michael Strautmanis, his general counsel and deputy chief of staff in the Senate. Straut, as we all called him, had met Michelle Obama in 1991 at Sidley Austin, where she was an associate and he was a paralegal who'd worked his way up from bike messenger and who, with Michelle's encouragement, would soon go on to law school. Over time he'd become close to both Obamas. He was fielding the same kinds of calls as me, and had decided emotions in the black community were reaching a boiling point.

Straut and I agreed it was time to draw Barack into the conversation. In his email, sharing with Barack the very critical feedback he'd received, Straut laid out the facts: Barack wasn't doing enough outreach with black voters; there was no media strategy around the issue of race; campaign resources were not flowing to black-owned businesses; and there were not enough black staffers in visible senior positions on the campaign. Barack had been so focused on executing the Iowa strategy that Straut's message took him by surprise.

When we all returned to Chicago, Barack convened a meeting at my home with all of his senior campaign staff to hash out a plan to make the campaign more inclusive and reflective of his values, and more effective in reaching voters of color. In addition to his team, Barack also invited Marty Nesbitt and Chris Edley, a UC Berkeley law professor who'd taught at Harvard when Barack was a student there and had since become a close friend.

Chris took on the role of bomb thrower. "You're a bunch of white guys who aren't hearing any outside voices," he said to the team. The reaction was stony silence. I was stunned at Chris's blunt language, but he wanted to let us know exactly what he thought. It made everyone squirm, which was exactly his goal. Even among the most trusted members of Barack's team, completely devoted to electing the first black president, it was hard to talk about race. But Barack insisted we do so, and it had to start in that room.

As uncomfortable as that meeting might have been, it did shake things up. Up until that point I didn't have an official role in the campaign. I was a surrogate out raising money because his supporters knew of our close friendship. Barack asked if I would take on a more formal role as senior advisor to the campaign. He also asked the same of Pete Rouse, his chief of staff. He wanted to make sure his team had our very different perspectives in the room where decisions were being made. He also thought we could help David Plouffe troubleshoot and augment the campaign's outreach with me taking on outreach to the communities of color, and he asked Straut to jump in and help me with that effort. That included being a sounding board of support for the black staff on the campaign who were also hearing the same complaints as Straut and I.

I understood why David Plouffe, as campaign manager, might have hesitated to have Pete and me, two people with independent relationships to the candidate, more involved and potentially second-guessing his decisions. But we all made an effort to coexist and never forgot we were working for the same mission. As David said to me once, "Do whatever you need to do to get this guy elected." Still, our difference of opinion on outreach, particular to the black vote, remained a source of tension. David Plouffe was one of the most seasoned political strategists on the team, and he fervently believed that if we didn't win Iowa, we would never be able to catch up with Hillary Clinton's machine. Everything else was secondary in his plan. And, as it turned out, he was right.

But many black leaders, understandably, were anxious to have Barack show up to their events and talk about issues that were important to the black community. A few prominent leaders, however, made demands for senior titles, chartered planes, dedicated staff, bloated budgets, advertising buys—seemingly more focused on their own self-interests over what would have been helpful to the campaign. Evidently, that is what had been made available to them in the past in order for them to act as intermediaries. But Barack's campaign strategy was different, and it took awhile for them to adjust.

A few well-known leaders in the black community, such as Reverend Joseph Lowery—a well-respected minister in the United Methodist Church and civil rights icon from Atlanta, Georgia—embraced Barack early on in the campaign. In March of 2007, Reverend Lowery preached from Brown Chapel A.M.E. Church in Selma, Alabama, on the fiftieth anniversary of the famous march for voting rights across the Edmund Pettus Bridge known as "Bloody Sunday." Reverend Lowery said that someone like Barack running for president was crazy—good crazy. Well, he took that funny refrain to the campaign trail, and I joined him for a round of several church visits one Sunday morning. His energy and enthusiasm for Barack were contagious and there's no doubt that he helped persuade many in the black community who were hesitant to take a leap of faith and support Barack's candidacy.

Another black leader who understood Barack's potential early on was Reverend Al Sharpton from New York. He was known for his fair share of controversy when he was younger, but he believed that Barack should be the future, not just for black America, but for America as a whole, without feeling envious or begrudging Barack's popularity. Sharpton knew he could be a lightning rod, so at the start, he quietly worked behind the scenes, pushing back on those in the black community who tried to throw shade on Barack and his campaign. The senior campaign staff was skeptical of Sharpton's motives, but he and I developed a relationship while navigating numerous tricky and sensitive situations, and I came to find his advice and counsel extraordinarily helpful in both of Barack's presidential campaigns and throughout the eight years I worked in the White House. During some campaign meetings with black leaders—and then, after the first election, very vocally in the press—he was often the voice in the room that reminded us that as a black president, especially with the extra burden of being the first one, Barack had to clearly demonstrate his commitment to *all* Americans. He also would masterfully describe how many of our priorities, such as health care and public education reforms, disproportionately benefited the black community even when not identified specifically as such.

Nonetheless, at the outset, most of my meetings with black leaders were hard. My responsibility was to explain the importance of our Iowa strategy and the many ways in which Barack's national agenda would help the black community. Straut and I organized a weekly call with key black allies who were surrogates for Barack on the campaign trail. The calls gave them status reports on the campaign and also opened up a channel for them to give us feedback and advice that I could pass on directly to the candidate. Eric Holder was a regular on those calls—and our sidebar texts, sometimes hilarious, and the time we spent campaigning together, led to a close friendship to this day. But the calls weren't enough. Black people wanted *Barack*, and David Plouffe continued to resist pulling him out of Iowa. The compromise we reached was to ask Michelle to go to South Carolina as a surrogate.

On November 20, 2007, I traveled with Michelle to Orangeburg, South Carolina. On the plane ride, we discussed the deeply rooted fear in the black community of what might happen—the fear of pushing too hard, too fast and provoking backlash. That day, she gave what came to be known as her "fear speech." Speaking to hundreds of black voters, she uncharacteristically moved off script and ad-libbed. "I want to talk not just about fear but about love," she said. "I know people care about Barack and our family. I know people want to protect us and themselves from disappointment, failure. I know people are proud of us. I know that people understand that Barack is special. You don't see this kind of man often. I equate it to that aunt or that grandmother that bought all that new furniture—spent her life savings on it—and then what does she do? She puts plastic on it to protect it." Everyone understood her powerful point: if I'm not afraid, you shouldn't be either. Don't treat him like our precious couch. She was loved by the crowd, who connected with her willingness to break it down in a way that was authentic and resonant. Her impact was like no other candidate's spouse, a fact not lost on our opponents.

Meanwhile, as the Iowa caucuses approached, it was all hands on deck for the final push. Extended Obama family, close friends, and supporters from Chicago and around the country arrived a week or so in advance to knock on doors and make phone calls. David Plouffe, who had the flu and a 104-degree fever, was so gaunt he looked like he hadn't eaten in weeks. But by sheer force of will he was plowing through, using every last bit of strength to push Barack over the finish line, which was really just the starting line.

Our great fortune in Iowa included the bright young folks on our team who had worked night and day. One in particular made quite an impression on me. Born to Ethiopian immigrants, Yohannes Abraham was a Virginia native who joined the campaign right after he graduated from Yale University. We met in Des Moines, where he was my as-signed driver on a cold, snowy Sunday morning in 2007. I wasn't pay-ing much attention to our route until I realized that we had passed the same gas station twice. Still, I didn't say a word. A few minutes later, Yohannes, visibly nervous, said he needed to pull over to make a phone call. After a long wait, finally, someone picked up.

"Wake up, man!" he said into the phone. "I need you to wake up. Do you know how to get to the church?" asked Yohannes, who then care-fully listened to the response.

We were off, but ten minutes later he pulled over again.

I had a reputation on the campaign for being very punctual, and, despite the frigid temperatures, Yohannes began to perspire as he called back that same person. "Man, I have Valerie Jarrett in the car with me, and those directions weren't right!"

Finally we got on the right course and managed to arrive amazingly close to on time. Yohannes came rushing around to the passenger side of the car to make sure I didn't fall on the ice. When I saw his worried expression, it made my heart melt. We chatted at length that day and I thought he was a special young man. I checked in on him from time to time throughout the rest of the campaign to make sure he was OK. We kept up with each other during the first term when he worked in the White House Legislative Affairs Department, then for the Democratic National Committee, and finally as deputy political director for the 2012 reelection campaign. Five years after that snowy day in Des Moines, I hired him as my chief of staff in our second term.

On the night of the caucuses, January 3, 2008, Barack, David Plouffe, Reggie Love (Barack's aide), and I arrived at one of the caucus locations, a huge public high school in Des Moines. We were allowed to enter the building but not the room where the actual caucus was taking place. The parking lot was completely packed. I had never been to a caucus. But David, who had been to many, said it was unusual to see such a big crowd. We sensed something special was happening that night.

All four of us could feel it. Inside the school, everyone wanted a photo with Barack. In the all-white crowd, I noticed one black woman in the back. She had a baby in a stroller and was holding a three-year-old by the hand. I approached her to ask if she wanted a photo with Barack. "Yes," she said quietly. I led her through the crowd and moved her into a position where he could see her. He put his arm around her and took a photo with her family. I often smile when I think about her. I am sure she has told her children many a time about that night and shown them the photo.

When we returned to the car, Barack was very quiet. I glanced over at him, and tears were streaming down his face. He turned to look out of the window, lost in his own thoughts. I'm sure his emotions were partly due to exhaustion. He had been campaigning full steam for nearly a year, and had done rallies in five cities the day before. But the emotion was also an expression of his profound gratitude for all the supporters and campaign staff who'd worked so hard for, and believed in, his unlikely victory. At least, that's what I imagine he was thinking, because that's what I was thinking, and I was choked up, too. We all rode back in silence.

We arrived at a restaurant and joined friends and family for dinner and hadn't even finished our entrées when the folks from the campaign boiler room rushed in to tell us that the results were coming in much faster than expected. And it looked like Barack was going to win. This mostly white and rural state voted for Barack Hussein Obama. When he gave the DNC keynote speech in 2004, I knew he could inspire the country, but when he won Iowa, I knew he could win the presidency.

Four days later, everything we'd built came crashing down in a totally unexpected defeat in New Hampshire. Several candidates had dropped out after Iowa, and our sole focus was Hillary Rodham Clinton. Senator Clinton's victory in New Hampshire shook us up. We had been so far ahead in the polls there that it never occurred to us that

Barack would lose. He didn't even have a concession speech written. So much for polls.

I had met Hillary Clinton, briefly, only twice before the campaign, but I knew she'd be a formidable opponent—and she was. Every single day she was out there on the campaign trail. Even though she was confident that she was the inevitable nominee, she was going at it full throttle, doing all she could to win.

She was a machine. *Indefatigable* doesn't begin to describe her, and I respected her for that. But the traits people admire in men are traits that are too often resented in women. Senator Clinton was in that terrible no-win paradox with which so many powerful women have to contend. It's important to appear strong, which to some means being unemotional. But if you're too unemotional, then you have no heart. It's one of many unfair realities so many women face. Part of finding our voice is learning to not worry so much about how we appear; instead, it is about being comfortable in showing who we are.

Gender aside, voters are looking for authenticity in their candidates. That was a real strength of Barack's and Hillary was criticized for lacking it. And while there may be other factors that contributed to Barack's loss in New Hampshire, I attribute it in no small part to Senator Clinton tearing up on TV the day before the primary. The next day after an early-morning rally on Dartmouth's campus, I climbed in bed for a rest before the evening I was convinced would hold his victory speech. I turned on the news just as the story came on about Hillary responding to a question about how she felt about all the attacks against her. When I watched her choke up during her answer, I thought, *Uh-oh.* Because I was moved, and if she could move me, she could move anybody. It was a rare moment where she let down her guard and showed a very human side. It could have easily backfired or come off as a ploy or stunt, but it didn't, because everyone could tell it wasn't.

After a few unsettling hours, we were informed of his defeat. Barack, Michelle, and I, together with a few shell-shocked campaign aides, gathered together to leave the hotel for the Nashua High School gym, where his disappointed supporters, gathered in expectation of a victory speech, had heard the news. As we somberly clustered inside the elevator, Michelle was staring straight ahead in stony silence. Barack looked at her. "We'll be fine," he said. "It can't be too easy." Michelle never said a word.

When we arrived at the gym, and the advance team wrangled the staff, I stood with Massachusetts governor Deval Patrick and Illinois senator Dick Durbin. We all just shook our heads, too numb to speak. But Barack dug deep. He drew on a reservoir of strength and resilience in order to embrace his defeat as a teaching moment. In less than half an hour he transformed the speech he'd hoped to give into a concession speech that inspired his supporters to redouble their efforts for the journey ahead. The impact was greater than any victory speech could have had that night. It was a history lesson about the American character, grit, and resilience. "When we've been told we're not ready or that we shouldn't try or that we can't," he said to the roaring crowd, "generations of Americans have responded with a simple creed that sums up the spirit of a people: Yes, we can. Yes, we can. Yes, we can. It was a creed written into the founding documents that declared the destiny of a nation: Yes, we can.

"It was whispered by slaves and abolitionists as they blazed a trail towards freedom through the darkest of nights: Yes, we can.

"It was sung by immigrants as they struck out from distant shores and pioneers who pushed westward against an unforgiving wilderness: Yes, we can.

"It was the call of workers who organized, women who reached for the ballot, a president who chose the moon as our new frontier, and a king who took us to the mountaintop and pointed the way to the promised land: Yes, we can, to justice and equality.

"Yes, we can, to opportunity and prosperity. Yes, we can heal this nation. Yes, we can repair this world. Yes, we can."

"Yes, we can" was Barack's ultimate expression of hope and change, and out of that crestfallen moment, his famous phrase, the campaign slogan that would carry us through to the end, was born.

Despite Hillary's victory, we felt like the momentum coming out of his speech in New Hampshire was real. At the same time, a high profile black businessman close to the Clintons gained attention after publicly putting Barack down with a thinly veiled reference to Barack's already acknowledged drug use in his youth. Nevertheless, in the weeks that followed, we rode to victory in South Carolina by a wide margin. Thanks to the confidence in Barack now held by black voters, the generational and cultural divides that had hurt Barack in his campaign against Bobby Rush had begun to fade away. Michelle's "fear speech" had proven so popular, the campaign had made DVDs of it and played them at small and large gatherings throughout the state. Victory in Iowa had helped immensely. The fact that such a predominantly white state had voted for Barack gave many white and black people the hope that maybe, possibly, this unlikely quest might succeed.

Two days after South Carolina, Senator Ted Kennedy of Massachusetts, along with his niece Caroline and his son, Representative Patrick Kennedy, of Rhode Island, gave Barack their official endorsement. "With every person he meets, every crowd he inspires, and everyone he touches," the veteran senator said, "he generates new hope that our greatest days as a nation are still ahead."

That was huge. Together with Iowa and South Carolina, those endorsements shifted the momentum exponentially. Beholden to the political power of the Clintons, many congressional leaders and high-profile Democrats had endorsed Hillary early on or withheld endorsements all together, including members of the Congressional Black Caucus. Representative John Lewis of Georgia, the longtime civil rights activist and leader, initially supported Hillary. Then, after a great deal of soul-searching, he switched his endorsement to Barack. We felt like we had our mojo, and I'm sure Hillary's campaign was feeling the pressure. But maintaining widespread support among black voters, without alienating white ones, continued to mean striking a delicate balance. When Barack said the campaign couldn't be "too easy," none of us envisioned just how hard it was about to become.

R everend Jeremiah A. Wright Jr. was the head of Chicago's Trinity United Church of Christ. Before the 2008 presidential race, Trinity was known to most as a mainstream church that attracted the city's prominent black lawmakers, judges, business leaders, and other professionals. The Obamas had been members of the congregation for years and Wright had married them and baptized their daughters.

From the moment Barack began exploring a presidential run, conservative right-wing pundits started digging into his relationship with the Afrocentric, activist reverend, hoping to drum up fears that Barack had a hidden racist agenda. None of that broke through to the mainstream media early on, but just before Barack was set to formally announce his candidacy, *Rolling Stone* published a piece highlighting some of the pastor's egregious quotes. Reverend Wright had been scheduled to give the invocation at the announcement, but after the article appeared, Barack made the hard decision to disinvite him; he didn't want the press focusing on Reverend Wright's controversial statements during the occasion, nor did he want to subject his pastor to harsh attacks from his opponents. The night before the Springfield announcement, Barack called Wright to cancel, and the reverend didn't take the news well. He must have fumed for over a year, eventually telling *The New York Times*, "When his enemies find out that in 1984 I went to Tripoli [to visit Colonel Mu'ammar al-Gadhafi] with Farrakhan, a lot of his Jewish support will dry up quicker than a snowball in hell."

That quote was published on March 6, 2008, just as the campaign's national momentum was building, and it would soon be overshadowed by the far more incendiary comments unearthed by the press just a week later. In a sermon from 2003, Wright had said from the pulpit, "The government gives them the drugs, builds bigger prisons, passes a three-strike law, and then wants us to sing 'God Bless America'? No, no, no, God *damn* America!" The sermon was available on videotape, sold by the church, easily available to anyone. I was stunned that our campaign research team had not unearthed it. Like all presidential campaigns, we had done opposition research on our own candidate. Yet no one had gotten around to vetting the candidate's pastor.

Barack, who'd been zigzagging across the upcoming primary states, arrived back in Chicago on the Friday that ABC broke the news of the tapes. He called his senior team to decide how to address the issue. Joshua DuBois, the campaign's religious affairs director, and I were the only black staffers there. We felt strongly that the senator should give a speech to help people put his relationship with the pastor in context. In black churches in America, there's a tradition of fiery rhetoric that serves to validate the pain of a people who have long suffered injustice in order to motivate them to rise above it. Everyone else on the senior team either stayed silent or expressed grave reservations, no doubt unsure themselves what the candidate could say to make sense of the reverend's comments. In the end, Barack decided he owed the American people an explanation, and the sooner the better. He cleared his calendar on the following Tuesday and chose the National Constitution Center in Philadelphia as the place to address the issue. That was only four days away, and he had a full schedule up until Sunday afternoon. He knew only he could write such a deeply personal speech. On the road late Monday night, he was still searching for the right words. Then he remembered Ashley.

Two months earlier, on the night of the South Carolina primary, we left Michelle, Susan Sher, and Tina Tchen in a cramped hotel room toasting his victory with champagne, and flew to Atlanta. On the plane, Barack was working to find the right words for a different speech on race, one he'd been asked to deliver at the historic Ebenezer Baptist Church on Martin Luther King Jr.'s birthday. Seeing that he was frustrated, I decided to distract him for a bit with a story I'd heard in the field. From its start, his campaign had been structured around field organizers, most of them fresh out of college or in their early twenties.

It was a huge investment of time and human capital and the key to Barack's grassroots strategy. The organizers were each assigned to a community where they'd build relationships with as many people as possible. If necessary, they'd start just by cold-calling lists of community leaders. When surrogates such as me attended events in their territory, the field organizers set the agenda. They told us where to go and with whom we needed to meet. They were our bosses for the day.

A couple of weeks before the South Carolina primary, I met a young field organizer at the city of Conway's local library, where we were holding a "persuasion event," a roundtable intended to win voters over, as opposed to a big rally with those who were already in. We all sat at a large C-shaped group of tables with about forty people, and the young organizer, who was white, kicked us off. She said she wanted the audience to introduce themselves first so I could tailor my remarks to their key issues. She said she'd go first. "My name is Ashley Baia," she began, "and I want to tell you why I support Senator Obama." Then she told us about when she was a nine-year-old growing up in Venice, Florida, and her mother lost her job due to uterine cancer, an illness that forced her to miss too many shifts. When she lost her job, she lost her health coverage, too, and they were forced into bankruptcy. Knowing her mother was worried about money, Ashley asked herself how she could help out. She decided to cut down on their food costs by convincing her mother that she wanted to eat only mustard and relish sandwiches for lunch, which she did every day for a year. Her mother eventually went into remission and, thankfully, survived. Ashley had joined the campaign, she said, because she knew Barack's mom had died from cancer and believed he was committed to helping people like her own mother hold onto their health insurance when they needed it most.

Everyone was visibly moved by Ashley's story. I suspect I wasn't the only one fighting back tears. She then gracefully turned the conversation to the others. As we went around the room, people mentioned a range of issues they'd like me to address, from veterans' benefits to job creation to public education. After most had spoken, we came to an older black

Always happy in the huge swimming pool a block from our home in Shiraz, Iran. My mom taught me to swim before I walked, 1958.

With my protector, Doddy, at my side I was fearless, Shiraz, Iran, 1957.

My favorite playground, Persepolis.

Pudden, Mom, and me having a bite in Tokyo, Japan, 1959.

Love my daddy.

My first trip to Giza, Egypt, in 1959.

My grandmother
Laura Bowman.

My grandfather
James Edward Bowman.

The Dibble-Taylor family at the end of 1927. FRONT ROW: Helen Dibble (my great-aunt) and her daughter Helen, Henry Taylor (my great-uncle), Beatrice Robinson (my great-aunt) with her niece (my aunt Lauranita Taylor). BACK ROW: Dr. Eugene Dibble, Edward Taylor (my great-uncle), Robert Rochon Taylor (my grandfather), Laura Dorothy Taylor (my grandmother), Robert Robinson Taylor (my great-grandfather), and Nelly Taylor (my great-grandfather's second wife).

My parents on their wedding day, June 17, 1950.

Mayor Richard J. Daley presenting a key to one of the first families who moved into the Robert Taylor Homes in 1962. My grandmother Laura Dorothy Taylor is in the back.

Three generations celebrating at a party honoring my mom in 1945: Lauranita Taylor (my aunt), Laura Dorothy Taylor (my grandmother), Barbara Taylor Bowman (my mom), and Laura Jennings (my great-grandmother).

My parents walk me out of our home on my wedding day, September 3, 1983.

Laura and her papa (my father) at the Erikson Institute graduation in my parents' yard, June 1988.

The self-described best day of Laura's childhood at Euro Disney, Paris, France, 1992.

In a 1995 trip to Egypt, I convinced a reluctant Laura to climb up a camel. The scary part was actually getting down.

On the beach with Laura at our favorite vacation spot: Martha's Vineyard, August 1998.

Michelle, Barack, and me at the Chicago Urban League Annual Golden Fellowship Dinner, November 2005.

Waiting backstage with Senator Obama during the 2008 presidential campaign.

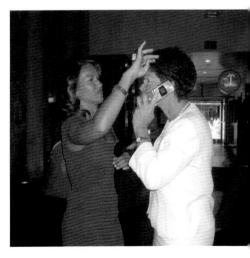

Laura touching up my hair before I do a press interview at the Democratic National Convention in August 2008.

Laura and I traveled to Indiana with Senator Obama on Election Day, 2008.

Standing on the platform with Laura on Inauguration Day, January 20, 2009.

Maude Baggetto, Rebecca Williams, and me at the Illinois inaugural ball, January 20, 2009.

In the Rose Garden, spring 2009—I cannot
believe we are having a senior staff meeting here!

The president's spontaneous
celebration on the Truman
Balcony on March 21,
2010—the night that the
Affordable Care Act passed.
Susan Sher is on the left;
Nancy-Ann DeParle is on
the right.

At the party, President
Obama met Ann Widger for
encouraging Natoma Canfield
to share her story about the
importance of the Affordable
Care Act. Michael Strautmanis
(my chief of staff) and I are
listening in.

Always a thrill to ride on Marine One with President Obama. Here, Anita Decker Breckenridge, Jen Friedman, and I listen as the president shares a funny story.

Ben Rhodes and I share the same birthday, more than a few years apart, and we celebrated with surprise cakes from President Obama on Air Force One, November 14, 2009.

Mom and Dad still laughing together after sixty years of marriage, October 2010.

Laura and Tony on their wedding day, June 16, 2012.

President Obama and my mother dancing at Laura and Tony's wedding, June 16, 2012.

The extended Taylor family gathered on February 12, 2015, at the National Postal Museum in Washington, DC, to celebrate as the United States Postal Service inducted my great-grandfather Robert Robinson Taylor into the Postal Service's Black Heritage stamp series for his lifetime achievements.

President Obama always made time to joke with his First Lady.

President Obama, Laura, Tony, and I watching the returns the moment MSNBC called the presidential election on November 6, 2012.

Touring the LBJ Presidential Library with President Obama and Marty Nesbitt after the fiftieth anniversary of the passage of the Civil Rights Act, April 10, 2014.

Old friends, Elvin Charity and Susan Sher, sitting with me at the White House in 2009.

I was thrilled to meet Pope Francis in the White House, September 25, 2015.

Listening to quiet words of inspiration from His Holiness the Dalai Lama at the National Prayer Breakfast on February 5, 2015.

Michelle Obama giving Tina Tchen and me her impressions of the extraordinary girls we met at a Let Girls Learn event in Cuba.

Kicking back with President Obama in Philadelphia on June 30, 2011, waiting for his long introduction to finish. Ever-present Joe Clancy, who headed the president's United States Secret Service detail, and Marvin Nicholson in the background.

Words of encouragement from First Lady Michelle Obama before President Obama's final State of the Union address.

As we commemorated the 2016 Black History Month, President Obama met with new and old leaders of the civil rights movement, sitting here between Brittany Packnett, co-founder of Campaign Zero, and the legendary John Lewis. Rev. Dr. C. T. Vivian moved everyone to tears describing how proud he was of President Obama.

One thing the president and I definitely share: a taste for delicious ice cream!

Three generations of Bowman/Jarrett women:
Laura, Mom, and me.

gentleman. He said he didn't need to hear from me at all. "I am here because of Ashley. I know her. I trust her," he said, "and because of her, you have my vote." Ashley smiled, and the introductions continued, but I knew right then I would always treasure that moment.

As I finished telling the story to Barack on the plane to Atlanta, he stared out the window with a faraway look. At first, he said nothing. *Classic*, I thought. *I'm going on and on, and he isn't even listening to me.*

But after a moment he turned to me and said, "That's the ending of my speech. That's what this campaign is all about. That older black man in South Carolina didn't come out to a library for me; he came there because he trusted a young white woman from Florida named Ashley. The image of those two people connecting is what my campaign is all about: building relationships that, without my campaign, would never happen." In the speech honoring Dr. King's birthday, he told the story of Ashley and that man and why it was so fundamental to his campaign, and on the evening before addressing the Reverend Wright controversy in Philadelphia, he decided to use it again in his "more perfect union" speech that became known simply as the "speech on race."

It made sense to me that he used that anecdote to end both. The promise of his campaign, his very purpose, didn't transcend race, but necessarily reckoned with it. It wasn't that our country would suddenly become "postracial," but rather that the big tent Barack Obama was determined to create was a place where people who had traditionally felt disconnected from one another could find a common bond. I saw this theme played out all across the country. On another trip to Atlanta, I visited a campaign office where a young black woman was helping an elderly white man sign up online to volunteer. Countless unlikely relationships, several of which even led to marriage, grew out of the Obama campaigns.

I sat with Michelle, Eric Holder, and Marty Nesbitt in Philadelphia, and I was, as usual, a nervous wreck. I had encouraged him to give the speech, and we all knew this was a make-or-break moment. Despite the incredibly high stakes, in the minutes before his speech, Barack was walking around amiably chitchatting with Eric about basketball.

The speech, as we now all remember, was a triumph. Just as he had with the concession speech in New Hampshire, Barack took the energy that had forced the campaign into a downward spiral and harnessed it to lift everyone back up again. Afterward, when Eric mentioned that we couldn't understand how he was talking sports before such a big moment, Barack just shrugged. "I knew I had been honest," he said, "and I was willing to trust the American people to hear me out." He was confident not just in himself, but also in the goodwill and decency of others.

His speech worked, for a while. But the campaign's all-out effort to tamp down Reverend Wright's divisive rhetoric only made the pastor angrier. In late April, the week before the Indiana primary, for reasons I will never understand, the reverend addressed the controversy three times in four days. It started on a Friday with an hour-long interview with Bill Moyers, where the reverend described his reaction to Barack's public condemnation of his incendiary sermons: "He's a politician, I'm a pastor. We speak to two different audiences." Two days later he gave an animated speech to twelve thousand people at the NAACP Freedom Fund Dinner in Detroit. "I am not divisive," he said to laughter and applause. "The word is *descriptive*."

More like combative. I watched his remarks over at Marty and Anita's home, while on a nightly phone call with senior campaign staff. Not good, we all thought.

Reverend Wright then doubled down the following day when he spoke at the National Press Club in Washington, DC. *Time* magazine called it "the kind of performance . . . that can only be described as political disaster." Wright ridiculed the audience, opined that perhaps the U.S. government had introduced AIDS into the black community, and performed an odd dance with his head and hands that likely referred to the sermon wherein he claimed the United States had brought the terrorist attacks of September 11 on itself. His memorable words were: "America's chickens are coming home to roost."

Exhausted mentally and physically, I watched this early-Monday-morning meltdown on the TV. As soon as it finished, Barack, who hadn't watched it, called. "How was it?" he asked.

Gingerly searching for the right words, I said, "I think it's going to be a problem."

Within minutes, we were inundated with panicked calls from other members of the team: This was an existential threat to our campaign. A black president with a racist, anti-American pastor? The consensus was we were toast. Barack finally came to the painful conclusion that he had to actively disavow his pastor and spiritual leader. Before that, he had tried to separate the incendiary sermons from the man who had done a lot of good in the world. This was no longer enough, so on April 29 he held a press conference to renounce Wright in no uncertain terms. It was hard, but it would have been even harder to let down all the young people like Ashley and Yohannes by letting Wright's inflammatory remarks destroy his campaign.

A week later, the night before the Indiana primary, Barack was at an all-time low, battered by the press relentlessly cycling through the Reverend Wright controversy. That night I had traveled with Eric Whitaker and Marty Nesbitt, to join him for an event at the American Legion Mall in Indianapolis, where Stevie Wonder was performing. The weather was grim, with a light, misty rain that was just enough to ruin my hair but not enough for an umbrella. We arrived just as the legendary performer was finishing up, which was always the case. Making the most of Barack's every waking minute, there was never enough time in the schedule to arrive early to enjoy the entertainment.

Still, as down as we were, I was thrilled to be meeting one of my favorite musicians, and as he came offstage we were introduced. His first words to me as he leaned in close were "I smell cigarettes on Obama. You need to tell him to stop smoking."

What? I meet Stevie Wonder, and he's warning me that he can smell cigarettes?

Barack was a closet smoker. I'd never seen him smoke, not even once, and to this day I never have. But, like Stevie, I had smelled it on him before. Barack never lied about it, but he didn't publicize it either. The closest I'd ever come to a conversation with him on the subject was one day while we were driving together in Iowa. His press secretary, Robert Gibbs, forwarded me an email from a reporter claiming to have it on good authority that Barack smoked. I simply handed Barack my phone with the message from Robert on the screen. He read it and handed my phone back, never saying a word.

All right, I thought when Barack ignored the email, *you're on notice.* A lot of the young kids on the campaign smoked, and I felt that his smoking might be tacitly giving them permission. I didn't like that, but you have to pick your battles. (We didn't discuss the subject again until two years later, after the Affordable Care Act passed. That's when he told me he had quit during the process. "Now?" I said. "You couldn't have found an easier time?")

As I watched Barack give his speech outside that night in Indianapolis, I wondered if the bad weather and my chat with Stevie were signs. Were we nearing defeat? After the event, Eric, Marty, Barack, and I were sitting in a conference room, waiting until it was time for the next event, a midnight stop by a local plant to shake hands with workers during their shift change. In the fluorescent-lit, nondescript room, Barack, who normally sat up straight so that even his posture projected optimism, was slumping and shaking his head. We could tell he was troubled, worried about disappointing everyone around the country who had worked so hard on his campaign. The campaign staff had spent more than a year away from home, sometimes sleeping five to a room, eating burgers, fries, pizza, and unhealthy snacks and drinking Diet Coke and Red Bull, to get Barack elected. And also thousands of volunteers who gave up evenings and weekends to make calls, raise money, and knock on doors. But as we neared the end of the primary season, there were fewer and fewer paths to victory. Every delegate counted, and every loss felt monumental.

For a half hour, Marty, Eric, and I tried to lift his spirits. We became sillier and sillier until Marty, out of nowhere, did his best impression of the chickens-have-come-home-to-roost dance that we'd seen the reverend do on TV. It was so absurd that we all burst out laughing, even our beleaguered candidate. The release was short-lived. David Axelrod walked in looking very somber. "I have very bad news," he said. "Poll numbers have you down by as much as twelve points in Indiana." Deflated, we packed up and drove to the factory.

While Barack was out shaking hands, Marty and I distracted ourselves with a debate about what we would call him if he became president. Marty said he'd continue to call him "Barack." I said we would call him "President Obama." Returning to the car in the middle of our argument, Barack asked, "What are you two fussing about?" I told him, and without any pause he said, "If by some miracle we win this thing, you'll call me Mr. President."

Barack did end up losing Indiana by a hair, exceeding our expectations, but, thankfully, the North Carolina primary was the same day and those returns came in first, and that's where we were with a jubilant crowd when the results came in that he won that state—both primaries giving his campaign a boost. *Newsweek* captured the moment in a cover photo of David Axelrod, Barack, and me watching the news break of the results.

After that late-April press conference, Barack didn't really talk much about Reverend Wright, but Wright continued to cast a shadow. To me, it didn't make any sense that Barack's pastor was willing to be responsible for his defeat. Not only was it personally hurtful but, given that the reverend had fought so hard for the advancement of black Americans, why would he try to ruin the chance for the first black man—and his parishioner—to be elected president?

The public and the press eventually moved on, and the campaign rebounded. Everyone's mood improved. At long last, by June 3, Barack Obama had won enough states to lock up the Democratic nomination for president. The evening he clinched the nomination, we traveled to St. Paul, Minnesota, where Barack addressed a cheering crowd of seventeen thousand people. "You chose to listen not to your doubts or your fears," he told them, "but to your greatest hopes and highest aspirations." This was the event where Michelle greeted him on stage with a fist bump, which spun up their critics. Just the beginning. But backstage, I also tracked down Ashley Baia, the young field organizer from South Carolina who was staffing the event, and introduced her to Barack and Michelle. They were as delighted to meet her as she was to meet them.

But we were not out of the woods yet. The specter of race still hung over the campaign, and a month earlier, a ginned-up controversy about Michelle that had been brewing in the background of the Reverend Wright catastrophe. Michelle had made herself available to campaign in the primary, but only for day trips; her one condition was that she had to be home in Chicago in time for dinner and to put the girls to bed. So within those parameters, she had been traveling the country, drawing unprecedented crowds wherever she went. Thousands showed up at her rallies, which very quickly were standing room only. No other candidate's spouse had ever generated Michelle's buzz and enthusiasm. And Michelle delivered. She energized her supporters and motivated them to get involved by knocking on doors, making phone calls, and giving donations. Her passionate oratory and down-to-earth touch converted skeptics. We called her "the closer." But because she was such a positive and popular force on the campaign, she also became a threat to the Republicans, who went after her with as much force as they would a candidate. We should have anticipated that if Barack gained traction, and she was viewed as an asset, she would come under attack. We didn't.

The problem had started in February of 2008, after a set of remarks Michelle made in Madison, Wisconsin, while campaigning for the state's primary. "Hope is making a comeback," she said. "It is making a comeback, and let me tell you something: For the first time in my adult lifetime, I'm really proud of my country, and not just because Barack has done well but because I think people are hungry for change. And I have been desperate to see our country moving in that direction and just not feeling so alone in my frustration and disappointment. I've seen people who are hungry to be unified around some basic common issues and it's made me proud." It seemed fine to us—full of hope and promise for the future.

Conservative pundits jumped all over one fragment of the speech: "For the first time in my adult lifetime, I'm really proud of my country." What Michelle was talking about was her pride at the incredible unity Barack's campaign had generated across boundaries of race, gender, age, and geography. But the comment was taken out of context, and the backlash was vicious. The right-wing media asked if she was proud of the Civil Rights Act or World War II. Rush Limbaugh was typical in calling her comments "unhinged." When Cindy McCain, wife of Republican presidential candidate Senator John McCain, told reporters, "I have and always will be proud of my country," the story spread to every news outlet in the country.

The caricature of Michelle as an "angry black woman" continued to fester and grow. In June, the notorious Republican operative Roger Stone told Fox News that a video of Michelle using the term "whitey" was going to be made public soon, lending credence to a preposterous internet hoax. No black person has said "whitey" since *Sanford and Son*. Of course, no tape ever materialized because no tape existed, but that hardly seemed to matter.

The next insult came on July 21 when *The New Yorker* put on its cover a cartoon of Michelle, sporting an Afro and carrying an assault rifle, giving a fist bump to Barack, garbed in a Muslim headdress— both of them standing in an Oval Office decorated with a portrait of Osama bin Laden with an American flag burning in the fireplace. *The New Yorker* said it was a parody, but it was outrageous and fed into the worst caricature of them being spread by the right wing. The backlash was coming on multiple fronts, swiftly and painfully.

Between January and July, Michelle's frustration had continued to mount. Every day the communications team sent out a roundup of news clips, and like the good student she was, my guess is she read most of them, and the distortion was devastating to her, and to all those who loved her. As someone who had devoted her career to service, Michelle has no patience for the underbelly of politics. Her ambivalence about Barack's career, going all the way back to the state senate, hadn't simply been about issues of family and work-life balance. Her father, a precinct captain, had been deeply involved in Chicago's ward politics, and she'd seen how petty and small, even destructive it could be—the darker side of it, how someone's reputation and character could be destroyed by their opponent's ruthless pursuit of power. Now she was on the receiving end of that herself. This extraordinary woman, talented and accomplished in her own right, now felt she was becoming a liability to her husband's campaign.

Where the rest of us fell short was in putting her out on the trail in a prominent role without the appropriate support. She was understaffed. The pressure on her was enormous, and her small team was worried. They kept trying to convince senior staff from the campaign to go on the road with her to help, but they were so swamped with Barack's schedule that they were caught unaware by the growing smear campaign against Michelle.

Preposterous allegations about Barack had been circulating since day one, the whole birther nonsense and the fiction that he'd attended a madrassa because he was a Muslim. On the campaign, we made a calculated decision not to give the rumors more oxygen by addressing them. Instead we focused our energy on legitimate concerns, like defending Barack's voting record in the Senate. No one in the mainstream press was buying into the ridiculous lies either. But what we learned over time was that just because a baseless rumor wasn't in *The Washington Post* didn't mean a lot of people weren't hearing it, over and over again. Repetition without pushback led many people to believe the absurdities. Because this was the first presidential campaign that had to contend with the growing use of social media, we were unprepared for the convincing power of lies spread in new ways. It took us a long time, too long, to realize that by not calling out these lies and nipping them in the bud, we allowed them to gain traction.

Eventually, David Axelrod and I traveled with Michelle to one of her events in May, where he taped her stump speech. Afterward, we met with Michelle. (Anita Dunn, the campaign's communications director, joined by phone.) David asked Michelle, her team, and me to watch the tape together. When it was over, there was complete silence. The words in her speech weren't angry, but her demeanor made them seem as if she was. She started to cry, while I held her hand; seeing her so upset made me want to wrap her in a blanket and take her somewhere safe.

Michelle turned to us and said, "Why didn't you tell me?" and she was right. We all knew what she was trying to say and what a message of hope and optimism she wanted to deliver, and we had simply counted on the audience seeing that as well. Michelle was trying really hard, but she wasn't a trained professional campaigner. We had an inkling of the problem but hadn't wanted to hurt her feelings. Plus her heartfelt delivery was refreshing and honest. Watching that video together, and seeing her reaction, was a wake-up call that we'd let our personal feelings cloud our professional responsibility to both her and her husband's campaign.

Looking back, I'm not sure why we thought we had to treat her with kid gloves. She was a strong, accomplished woman. She'd weathered two years at Sidley Austin, one of the most prominent corporate law firms in the country, as well as Chicago's rough and tumble city hall. She'd launched a grassroots leadership program at Public Allies. She had run a volunteerism program at the University of Chicago and was in charge of community relations at its medical center. She had shown a natural ability to deal with challenge and controversy with professionalism and grace throughout her career. So it was no surprise that after a few tears, rather than retreat from the campaign and return to her more normal life, she brushed herself off and said let's bring in more help. At Anita's suggestion, the campaign hired Stephanie Cutter, a seasoned political consultant. She clicked with Michelle and her team. She said what most people knew of her were sound bites, not her story. "They don't know who you really are. So let's introduce you . . . again."

Michelle decided the best place with the largest audience would be the Democratic National Convention in August. She worked on her speech tirelessly, determined to share her story on her terms, rather than letting others define her. She practiced her delivery over and over, knowing there wouldn't be a better opportunity to get it right.

I arrived with Laura at the convention the day before it began to do press and take care of our supporters. I didn't have that much experience with national media, so seeing Laura's supportive face off camera helped put me at ease. The first day of the convention was chaos. Traffic was so bad on our way to Denver's Pepsi Center that Laura and I had to flag down a rickshaw that could weave in and out of the car jam in order to make my live "hit" on TV on time. *It shouldn't have come to this*, I thought as the driver pedaled in the August heat.

The night Michelle spoke was pure magic. Confident and comfortably herself, she told her story, and everyone who heard her was mesmerized. She talked about her upbringing and values with raw honesty, heart, and passion. Her brother, Craig, who was sitting next to me, said, "*That's* Miche." He was right. The reviews raved about her. She'd weathered the storm to come out stronger and more admired than ever. But that rough patch portended that there would never be clear sailing ahead.

From his 2004 keynote in Boston to his rousing "Yes, we can" rally in New Hampshire to his honest and uplifting speech on race in Philadelphia, Barack Obama had found the voice that would enable him to unite people from every background across the nation. Now Michelle had found her voice as well, and together they told the nation a compelling story for which so many people were truly hungry.

With that momentum going into the general election, we felt like it was ours to lose. The primary season had gone on for nearly a year and a half, and Barack had already campaigned throughout most of the country, giving him a strong foothold in many blue and purple states. He had even visited red Idaho, where the president of the state university told me at a five-thousand-person rally on a Saturday morning, "Usually Democratic candidates campaign here by flying over, looking down, and waving."

By finding their voices, Barack and Michelle had inspired others to use theirs to carry their message. While I had learned to speak up and assert myself in my private and professional lives, speaking in public had never been my forte. I still shake my head when I think back on the first speech I gave as commissioner of the Department of Planning and Development. Elvin Charity was the board chair of Friends of the Chicago River, and he had invited me to address a small group of supporters, so small they fit in a conference room in Elvin's law firm. The situation couldn't have been friendlier. The topic of the day was my new department, and since I had created it, what could be easier for me to talk about? But I was so nervous, and my hands sweated so much, that I smudged the ink on my handwritten note cards, so much so that I couldn't read a word. I made it through, but was reluctant to try it again.

Greg Longhini, my press secretary, whom I tried to fire when I began, thinking there was no need for me to do press, kept pushing me to do more and more interviews with the media and public appearances. After a few bad press stories he convinced me that the only way for me to define my message was for me to be the one who delivered it. And of course he was right. Which is not to say the butterflies in my stomach ever flew away for good. With each new challenge, they return, and speaking on behalf of a presidential candidate was certainly a new and daunting task. But when the campaign called on me to be a surrogate, I had to just push through. I discovered that I was more at ease when I told stories about people I'd met, like Ashley. I began traveling the country independent of Barack or Michelle, and by the general election phase of the campaign, my name recognition and relationship to the Obamas had grown enough nationally that, with hard work by our organizers, I could draw a crowd. Because I knew Barack and felt passionately about his ability to lead, I began to really enjoy it. I would arrive at events early and stay until I had shaken every single hand and answered every question.

As Election Day neared, all signs pointed to Barack's victory, and I was euphoric. And on the night of November 4, as the polls began to close and the results poured in, over a million people descended on Chicago's Grant Park to hear him speak. Laura and I had left the Hyatt Hotel ahead of the Obamas' motorcade, and while riding to the event, we heard the official news that Barack Obama had been elected the forty-fourth president of the United States. When we arrived at Grant Park, we made our way backstage so that I could see Barack before he went onstage. But when he surfaced at the top of the stairs of the platform, my mind filled with so many memories of our journey together. As I walked toward him I still didn't have the right words to say. What words possibly could sum up all I felt? Perhaps he felt the same way, because he walked over to me in silence and just hugged me. We didn't say a word.

A few days after the election, the Obamas appeared on *60 Minutes*. I watched the segment from the rehab center where my father, who had been gravely ill, was recuperating. My mom was on one side of my father's bed and I was on the other as we watched our newly elected president and First Lady in awe. They were as relaxed and down to earth as the young couple I had met seventeen years earlier.

At the end of the interview, my mother looked over at me. "How did you know that he could win?" she asked. "Not that he would, but even that he could?"

"Because of you two," I said, a bit of surprise in my voice. "Because you both raised me to believe that if you work twice as hard as anyone else and sacrifice for what you believe in, and luck is on your side, the sky's the limit."

She shook her head and said softly, "I never believed any of that." My dad chuckled and said he agreed with her.

I stared at them in disbelief. For the first time I realized my parents had raised me aspirationally, instilling in me a set of core beliefs that they didn't actually hold themselves. Their gift to me was not to shackle me with their reality, but to prepare me to own the full potential of mine.

· *Chapter 9* ·

Drinking from a Fire Hose

I woke up at the crack of dawn on February 22, 2008, during the campaign, in a hotel room in Austin, Texas. As usual, I had no idea which hotel I was in or my room number. It was the morning after one of Barack's primary debates with Hillary Clinton. I looked over at the telephone, searching for our hotel's name, more out of curiosity than necessity.

I hit the gym for a quick workout and read the press clips from the debate while walking briskly on the treadmill. Afterward, I grabbed a quick bite to eat with Eric Whitaker, who was traveling with us, and he and I piled into the service elevator to wait for Barack. At seven thirty sharp, Barack sauntered in, mumbling a barely audible hello.

I smiled to myself about his punctuality, but have I mentioned that Barack is not a morning person? I am, and it took me a while to learn to modulate my chipper morning voice until he had been up for a while. That day Barack had a cold, so he was even quieter than usual. An older black man was operating the hotel elevator, and once we were all in and heading down, he cleared his throat to speak. *Oh, no,* I thought, holding my breath. *This is not the time to strike up a conversation.*

"Senator," he said, "I'd like to give you a gift."

Since I'm nosy, I peered around Barack's shoulder to see what it was. It was a patch from a military uniform. Recognizing what it was, Barack said, "Oh, sir, I couldn't possibly accept that."

"No," the gentleman said, "I insist."

They went back and forth a few times until finally he said to the senator, "Sir, I've carried this patch with me every day for forty years. It has given me the courage to defend our country. It has given me the strength to go through some extremely tough times. And I want you to have it," he added with a smile. Barack thanked him and gave him a signed copy of *Dreams from My Father*. He often gave out copies to thank people for their help along the campaign trail.

The whole thing was too much for me. I immediately burst into tears. And I don't mean a few drops. I was heaving and sobbing, and tried to muffle the noise in the small elevator. Eric cried, too, but more quietly.

For the rest of the day, I kept thinking about what the man had done, trying to imagine how Barack processed such an act of selflessness. This was long before people started handing him their babies to hold as they crowded to the front of rope lines. Later that afternoon, when Barack and I had a quiet moment alone together, I asked him what he did with the patch. He said he put it in his pocket. *Typical guy*, I thought, *absentmindedly stowing away this precious object*.

"No," I said, "I mean, how did it make you feel?"

"Valerie, I put it in my pocket," he responded. Then he reached into his pocket and took out about ten or eleven other trinkets and keepsakes. "I put it in my pocket with these." He then proceeded to tell me the story behind each one: the name of the person who had given it to him, if he knew it, where they were at the time, and why it was special enough for him to carry it around. He looked at them each night when he emptied his pockets and again as he put the items back in the next morning. To this day, he selects a few from among the many he received over the course of his public life, depending on his mood and need for inspiration, to keep him company each day.

After the president was sworn in, I reflected back often on the people we'd met on the campaign trail—that man in the elevator, Ashley in South Carolina, a 112-year-old black woman waiting patiently in a rope line, Yohannes in Iowa, Edith Childs, who began the "Fired Up, Ready to Go" chant in South Carolina. I used their stories to show the sacrifices people were willing to make to be a part of a movement. And on my first day of work at the White House, I decided to use the story of the man from the elevator we met that day in Austin as a way to keep myself grounded and remind me why we were there.

On a typical morning at the White House, I would arrive well before sunrise, and as my car idled, waiting for the Secret Service gate to raise, I would take a moment to look up at the Washington Monument rising majestically above the tree line south of the White House grounds. I would watch the light at the top of the monument blink three times, then close my eyes and say to myself, "Remember, you only have the privilege of being here because of people like that man who gave a struggling candidate his military patch, so focus on making him proud."

Tom Brokaw had been the first to call it. Early on in the campaign, he told me, "If your friend wins, your life will never be the same." A mutual friend had introduced us at a dinner at RL, one of my favorite restaurants in Chicago. I'd admired Tom Brokaw for as long as I could remember, but I told him the idea of my life changing was not likely. I already had a great life in Chicago.

Then, the Thursday after the election, my cell phone rang: it was Tom Brokaw. "I want to congratulate you on your friend's incredible victory," he said. "Do you remember when I told you eighteen months ago your life would change? How about we begin this Sunday with you coming on *Meet the Press*?"

I had done national television at the convention and then again on election night, but nothing with nearly as high a bar as the most popular Sunday-morning show in the country. My stomach started its usual churning but, after talking it over with Barack, I agreed to fly to DC to appear on the program. Walking onto the set, sitting at that famous desk I had seen countless times on my own TV, watching the count-down clock tick down, I was scared out of my wits. Tom, seeing my expression, reached over to me, put his hand on top of my hand, and said, "Valerie, I'm not going to ask you any question to which you don't know the answer. Relax, and let's have some fun."

Oh, boy, did I ever. I forgot about the millions of people watching back home, and my nervousness melted away, and I felt like it was just Tom and me having a casual chat. Perhaps a little too great. On the way back to my hotel, my cell rang. It was Barack.

"Were you flirting with Tom Brokaw?" he asked.

"Maybe just a little," I said.

At that point, *Meet the Press* seemed like it might be the high-water mark of my participation in Barack and Michelle's political life, though people had been trying to make me think otherwise for months. At the Democratic Convention in Denver, Michelle's brother, Craig, had said to me, "You know, you're going to have to go to Washington with them. They're going to need a friend who's willing to look out for them." I was touched by his sentiment, but to move away from my family, leave my CEO job and other board commitments just to be the "First Friend" when I could do that by flying in to DC regularly from Chicago, did not make sense to me. Then, further into the general election, Barack and I were alone during a long flight, discussing how well the home-stretch of the campaign was going, and he said, "If I win, I'm going to ask you to come with me."

I didn't want to jinx it. "Let's wait to talk about it after you win," I replied.

But after *Meet the Press*, I still had no clear indication of what role I might play in the White House. My goal during the campaign had been to help Barack Obama win the election, not to get a job in his administration. Besides, by then I was eyeing political office myself.

A few weeks before Election Day, I'd gone to an event honoring Bishop Arthur M. Brazier, pastor of the Apostolic Church of God, a megachurch located in the Woodlawn neighborhood of Chicago, just south of Hyde Park. An iconic civil rights leader and one of Barack's earliest supporters, Bishop Brazier was also my dear friend, and we had spent years working together on the redevelopment of Woodlawn. I sat on the dais for several hours with Senator Dick Durbin, who early in the evening said to me, "When Barack wins, why don't you throw your name into the hat?" Illinois governor Rod Blagojevich was going to appoint Barack's replacement in the Senate, and Senator Durbin wanted to recommend me.

I was ambivalent, but he went on to make a compelling case for why I should think about doing this. With Barack in the White House and the Democrats in control of the Senate, Majority Leader Harry Reid could use another person he could trust from the president's home state. I was also a lawyer, so understanding the legislative process would be easy. "You're perfect for the job," Senator Durbin said, "and I'll support you."

It was an intriguing pitch, but it wasn't until after the election, while contemplating my future, that I came back around to the idea. I understood the job of a senator, unlike the White House, where I didn't have a clear sense of what my role might be. Whatever I was going to do, the pressure to make a decision was mounting.

A couple of days after the election, I received a call from the head of one of Illinois's local unions, who'd reached out to say he had an "intriguing idea" to discuss with me. The president-elect (I loved the sound of that title) had asked me to be one of three co-chairs of his presidential transition team, so I had no time to spare. I asked the leader to come for an early-morning meeting at the temporary transition headquarters in our friend John Rogers's office while we waited for his official transition office to be ready. At our meeting, this union leader told me he'd heard that I might be interested in the Senate position and wanted to gauge my interest. He also said he'd heard that Blagojevich was interested in nominating me, but that he, who was at the end of his second term, wanted to be appointed secretary of health and human services. I laughed at the idea that Blagojevich would be appointed to any spot in the Obama administration. It was a nonstarter as far as I was concerned. Moreover, we were already aware from the press that a federal investigation was casting a cloud over the governor.

"That's ridiculous," I said.

"Hey, don't shoot the messenger," the union head replied.

Blagojevich was eventually convicted in a wide range of corrupt schemes, including trying to use the offer of the Senate seat in exchange for a job for himself.

What I didn't know at the time was that the Obamas already had other plans for me. Michelle suggested to her husband, "Make her a concrete offer so she knows what you have in mind for her specific responsibilities. Being your friend or a generic senior advisor will not be enough." So he asked his organizational genius, Pete Rouse, to think through what would make sense given my skill set. After Pete offered his recommendation, the president-elect called me at a hotel room in New York, where I had flown after *Meet the Press* for a business meeting. He began by saying, "I know the Senate and I know you. You belong in the White House with me. You'll be happier, and Michelle and I will be happier." He then offered me the position of White House senior advisor and assistant to the president for intergovernmental affairs and public liaison, which we later renamed public engagement.

A wordy, cumbersome title, but what it meant was that I would continue to give him my opinion and assistance wherever I could be helpful as a senior member of his team, and I would also oversee the White House offices responsible for relationships with our nation's governors, mayors, attorneys general, and state legislators—essentially all the elected officials in America except for members of Congress. I would also be the gateway through which a wide range of advocates and businesses, as well as ordinary citizens, could engage with the White House. Giving state and local elected officials a voice in Washington and bridging citizens to the highest levels of government? Who could ask for a better job? In fact, after I hit the ground running, I often joked with President Obama that my job was far better than his.

I accepted the position on the spot, but as is life, a bit of drama followed. Rahm Emanuel, the president-elect's newly named chief of staff, had other ideas. Rahm was very open with me about the difficulty of having Hillary Clinton so involved in her husband's administration. That experience had left him wary of having anybody in the White House closer to the president than he.

Rahm is a longtime Chicago politico, and we'd always been quite friendly, having worked closely together when he was vice chairman of the Chicago Housing Authority Board. My boss, Daniel Levin, had also been a big contributor to Rahm's congressional campaigns. I had felt comfortable enough with him to solicit his endorsement of Barack during the 2008 presidential primary campaign. It was a tricky piece of business since his relationship to the Clintons went way back. Over lunch with Rahm at the East Bank Club during the heated primaries, I'd really pushed it hard. But he didn't want to get involved. "I'm just holing up under a table," he said, laughing. I understood and laughed, too. As we were walking out of the club's restaurant, who walked in? Barack Obama. He chuckled at the sight of us, asking, "Valerie, have you been pressuring this guy?"

Rahm wasn't the only person to throw cold water on the idea of my joining the administration. After the Democratic convention in August, while Barack was campaigning in Las Vegas, he set up a meeting with a group of former Democratic presidential chiefs of staff to ask for their counsel. If he won, he wanted to be prepared. One person who joined the meeting via conference call offered this piece of advice: "Don't bring any of your friends from Chicago." I thought, *He must be talking about me.*

I'd experienced plenty of infighting and jockeying for power in city hall. I said to Barack, "Look, he's your chief of staff, and he is clearly uncomfortable with me. I've worked with people like that before, and I don't want to do it again."

Having sat through many a story from me about my city hall days,

Barack already knew exactly what I was talking about. "I guarantee to you that I will have your back," he said. "You're not going to have that problem in my White House."

"Given how Rahm feels, yes, I will."

"No, you won't."

I said yes, but an uneasiness lingered.

Two days later, on my fifty-second birthday, after a last-minute effort by Rahm to scuttle my appointment, President-elect Obama publicly announced that I would be joining his White House team. Not a bad birthday gift from a dear friend who was about to become the most important man in the world.

I brought in the best people I knew to help me. Michael Strautmanis organized my offices during the transition, and I had known all along that he'd be perfect as my chief of staff. Having worked with him so closely throughout the campaign, I knew his work ethic and core values, as well as his long-standing relationship with the Obamas. To run my Intergovernmental Affairs office, I brought in Cecilia Muñoz, a Detroit native with Bolivian parents who had supervised legislative and advocacy efforts at the National Council of La Raza (now known as Unidos US), the country's largest Latino advocacy group. Because of her credibility with immigration advocates, she also headed up our efforts in immigration. She was reluctant at first, a mom of two teenage girls, but I assured her I completely understood her priorities, and we would make it work. And to serve as director of public engagement, I hired Tina Tchen, a tough-as-nails fearless former litigation partner at the Chicago office of Skadden, Arps, Slate, Meagher & Flom, with a national reputation as an advocate for gender equity. Tina wasn't used to losing any battles, and I knew we shared the same work ethic and values. In a coffee shop in the Aon Center in Chicago, with Susan Sher there to back me up, I gave Tina all the reasons why, despite her comfortable life and lucrative career in Chicago, she should join me in DC to work in the White House. To which she simply replied, "You had me at hello."

Inauguration Day was bitter cold, even worse than the day Barack Obama announced his candidacy, but the moment I walked out of the door of the Capitol I literally gasped and held Laura's hand tightly. We saw people filling every square inch of the mall. The depth and breadth of the crowd was overwhelming. An estimated 1.8 million people, the largest crowd ever at any event held in Washington, DC, showed up from across the country and around the world for this historic moment. Laura and I sat a few rows back on the platform, close enough to see Barack and Michelle's expressions as she held the Lincoln Bible while he took the oath of office. I tried to imagine what they were thinking. My thoughts were of the people like my parents who for so long feared this journey was impossible. Our country had turned an important page, and optimism and pure joy filled the frigid air.

As the Obamas watched the parade from the viewing stand in front of the White House, I was inside, moving into Hillary Clinton's and Karl Rove's former West Wing office. Because I hadn't asked ahead of time where it was, I had to wander around the hallways of the first and second floors until I found my name placard by the door of a spacious office on the second floor. I went to the window to check out my view. The parapet around the building came up so high that it obscured almost my whole view except for a bit of the Washington Monument and the sky. I guessed the design was for safety concerns. A sobering reminder on my first day.

The decor was bleak, so I went scavenging through the empty offices for some additional furniture. I took a desk from one person's office and a couch from somebody else's. First come, first serve. Nothing really matched, but I didn't feel the need to make my office any fancier than it was. Several times over the next eight years, various people in operations offered to repaint my office's dingy yellow walls or upgrade the furniture, but I never took them up on it. It was privilege enough just to occupy any office in the West Wing; it didn't matter what it looked like. But it did matter to me what I did there. One of my roles was to be a bridge, broadly speaking, between the voices inside and outside the White House. The two offices I ran served as the primary points of contact between the executive branch and all elected officials other than Congress, advocacy groups, experts, and other stakeholders, including the general public. And to do that effectively required us to listen and engage—the same skill set I had honed when people like Mrs. Adams showed up at the mayor's office, or when I tackled redevelopment in Chicago's neighborhoods and worked on transit services in Chicago. Whether it was meeting with LGBTQ activists about the repeal of "Don't ask, don't tell" and their inclusion in federal job-discrimination guidelines, or with civil rights activists about reforming the criminal justice system, or reaching out to a governor after a natural or man-made disaster, we were there to ensure that the federal government was meeting the needs of people on the ground.

In the Office of Intergovernmental Affairs, we set the task of introducing ourselves to as many of the nation's mayors, governors, and other elected officials as possible. The president wanted them in the loop, and so we took their pulse on every issue. My phone line was always open to call me directly so that they could cut through bureaucracy. If we were working on any piece of legislation that had an impact in a state, we'd touch base with governors to see how they felt about it. That included everything from funding for affordable housing to Arne Duncan's Race to the Top education strategy to our campaign to end homelessness for veterans. On health care reform, given the impact that Medicaid expansion and the insurance exchanges would have, I worked closely with the governors to ensure their voices were heard.

The Office of Public Engagement, was originally started under President Richard Nixon as the point of contact between the White House and lobbyist groups, but we designed the office to interact with all people, not just special-interest groups. To start out, Tina Tchen tracked sixty-plus buckets of constituency groups, all represented by robust national organizations, categories ranging from "Progressive Labor

Unions" to "Business Associations"; from "African American," "Asian American and Pacific Islander," "Hispanic," "Military families," "Women," and "LGBTQ" to "Faith Community"; and from "People with Disabilities" to everyone's favorite assignment, "Celebrities and Athletes."

We were the first point of contact for any of these people trying to navigate the bureaucracy of the executive branch or advocate for a policy in the federal government. That ranged in scope from someone concerned about their small business getting relief from flood damage to advocates trying to reform the criminal justice system. And the relationship went both ways. We called upon our constituents when we needed a sounding board for policy initiatives or our legislative agenda. So, for example, when we were trying to decide which bill to push through Congress first, women's rights groups were instrumental in advocating for the Lilly Ledbetter Fair Pay Act.

The first six months were a blur of eighteen-hour days. In the wake of the financial crisis triggered by the collapse of Lehman Brothers in September of 2008, housing foreclosures had skyrocketed, the big banks were on the verge of a chain-reaction collapse, and two of the three largest U.S. automobile companies were in bankruptcy. We were dealing with a global economic crisis while trying to stay focused on our policy priorities and staffing up the administration. We all said it was like drinking from a fire hose.

None of us had a chance to settle in; maybe every new administration feels like that. I'd found an apartment and moved to DC so quickly that my movers packed up a trash can still filled with garbage. Boxes stayed piled up in my living room so long that I finally just covered them with a large blanket to avoid the daily reminder. One of the few boxes I did unpack was the one with photos of Laura. I didn't have time to buy a hammer and nails, so I put "all my little pumpkins"—as I called the images of her from various ages—along the floor.

My apartment soon also became littered with binders, each one stuffed with briefing papers for the president and his senior staff. I stayed up late into the night reading every single one and drafting many of my own. I was used to working hard, but now I was doing it on the biggest and most public stage in the world. I wasn't just dealing with the familiar pressures of being a black woman in a professional setting, I was also a close friend of the president's. Though I rarely said it out loud, I knew the stakes were higher for the first black president and First Lady. The pressure that caused motivated me to try to do my best every day, because I felt that any misstep by me would reflect poorly on them. At first, I used my voice carefully, knowing that it carried greater weight because people assumed that I had an inside track to the president's thoughts. Anytime I did a press interview, I spent hours thinking of every possible question and forced our already-overworked press office to go through multiple practice sessions with me. I gained a reputation for trying to overprepare—to the point that when the West Wing ran low on binders for the briefing memos, a staffer politely asked if I wouldn't mind returning a few. But overpreparing paid off. I felt confident in my opinions, and though I used it judiciously in the beginning, I had found my voice in the most important building in the country.

I convinced Susan Sher to not only accept a job offer in the White House counsel's office, but also to move into an apartment across the hall from me. She was a natural fit for the health care team given her experience as general counsel at the University of Chicago Medical Center, but it meant she had to move away from her husband, Neil Cohen, who was a judge in Chicago, a sacrifice for them both, of which I was acutely aware.

Rituals are important to me. Holidays, Sunday dinners, summer vacation at Martha's Vineyard. Perhaps because we traveled so much when I was young, I crave moments of certainty and predictability. Before moving to DC, I had lunch with the same circle of friends every Saturday at Gibsons Bar & Steakhouse on Rush Street. We always ordered ribs to share, dry, with sauce on the side, and a chopped salad for me. Once in a while we would try a new dish, but we always reverted to what was familiar. When I first arrived in DC, I felt yanked out of the traditions that had grounded me. We were working so hard that I did not appreciate how unsettling the disruption was in the beginning. But over time I began to crave new rituals and habits that would make DC feel like home. Having Susan across the hall was very comforting. Laura's best friend, Maude, joined my team, too, and spent many a night crashing in my apartment. Susan and I left our doors unlocked so we could roam freely back and forth. Whenever my mom came to visit, she would appear at Susan's door looking for her morning cup of coffee, since I'd quit drinking coffee years earlier and never had time to go to the store to buy any for her. Those first two years would have been exponentially harder for me without Susan and Maude there. Our living situation became like a dorm. After a grueling night, we drank wine and ate a lot of cereal, and every day felt more challenging than our hardest final exams.

In addition to Susan and Maude, I also relied on a close circle of girlfriends to give me the space to exhale. Kelly King Dibble (who had married my cousin Andrew) moved to DC at the start of the administration, along with Susan Kurland, who joined the Department of Transportation, and Karol Mason, who joined the Department of Justice and was the one law school friend I remained close with over the thirty years since law school. We had brunch every Sunday along with my cousin Renée McCoy, and sometimes Tina Tchen. It reminded me fondly of my Saturday lunch routine in Chicago. Sunday family dinner was often at my cousin Toni Bush's home; she picked up the ritual begun by my parents. People often ask how I kept my spirits up at the White House for all eight years, a record for any senior advisor in history. These special rituals are why.

My other way to relax was by spending time with the Obamas. Weather permitting, we would sit on the Truman Balcony, enjoying the weather and a martini (or two), with delicious hors d'oeuvres prepared by their extraordinary chefs; they used to make the most delicious mini open-faced BLTs with a hint of sugar. If it was just the three of us, or five with the girls, we'd sit at a round table that could comfortably hold ten. Their private dining room, which they'd redecorated to their taste (and at their personal expense), could accommodate many more, so different tables were used depending on the size of the group. The flowers, always freshly prepared by the in-house florist to match the decor, were works of art (and there were actual works of art, too; one night Susan Sher whispered to me in awe, "It's a real Monet!"). After dinner we would go back to the Truman Balcony or hang out in the West Sitting Parlor or the Yellow Oval Room. Or we might watch a movie in their private movie theater on the ground floor of the residence.

One time when Michelle had a group of her girlfriends over, the president came into the Yellow Oval Room to say hello to everyone. He stayed and chatted for a bit. Then he left, and when he came back a few hours later, we were all still in the same spots. "You're still talking?" he said incredulously. It reminded me of my parents' disbelief when I would spend hours talking to my high school boyfriends on the phone. We responded, in unison, that we never ran out of topics to discuss.

My other rock of support was the one person I couldn't have imagined going to the White House without: my longtime executive assistant, Katherine Branch. I was totally dependent on her. Several months after I became commissioner in 1991, I hired her as my assistant, and from that day, Kathy took care of me in every possible way, whether it was juggling priorities on my overpacked calendar or making sure I knew Laura was on the phone whenever she called. A single mother herself, Kathy was always protective of my time with Laura against the avalanche of demands. Kathy's response when I asked her to join me in the White House was the same as when I left city hall and asked her to join me at The Habitat Company: "Who?" she said, looking over her right shoulder, and then her left.

"You!" I said. "I'm talking to you!"

"*Me?*"

Kathy wasn't being humble or making a joke. She was genuinely in shock.

A West Side Chicago native, Kathy was twenty-five years old when we met. She'd dropped out of school after becoming a mother at sixteen, but she was resilient and determined to make a good life for her son. While working at a temp agency, as well as at McDonald's, she was placed in the city's Department of Planning and Development, where my chief of staff, Beth, recognized her talent. Four years later, she joined me when I moved to The Habitat Company.

One day while we were working at Habitat, Kathy stepped into my office to confide that she was having a very serious domestic upheaval. I'd sensed she was having trouble at home, mainly because she wasn't in her usual bubbly good spirits, and she slowly opened up and described in painful detail what she was enduring at home. I tried to be a helpful sounding board and source of strength for Kathy. Her spirit was broken for a while but she summoned the courage to take back control of the situation. If we had not been close enough for me to ask what was wrong, I couldn't have helped her.

Kathy's journey to the White House was truly her wildest dream come true, but she picked up a bias against her before we even left Chicago. People were incredulous that I would hire her to work at the White House. "How'd you get that job when you're so geechy?" someone asked her, using the slang word for Kathy's thick southern black accent. Inside the West Wing, Kathy was a black woman without a college degree surrounded by Harvard and Yale grads. Even some members of my handpicked team didn't appreciate her capability at first and tried to second-guess her. Over time they grew to trust her judgment, recognizing that nobody on my team there knew me better than I did. She had her own doubts, too. Was she really qualified to be there? "I don't know what I'm doing here," she said to me early on. I had to convince her to ignore the fancy résumés of her peers and recognize that she had at least two strengths that they didn't: she had actual experience in government, and she knew me very well. "You know more than you think you know," I said. "*Much* more."

Her tears dried up, and as she later said, "You made me feel like the smartest person in the world when I felt like the dumbest."

Kathy had known the president and First Lady longer than most people in the White House, from Michelle's early days in the Chicago Department of Planning and Development when Michelle's office was located near Kathy's desk. While I was at The Habitat Company, Kathy would pick up my lunch at the nearby East Bank Club, where, like clockwork, she would see Barack coming down the stairs from his workout while she was walking up. He would always give her a fatherly kiss on the forehead and say, "Tell Valerie I said hello."

On the first Friday after the inauguration, Kathy and I were in my office working on my already out of control schedule for the following week. Tina Tchen, my director of public engagement, popped in from her office next door. We had all known each other for nearly two decades, and we started rehashing our first week and incredulously laughing as we tried to absorb that we all worked there. You can always hear Tina's laugh a mile away. President Obama was taking his first stroll around the second floor and poked his head in to see what was going on. He grinned when he saw three very familiar faces, and invited us down for a visit in the Oval Office. Only Tina and I followed him out the door. He leaned back in and said, "Come on, Kathy!"

Two days earlier, on the first day of work, I walked into the famous office I'd seen only from a hallway behind a rope on a White House tour. I had studied every corner of the room, including its gorgeous ceiling, still trying to absorb all that had happened to land us there. I sat on the couch in the seat nearest him. When my eyes caught the president's as he sat comfortably in his chair, it was hard to keep my focus.

So now when Kathy and Tina just stood there, gawking, I realized I was still gawking, too. Michelle, who happened to stroll in, turned to Kathy and asked, "Kathy, what do you think about all this?"

"I'm still pinching myself," she said, speaking for all of us.

We sat around chatting like we always used to do until the president announced he had to get some work done. As if on cue, Tina, Kathy, and I simultaneously stood up.

"I'm not ready to go back," Michelle said.

In unison, the three of us sat back down.

Kathy stayed with me at the White House for the entire eight years, and over the twenty-five years that we worked together, she's proved to be one of the most determined, loyal, and inspirational people I've ever known. While working in the West Wing, she went back to school, taking classes online and at night, earning her BA in 2011 and, at the age of fifty, her master's degree. Kathy overcame immense obstacles to succeed at the White House, but she wasn't the only woman there who struggled.

About six months into President Obama's first term, I started to notice a troubling sign in the senior women in the White House. They weren't speaking as much, or as forcefully, in meetings as I knew they could. A few confided in me that they did not feel that their input, even in their areas of expertise, were being valued.

Every White House is intimidating. For the staff, stakes are always high. You're working for the most powerful person in the world, and the decisions he makes have global impact. It's the ultimate pressure cooker, and nobody has a tougher job than the chief of staff. All five who worked under President Obama had different skill sets, management styles, interests, and temperaments, and Rahm Emanuel, being the first, in some ways had the most challenging job of all of them. He walked into a crumbling economy, ambitious agenda, high expectations, and a team that was talented, but many of whom had never worked together before. His bombastic style of leadership was intimidating to many. He let off steam by *screaming*, which was unsettling not just for those to whom it was directed, but to anyone in earshot. He didn't blow up often, but when he did, it sent shock waves through the West Wing. He never actually yelled at me, but I found it hard to watch him make so many others squirm.

It's true that Rahm was an equal-opportunity screamer, but the women on staff absorbed it personally. (Perhaps the men did, too, but they didn't complain.) A few of the other senior men in those first years of the administration exhibited a similar bravado that, intentionally or unintentionally, also made the women feel at best left out, and at worst disrespected.

I had gone from being a CEO, where I was the decision maker, to a member of the team giving advice to the president. From my experience running a company, I learned that the strongest teams depend on the level of trust between their members, and that building trust does not happen instantaneously—it takes hard work and time. Although early on I'm sure a few of my colleagues may have felt uncomfortable, or even intimidated, by my relationship and access to the president and First Lady, as we all worked together closely, I sensed in most cases that the initial apprehension had faded away. I did remain sensitive to the issue throughout all eight years. If the president asked my opinion with the team or in private, I always gave it, just as we all did. But I never tried to re-litigate policy decisions, for that would have hurt my relationship with both the president and the team and have been disruptive to our rigorously structured decision-making process. There were, however, certain sensitive operational issues that I felt needed his attention. This was one.

I could see for myself the growing frustration among the senior women and felt, as the most senior woman in the White House, I had a responsibility to use my voice to make sure President Obama knew he had a problem. This was no time to remain silent. I told the president that the general macho atmosphere was causing women to feel un-welcome.

"If you notice," I said to him, "in meetings the women rarely talk. And when you aren't there to ask their opinion, they are becomingly increasingly mute."

"That's unacceptable," he said. "They're here to tell me what they think. That's their job."

"Well, they don't feel comfortable."

"Then let's all talk it through," he decided, never one to dodge a tough situation. He invited over a dozen of the senior women for dinner at the White House to discuss what was going on so he could better understand the dynamic and how he could help. Before dinner I visited each woman individually and encouraged her to be honest with him about her concerns, assuring her that the president cared about creating an inclusive culture inside the West Wing and wanted to bring out the best in us all.

The dinner was scheduled for November 5, 2009. Earlier that day, however, thirteen people were tragically killed and thirty-two others were injured in a mass shooting at Fort Hood, an army base in Texas. It was the first of far too many tragic mass shootings during our eight years. Over cocktails, a few women wondered if the president would even show up. But, not only did he come, he gave us his undivided attention for two and a half hours, staying long after the butlers had finished serving us a delicious three-course meal at the large formal table in the State Dining Room.

He went around the table, asking each woman to share how she felt and what changes she wanted to make. He listened to every one of the most senior women in the White House, including the deputy chief of staff, director of domestic policy, chair of the president's council of economic advisors, staff secretary, and communications director. They brought up the kinds of issues that are so common to women no matter what they do or where they work—that their contribution was not valued, and when they tried to speak up, they were dismissed or ignored. As time ticked by, I could sense a growing unease in the room that we were taking up too much of his time. But he didn't seem to be in a rush, which several women later told me they found extremely reassuring.

In the end, the president said he would talk to Rahm about what he'd learned at our dinner, because he wanted his chief of staff's help in improving the work environment. But he also wanted them to know that he could not afford for them to shrink or fade. If they were silent when they had opinions, they were not doing their jobs. "I handpicked each one of you," he said. "This is the White House. I expect you to fight to make sure your voices are heard. It's not about you. It's about helping me make the most fully informed decisions."

He asked for their patience while this was straightened out but said that if they felt that they needed another dinner with him, they should let me know. From then on I scheduled regular dinners with the senior women in the White House. At the end of each dinner, I asked if anyone needed another dinner with the president. The answer was always no. My question became a running joke, because we all knew it was better.

Which is not to say everything was perfect. There were still times when women on the staff would show up on my doorstep on the verge of tears and I'd say, "Come in and close the door. You can cry in here, but you can't let anyone else see you cry." And I also certainly showed up on their doorsteps, too. But for the women in the White House, having the president himself reassure them of their value, coupled with the strong bonds we developed with one another, gave us the courage and confidence we needed to make our voices heard.

Around the same time, Anita Dunn, President Obama's communications director, and a savvy Washington insider, married to Bob Bauer, the president's personal lawyer (who became White House counsel when Anita left the White House), started picking up signs of another "women's problem." The women who covered the White House for the press outlets didn't feel they were receiving enough attention either. She had run the communications shop during his campaign and knew the signs. Anita suggested I start hosting women from the press corps in my office on Friday afternoons as a casual way for us to develop a relationship without a deadline or specific goal. She thought it would help them and help me; these were important relationships, and a gesture to build goodwill.

I was intimidated at first, since I had not spent much time with the press, but I agreed to start doing informal get-togethers. Anita would bring up cookies from the White House mess, and it was very relaxed and fun.

We moved on to hosting regular dinners with the women in the press corps, often at Ris, a favorite restaurant of mine on L Street. We would reserve a big round table in a private room so everyone could hear one another, and we'd have off-the-record conversations that ranged from the news of the day to our favorite new movies to the challenges of being working moms. One of the reporters even brought her young daughter along when her babysitter fell through, and over the years I took delight in the reporter, feeling comfortable having her daughter there, reminding me of all the work events I took Laura to when she was a child. I also enjoyed having my own special relationship with her daughter as I watched her grow up. At the end of each meal, I always reminded the reporters to call me if they thought I could help them. "I won't leak confidential matters," I said, "but if you want to know what I think, I'm happy to tell you." They did, and I hoped that our rapport informed their stories.

As though helping the leader of the free world wasn't challenging enough, my arrival in Washington, DC, coincided with the onset of menopause and the arrival of hot flashes. I had always looked forward to menopause, because having spent my childhood in a warm climate, I'm always cold, especially in Chicago winters. No more periods and flashes of warmth all of the time? Sounded great to me. I thought because the word "flashes" was in the name, that they would feel like quick bolts of heat that would subside quickly. Nobody told me they could last *forever*, my pores opening up and sweat always flowing down my face and wrists. Why just those two parts of my body? Who knows. But they would arrive, without warning, several times a day, especially when I spoke publicly, and I was helpless to stop them. As a friend of my mother's once said, "Hot flashes are the devil." So true.

Tina had them, too, but just ignored the sweat and let it bead up on her face. I was much more self-conscious and tried discreetly to brush it away, convincing myself that it was visible only to me, even when my hair was so wet it stuck to my forehead.

In his car, President Obama always turned the temperature up to make it feel like a hot summer day in Hawaii. If I was riding with him, and a flash exploded, he simply turned up the air-conditioning and handed me his handkerchief, without saying a word or even looking in my direction. He just knew. Other times he would tease Tina and me in a good-natured way that only a man who knows you well, like a brother, has permission to do.

But the fact that Tina and I were two of the only women in this state was also an ever-present reminder of how young most of our colleagues were. I envied them in a way, coming right from a historic campaign to begin their careers at the top. But I also knew Tina and I had a far better appreciation for the extraordinary opportunity to work in the Obama White House. I also think our age gave us a thicker skin and made it easier to absorb the inevitable attacks that came our way. I certainly learned in my time in public service in Chicago how to take a punch without withering. Early on in my tenure at the White House, Rick Warren, the influential pastor of Saddleback Church, a Baptist church with twenty-two thousand members, came to see me. I was in a perpetually agitated state back then, and I began our meeting by ranting about some baseless attack by Republicans on President Obama that I can no longer remember. Pastor Rick listened and offered some gently measured advice. "Valerie, an essential quality of leadership is being able to absorb pain. Of course, that rang true. We talked about how we cannot let the pain make us numb or destroy our spirit. And that we are going to know so much that others don't. We agreed that you can't control what others do. Just how we react.

After he left my office, I went right down to President Obama and repeated his message. It really struck a chord with us, so much so that it became a regular expression between us. "Time to absorb some pain," we'd say to each other, exchanging knowing glances.

There was a whole generation of young people on the campaign, and now at the White House, who were my daughter's age. I cared deeply about these bright, earnest, young people. And because I cared about them, I came to think of them as "my children." I mothered them, in the professional sense, meaning I both was supportive and set high expectations. But I also mothered them, well, like a mother. One of the many ways my day was thrown off schedule was when one of the young staff came in to have a heart-to-heart. Sometimes it was a professional issue, sometimes personal, sometimes both. The White House was like any workplace in that we had women coping with the new demands of motherhood, people experiencing the loss of a loved one, and others grappling with hard career choices. I later found out that Kathy and my chief of staff would draw straws to see who was stuck with the awkward task of coming into my office where someone might be crying over a breakup to say, "Senior staff meeting is happening now!"

Every single aspect of our life in President Obama's White House was under intense scrutiny. When Common—a Grammy Award–winning artist who worked on *Sesame Street* and started a foundation to help young people in poor communities become leaders—came to the White House for an "evening of poetry" in 2011, it set off a firestorm because of some rap lyrics he had written criticizing President Bush. It was a bogus criticism and it didn't stop us from inviting him back multiple times. But it demonstrated the hypercritical atmosphere we were up against. When President Obama wore a tan suit, even that caused high drama, never mind when he put his feet on his desk or took his jacket off in the Oval Office.

Because the stakes were so high, we demanded the highest quality of work from the White House team in *everything*. Back in my corporate law days, I had a boss who scolded me when the correspondence with a client was not in perfect chronological order, but I became that exacting with my staff in many ways. One of my rules was "no acronyms." People love to use jargon, especially in DC, perhaps to show they were in the know, and they certainly saved time. Let's face it—the American Recovery and Reinvestment Act of 2009 was a mouthful, but nobody in the public understood what ARRP was. I instituted another rule about emails: if it takes more than two scrolls to read, it's probably a message you should deliver in person. And of course, be on time. I didn't have to say that rule out loud; people could just feel what I was thinking when they were not punctual. Those who were late to a meeting in my office knew they would have to endure the embarrassment of walking into one that had begun at the scheduled time with whoever *did* show up on time.

The most important rule, however, was to remember that everything we did or said at work or outside of the office reflected on the president of the United States. Perhaps not fair, but that was our reality. I made a point of delivering this message to each class of White House interns after Straut fired one of ours for relieving himself outside the Pentagon subway station. I also reminded my team that our memos for the president would actually be read by him. (Just as I'd discovered years earlier that Mayor Daley read mine.) My mantra was "Show up on time, try the best you can, learn from your mistakes, no surprises, and be good to your colleagues and all our visitors."

In addition to my job responsibilities, I became an informal conduit between the West Wing and the East Wing early on, once it became clear the lack of coordination between the two was causing problems. This shuttle diplomacy was initially intended to keep the president and First Lady from wasting their time with coordinating schedules. In the beginning, the First Lady's chief of staff wasn't invited to senior West Wing staff meetings. This made it more difficult for the First Lady's team to plan with the amount of lead time she required. Her office often felt jammed up, trying to juggle her schedule to accommodate decisions made by the West Wing. The right hand didn't know what the left hand was doing. Tensions flared up, for example, over the easily avoidable scheduling conflict of having the president out of town when his girls had an important school activity they wanted him to attend. Simple to avoid if we talked to each other and weren't all moving at the speed of light.

After the Affordable Care Act passed, Susan was promoted to the First Lady's chief of staff. Recognizing the communication problem, Rahm began inviting Susan to his morning meetings. Even with that issue solved, however, Susan and I still collaborated a lot, both formally and informally. Scheduling wasn't the only source of conflict with which we had to deal. There was also the issue of radically different management styles. Mrs. Obama required her team to give her information well in advance of any event or decision. Meanwhile, we would cram the president every night, sending him home with voluminous piles of paper he had to plow through to prepare for the next day.

There wasn't a single time in eight years when I remember the president walking into a meeting unprepared, he never once yelled at us, and he rarely complained. "You guys are killing him," Mrs. Obama kept telling Susan and me in different ways and at different times. Although he never complained to her, she certainly noticed when he climbed into bed at 2 a.m. Quite rightly, she viewed it as our job to look out for her husband, and that included not ignoring the toll the grueling schedule was taking on him. We'd relay her concerns to other members of the senior staff, and we'd try to do better. We would institute new reforms. Memos would be due to the staff secretary by a certain time of day so he wouldn't have to consume so much information into the wee hours of the night. But inevitably we slipped back into the old way of doing things due to the volume and urgency of time-sensitive decisions. The habit was impossible to break, though every chief of staff tried.

After the bumps on the campaign, Michelle Obama was determined to set her own pace and priorities in the White House.

One of the ways she tried to establish normalcy for herself and her family was to set dinner in the White House always at 6:30 p.m. Knowing how important those dinners were to the president and the First Lady, any evening that I was in the Oval after six, I started feeling anxious when the clock struck 6:10. I knew we needed to wrap by 6:25 so the president could make his two-minute commute with time to spare. When, late in the day, people brought up thorny problems that I knew would take considerable time to resolve, I'd think to myself, *How can I help move this along, and fast?*

O f course, the goal of all our hard work was not simply to have a better-functioning White House but to do so with the aim of serving the American people. It's no coincidence that the Lilly Ledbetter Fair Pay Act was the very first bill President Obama signed. The law, which made it easier for women to bring pay discrimination suits, had been wallowing in Congress for years. But Speaker Nancy Pelosi moved it along, as only she can do, once President Obama was elected. He wanted it to set the tone for his administration's priorities.

My office was responsible for working with the social office to manage any event tied to the vast array of our constituency groups. The Lilly Ledbetter signing was our first time organizing an event on the State Floor of the residence. For that and for all subsequent signings, we invited the stakeholders who'd been the most involved in its passage, which, because of limited space, turned out to be a lot harder than it looked. We were never able to satisfy the demand, and I had to review the final list of invitees to make many tough calls. Even among those who made the final cut, there were always people unhappy with their seats. Before each event my staff would tell me who was grumpy so that I could "show them some love," as we called it. I tried to arrive early and walked around the room to lay hands on and spend a little time with as many of our guests as possible. I wanted the attendees to enjoy themselves, to feel we appreciated their hard work since they were there because they had done the heavy lifting that gave reason to celebrate.

On that first bill, it was all hands on deck. We scurried around frantically at the last minute to make sure we were ready. Thankfully the White House social aides, who were part of the permanent staff, subtly guided us when balls started to drop. Many on my team, seasoned field organizers on the campaign trail who were used to executing complicated tasks flawlessly, were stressed out by the time the president emerged to sign the bill. Lilly Ledbetter, after whom the bill was named, looked resplendent in her signature red. She was an icon among women's rights activists for her selfless lobbying efforts. The law she had pushed would not benefit her, because she had already lost her Supreme Court case against her employer, Goodyear Tire & Rubber Co., for wage discrimination. But it would help countless women in the future.

After the signing, Tina and I felt triumphant on a number of levels. Hoping the Ledbetter Act was just a good start, we spent much of those first months trying to figure out the best strategy for continuing our lifelong fight for gender equity. We studied past administrations and consulted a wide range of women's advocacy groups. In the end, we recommended to the president that he codify a government-wide approach, using an executive order to create the first White House Council on Women and Girls. It was composed of senior officials in every agency and department. Each member of the Council and their teams would evaluate all of the programs, policies, and legislation through a gender lens.

This had never been done before, and when we pitched him on it, President Obama was fully supportive of the idea. He had always been surrounded by working women in both his family and at work, and he knew the playing field was far from even. He had watched both his mom and Michelle struggle to juggle their responsibilities at home and at work. He had seen his grandmother's disappointment when she was passed over for promotions that she deserved while forced to watch less qualified men—men often trained *by her*, leapfrog over her. And he was certainly raising his daughters to feel empowered to compete with any guy. And so, on March 11, 2009, President Obama announced the creation of the Council and named Tina Tchen its executive director and me its chair, positions we held for all eight years.

When he signed the executive order, I was expected to introduce him in front of a large audience at an event covered in the media by the White House press corps. The all-too-familiar butterflies were back in my stomach. The venue was the not-yet-familiar East Wing of the State

Floor, where I'd been only once before. Writing my speech had been easy, since the issue was deeply personal for me, too. But the thought of delivering it, in that grand and very public setting, with the president waiting in the wings, made me queasy. What if I fainted, as I nearly had at my friend Gwen's wedding decades earlier? I came close to suggesting that only the president speak, but what would be the optics of that for the empowerment of women?

And so I steeled myself, and as my name was announced, I walked into the room, carefully climbing the three steps to the podium. I wish I could tell you I was thinking of my family arc—my great-grandfather, no doubt nervous on the lonely train ride to MIT—or the generations of women who had fought so hard for Tina and me to have our important seats at such a powerful table, but no, I was thinking, *Don't you dare stumble*, since I tend to be clumsy. When I faced the audience I saw my mom, who just happened to be in town, seated in the front row, and I remembered what she often told me: "Just because you are nervous doesn't mean you have to show it." I also knew I had waited my whole career for a moment where I could use my strong voice to help empower other women and girls. I may not have given my best speech ever that day, but I made it through, and yet another "first time" was behind me.

There were countless more times that I spoke from that stage. I always worried about tripping, but not about speaking.

Then, just a few weeks later, my team and I had the privilege of helping the country take yet another historic step forward for women, when President Obama nominated Sonia Sotomayor to the Supreme Court. When he decided to appoint the Court's first Latina, and one whose life story is so quintessentially American, I was so proud that he was leaving his mark on history in this unique way. Then the hard work of her confirmation began.

While the White House Counsel's office took the lead on vetting the prospective nominee's writings, and the FBI conducted background checks, the Office of Public Engagement played an integral part in her confirmation process. We came in at the point when the president was considering multiple candidates. The original short list included three or four candidates. We were responsible for testing reactions to nominees with outside stakeholders. We would consult various national groups that focused on the Supreme Court and ask for their short lists, hoping our prospective names were on them; then we'd ask for views and preferences, all without tipping our hands. We never divulged our prospective names, wanting to protect the privacy of the candidates. Before making a decision, President Obama wanted to know all he could about a candidate so there would be no surprises. He had to be able to defend the nominee's complete record and make a compelling case for his or her confirmation. We didn't leak names to the press to flush out a reaction—known as floating trial balloons. I devoted a small number of folks from the public engagement team to the task, with one full-time quarterback to keep me up to speed. We had only a few weeks from receiving the president's short list to the time he wanted to make a decision on the selection.

That was only the start of my office's job. Once the nominee was announced, we followed up with a huge push to galvanize support by lining up advocates willing to work on her behalf. In the case of Justice Sotomayor, President Obama believed the highest court in the land would be better served by a brilliant and extraordinarily well-qualified woman who would represent a new perspective on the bench. Although she handled her confirmation hearing flawlessly, it was a nail-biter.

After being confirmed that August, Justice Sotomayor invited me, my mother, and Laura, who was in her third year at Harvard Law, to hear oral arguments at the Supreme Court's opening session on the first Monday of October. For three women of color to be sitting in the beautifully adorned chambers of the Supreme Court of the United States, watching the first woman of color ever appointed to that court, was extraordinary, an incredible testament to how far we had come. I'm sure that day helped motivate Laura to clerk for two federal judges.

But as heady as that moment was, the next morning I was up before dawn, climbing into my car with a stack of briefing binders under my arm, and as I pulled into the White House grounds, my car waiting for the Secret Service gate to go up, I looked up to see the red light on the Washington Monument blink three times, thought about that man from the elevator in Austin, and I knew we still had much more to do.

· *Chapter 10* ·

Pinch Myself Moments

The title of Senior Advisor to the President of the United States came with a host of responsibilities, but it also came with some incredible opportunities. Perhaps the most fascinating was that senior advisors, as well as the chief of staff, were able to travel with the president whenever we thought it appropriate.

And so, in the course of eight years, I attended state dinners at Buckingham Palace hosted by Queen Elizabeth, and luxuriated in the millions of flower petals covering the Rashtrapati Bhavan palace grounds in New Delhi, India; I devoured a "feast for a king" that King Abdullah of Jordan delivered to President Obama and his traveling party while we toured the ancient city of Petra, and I climbed the stairs to the Great Wall of China against a frigidly cold wind; I flew to Oslo, Sweden, for the failed attempt to secure the Olympic Games for the United States, and back again for the festivities when President Obama was awarded the Nobel Peace Prize; I rode with the Obama family late one night up the winding road in Rio de Janeiro, Brazil, that had been shut down in order for them to see the Christ the Redeemer statue emerge from a dense fog; I stood silently with the president in Nelson Mandela's cell on Robben Island; we toured Goree Island in Senegal, where we looked out to the ocean from the quarters where slaves had been held before being shipped off forever to faraway lands; I watched from a front row seat when President Obama and the First Lady were coaxed by professional dancers to do the tango in Argentina; and I partied with Tina Tchen late into the night in Cuba, celebrating the restoration of our diplomatic relations.

Early on, while we were all still getting our feet wet, several of the senior staff traveled with the president often so that he could be surrounded by a virtual White House, and we could keep him up to speed with briefs and timely guidance. So in June of 2009, when the president traveled to Saudi Arabia, Egypt, Germany, and Normandy, I made my first trip with him, together with several other senior aides.

Our first stop was Saudi Arabia, where our party was met on the tarmac by King Abdullah and his entourage and immediately swept into lunch in an extravagant ballroom at the airport. The moment we walked in, Alyssa Mastromonaco, who was the president's director of scheduling and advance, and I were keenly aware that the only women in the room had just come off of Air Force One, and when we sat to eat, it was clear there would be no welcoming conversation for us. In fact, no one from the Saudi delegation opted to sit next to Alyssa, so the seat next to her remained empty throughout lunch.

We stayed at the eighty-four-year-old Saudi king's ranch at Jenadriyah, a complex in the suburbs of Riyadh where the royal stables of over a thousand Thoroughbreds and Arabian horses are kept. In keeping with the lavish theme, each of us had our own expansive villa. When I walked into mine, I noticed a very large gift box. Curious, of course, I opened it immediately. Inside was a huge, green leather briefcase made from some kind of reptile skin. It struck me as odd, since nobody uses large, cumbersome briefcases anymore, so I texted Alyssa, who was staying in the villa next door, to see if she had received a briefcase, too.

"No," she texted. "I guess I was left out." Then, a half hour later, she texted me again. "My briefcase just arrived. Open it."

When I popped open the case, it was like a scene out of *One Thousand and One Nights*: Emeralds and diamonds, and lots of them, were sparkling up at me. There was a stunning necklace, earrings, a ring, two watches, and a bejeweled pen. I took a photo of the contents because they were so incredible. And because I knew that I couldn't keep any of it.

Before we left, we'd been prepped extensively on the protocols for each country on our itinerary, from the particulars of the arrival ceremony to social taboos to avoid. We'd even studied our dinner companions to make sure we could have useful conversations. Somehow, though, the gift issue had slipped through the cracks. No one had warned me this might happen, but I remembered the wise advice of my colleague Phil Schiliro, a former congressional staffer. "During your time here, people are going to offer you all kinds of things," he said. "If someone offers you a gift, and you think you would enjoy it, just say no." Phil, who had worked on Congressman Henry Waxman's House Oversight and Government Reform Committee under President George W. Bush, was keenly aware of what could trigger an investigation.

Alyssa, whose loot was in rubies and diamonds, reached out to the State Department, which has a whole official process to inventory foreign gifts; after being logged in, they're either auctioned off or stored. As a government official, you do have the right to buy the gift for its market value (in the United States, not the country of origin), but none of us elected to buy a bag filled with expensive precious jewels. We couldn't give them back, either, because that would have been an insult to the king. All we could do was hand them over to the State Department. As Alyssa and I walked our briefcases over to the State Department villa for cataloging, we ran into Rahm, who had also received a briefcase full of jewels. "This is great," he joked. "My wife's birthday is next week." I hasten to add, he turned his over to State, too.

The next stop after Saudi Arabia was Egypt. In all the traveling I had done in my life, no place mesmerized me like Egypt, a place I had visited a number of times. Usually on our way to other far away locations, my parents always made time to visit Giza. As a little girl, the Great Pyramids were just another playground of mine, the backdrop to the camel and donkey rides I adored. It wasn't until I was in high school that I understood their age and immense significance. I could never have imagined back then, or even when I visited with my husband, Bobby, that one day I would return for a private tour with the president of the United States.

At Cairo University, President Obama gave a visionary speech about a "new beginning" to three thousand people, who responded with a standing ovation and chanted his name. From there we took a helicopter to the pyramids in Giza.

"This is incredible," I said to President Obama, gazing down at the enormous city below. I'd never seen it from that view before.

"Sure," he said, looking out at the ground below with a serious expression. "As long as we don't get shot by a surface-to-air missile."

For the rest of the ride, all I could think about were the impossible logistics of securing a city of nineteen million people.

We landed safely and were then given a private tour of my favorite of the Seven Wonders of the World. We did the whole bit. Rahm, Reggie Love—still the president's special assistant and personal aide—and I even rode on camels. (Not the president.) Then we climbed up a ladder into the tomb in the largest of the three pyramids. It was a cavernous room two thirds of the way up, with nothing much to see. We had to climb backward down the same ladder to exit. The president went first. I followed him. Then it was David Axelrod, and last Rahm Emanuel. Rahm, being the competitive spirit he is, was moving really fast, causing David to panic. "Slow down!" he said. "Your ass is in my face!" Once we were all outside again, the president teased David, "Man, you sounded really worried back there." We all laughed at David's expense, but, as usual, he was a pretty good sport. And our tour guide, one of the world's expert Egyptologists, even showed us an etching of a man who, presumably because of the size of his ears, resembled the president.

In Germany we visited Buchenwald, the notorious World War II concentration camp, accompanied by Holocaust survivor and Nobel Laureate Elie Wiesel. I had never been to a concentration camp before and didn't know what to expect. Wiesel had been back to Buchenwald only once, many years earlier, but said he'd left the grounds, also his father's resting place, almost immediately because they were so poorly maintained.

But by then the German government had fixed up the property and so Wiesel agreed to go there with us. On the site of the barracks where he and his father were housed, there was a photo of him in one of the cramped four-level bunks. He stared at the emaciated image of himself. As I looked at the sunken eyes of the photo returning his gaze, I couldn't imagine the thoughts running through his mind. After the walk around the grounds, President Obama, German chancellor Angela Merkel, and Elie Wiesel addressed the press. Wiesel said, about the day his father died, "He [was] on the upper bed and I on the lower bed. He called my name, and I was too afraid to move. All of us were. And then he died. I was there, but I was not there." Despite his excruciating words, there was a remarkable absence of bitterness in his tone. As we all listened, he told his story, seeking not recrimination but understanding. I was deeply touched by this special man who had experienced so much hate, pain, and loss yet could still be a kind and gentle spirit.

From Germany we traveled to Normandy, where Allied soldiers had stormed the beach sixty-five years earlier as part of the largest naval, land, and air operation in history. Having never seen the landing beaches before, flying over them I was struck by how steep the cliffs behind them were. Our brave men had no chance against the enemy shooting at them from above, and indeed nearly thirty thousand Americans died as they poured onto the beaches from their boats. Before the ceremony, I walked through the nearby cemetery by myself and said a quiet thank-you to those who were buried there, and their families, for making the world a better and safer place.

The anniversary was marked by a military ceremony attended not just by heads of state—including French president Nicolas Sarkozy, Canadian prime minister Stephen Harper, British prime minister Gordon Brown—but also by President Obama's great-uncle Charles Payne, who had fought in Germany and who traveled all the way from Chicago to be at the event. President Obama gave a shout-out to Charles and to his deceased grandfather, who arrived in France six weeks after D-day. There was one moment of levity when Gordon Brown mistakenly called Omaha Beach "Obama Beach."

Amazingly, we did all of that, four countries in only five days, by sleeping all but two nights on Air Force One. Despite its reputation, the aircraft wasn't what I imagined it to be. It doesn't have the plush, white-leather interior you saw in *Independence Day*, for starters. The president's plane, while very big, is not fancy. It's functional. Naturally, the president had his own suite with a bedroom, office, and bathroom whose shower I coveted. And there are essential amenities, such as a doctor's cabin with an operating table. (When we all went to South Africa for Nelson Mandela's funeral, President George W. Bush and First Lady Laura Bush slept in the cabin's pull-out bed.) The compact senior staff cabin contained four chairs that could face one another or swivel around to their own fold-down desk spaces.

The first night on Air Force One, I chose a long leather couch along the wall in the conference room where I could lie flat, because I suffered from chronic lower back pain. Unfortunately, David Axelrod slept on the other end, and we kept accidentally playing footsie all night. The next night on board, I tried sleeping in my chair, but it was too slippery. Then the floor in our cabin, which was freezing cold. Finally I settled onto the couch in the main hallway between our cabin and the kitchen. Covered in a soft cloth, it was so comfortable that I did not hesitate to sleep out in the open in front of everyone walking by. I felt like Goldilocks finding that bed. It was just right. From then on, through both terms, when I slept on Air Force One I dared anyone to try to poach my couch.

One of the thrilling parts of flying on Air Force One is having the phone operator announce your name as "calling from Air Force One" when your call is connected, which is why every staffer and guest calls their family the first time they're on board. But the best part of Air Force One was the military personnel who operated it, from the pilots to those who made sure our technology functioned seamlessly, to those who kept us well fed, all attending to our every need with precision and professionalism, not just in their skill but also their demeanor. Their job, which they did at the highest level, was to make our jobs easier. One of them impressed the president so much that he promoted him to oversee the household staff in the White House, and at the end of the administration, he retired from the government and went to work directly for the Obamas, which he does to this day.

The same was true of the military staff on Marine One, the president's helicopter. I actually preferred flying on Marine One to flying on Air Force One. (It sounds absurd to even admit to a preference, right?) Air Force One is an amazing plane, but once you're up in the air, the view outside isn't so different from any other plane; it flies and lands like any other, just faster and smoother (thanks to the best pilots in the world). A helicopter, on the other hand, takes you places and shows you scenes from a vantage point very few people ever see.

Everyone has watched on television as presidents walk across the South Lawn, wave at the crowd, and climb on board Marine One. It's very different to be there in real life. To watch President Obama's first takeoff, I walked over several minutes before his scheduled departure from the West Wing along the colonnade and then inside the residence to the Diplomatic Room, referred to as the Dip Room, which was the entrance to the residence used by the first family and often by visiting dignitaries and friends. An invited crowd often gathers along the walkway on either side of the Dip Room to watch takeoff and arrival. Since it was President Obama's first one, I invited myself.

Just as I was about to walk out of the Dip Room door to join the other guests, one of the Secret Service agents awaiting the president's arrival warned me, "Ma'am, it's pretty windy out there." I smiled and kept walking. How windy could it be? It turned out to be one of those matter-of-fact understatements I grew to appreciate. It's not just windy. It blew in a way that kicks up every loose piece of dirt and swirls it around with every rotation of the propeller. That day I was too proud to duck back inside, but from then on, if I wanted to watch, I did so from a much more comfortable distance.

When the president walked out with his confident stride, we all cheered. I even teared up. He had earned this incredible opportunity, and I was thrilled knowing I was going to be there for the whole ride. The majesty of Marine One landing and taking off from the South Lawn is unmatched. The pilots land precisely on their target, and when they take off they steer the helicopter straight up, turn smoothly in place, and then go soaring off southward toward Andrews Air Force Base. It's incredible to watch from the ground. It's even better to be on board.

I was so excited about my first Marine One trip a couple of weeks later. But I hadn't anticipated the challenge of walking to the helicopter, sitting about twenty-five yards from the Oval Office and a little closer to the Dip Room. In high heels it was treacherous! The president would always walk out first, with the staff following well behind so as to not obstruct the cameras' view of him. "Staying out of the shot," we called it. As I began to walk out, my heels sank into the grass; I hoped that they would ease out of the dirt without getting stuck, fearing I would walk out of my shoe or stumble and fall. When I grabbed the handrail to climb the stairs, I said a little prayer in relief that I had made it.

It never became less scary. The staff tended to walk in clusters, with an unwritten commitment to catch one another if any of us stumbled. I also mostly gave up on wearing high heels. I never stopped saying my little prayer upon reaching the stairs, but one day I exhaled in relief too soon. On the third step up, a large gust of wind came along and scooped up the back of my dress. Fortunately, in a moment of grace, Rahm, on the stair right behind me, grabbed my skirt as it sailed up and pulled it down, keeping me from flashing the entire press corps. President Obama, watching from his window inside, burst out laughing at my near catastrophe.

On that first flight, a few minutes after we were in the air, President Obama said, "Look out of the window."

"Yes," I said, "it is all very pretty."

"No, no," he said with a knowing expression, "wait a moment."

And then, a few seconds later, the Washington Monument came into view. My God, we were close! It felt like it was only a few feet away, almost as if we could reach out and touch it. My stunned expression made the president smile, having predicted my reaction.

I had two favorite places to fly on Marine One. The first was over the Tidal Basin in the spring, with the blossoming cherry trees below looking like pink clouds hugging the ground. The second was around the Statue of Liberty at night, seeing it all lit up like a beacon of hope, when we took a shortcut to avoid creating a traffic jam from the airport to Manhattan. The pilots often circled around so we could catch a second look. I tried numerous times to capture her elegance in a photo but could never do her justice.

My work for the White House took me around the world and back, many times. Very early on we heard that the Dalai Lama wanted to visit DC and call on President Obama. At the same time, we were trying to manage our relationship with China, and it would have caused diplomatic problems if the Dalai Lama, who China considered to be an enemy, came to visit the White House before they did. We had to try and think of a delicate way to ask the Dalai Lama to postpone his trip without giving offense. The national security team came up with the idea that I should go and hand-deliver a letter from the president to the Dalai Lama in Dharamshala, India, where he and thousands of other Tibetans have lived in exile for fifty years. The letter invited him to come in six months. We felt that the symbolism of someone close to President Obama making this trek would smooth over any ruffled feathers with the Dalai Lama, while not provoking any negative reactions from the Chinese.

So, in September of 2009, Straut and I found ourselves on a plane bound for Dharamshala, which is not an easy place to reach—our first overseas adventure together. We flew first to Germany and changed planes there because we needed a plane that did not say THE UNITED STATES OF AMERICA to fly over parts of the Middle East. I can remember flying over Afghanistan and thinking, *Well, no wonder we can't find Osama bin Laden.* Because there were thousands of caves in the mountains below. We landed in Delhi, then took another plane as close as possible to Dharamshala and drove the rest of the way.

We arrived a couple of days before the Dalai Lama, who was on his way back from Europe. He'd arranged for us to tour an orphanage filled with over five thousand children, all sent by Tibetan families to escape persecution in China and to be closer to their spiritual leader. The children were so well loved and happy. One of them grabbed my hand and took me to her immaculate room and showed me her stuffed animals. The woman giving me the tour had a special way with the children because she had been an orphan herself decades earlier. I visited with nuns who'd been incarcerated in Tibet because of their commitment to the Dalai Lama, and met with the men who'd escaped the Tibetan village and hid in the surrounding mountains while the Chinese government searched for them. We met with the Buddhist monks who tended to the ancient manuscripts secured safely away in their monastery, and they told me the history of the Dalai Lama and why he meant so much to his people.

When I returned to DC, I told the president that the Dalai Lama had changed my life. If his spirit could be so positive and hopeful in the face of fifty years living with his people in exile, I should have no complaints. Several months later, when the Dalai Lama did visit the president, I was so excited to see him again. After dealing with the frustrations of trying to work with the Republicans in Congress, I needed another infusion of his hopeful spirit. After President Obama greeted the Dalai Lama, he re-introduced him to me and told the Dalai Lama that I had said he had changed my life. The Dalai Lama's eyes danced with delight, and, pausing first for effect, he announced with a belly laugh, "She exaggerates."

He had the same generous spirit I saw in Elie Wiesel when we had visited Buchenwald, a spirit I'd also seen once before back in city hall in Chicago, when we received a visit from Nelson Mandela. My political activism at Stanford had been limited to one rally where a group of us marched to protest Stanford's investments in South Africa during apartheid. Similar protests were going on all over the country. I followed the story of Mandela's incarceration on Robben Island, and he became a hero of mine, as he had become for so many people. About three years after he was released, he visited Chicago and came to city hall to meet Mayor Daley. I positioned myself right outside the first elevator used for the mayor and for visiting dignitaries, in the hopes of catching a glimpse of him when he arrived. When he got off the elevator, I put out my hand and said, "Sir, it's my honor." He shook my hand and, giving me the briefest glance, smiled.

Years later I accompanied the Obamas to South Africa. They'd both had the opportunity previously to meet him in person, but he was too ill to meet with us that day. So we visited Robben Island and stood in the tiny cell where he'd been imprisoned for twenty-seven years, and we walked around the quarry where he'd been forced to labor in sun so blinding it damaged his eyesight. I tried to imagine how he could emerge from that horrendous experience with such grace intact—Elie Wiesel and the Dalai Lama, too. All three men had endured terrible ordeals, and not only had they not lost their will to live, but they never let those experiences warp their spirit or undermine their belief in the potential of all people to be good. Their empathy, warmth, and compassion always remained unshakably intact. They all had a genuine love for their fellow man, regardless of how their fellow man felt about them.

One of my greatest privileges was notifying people when President Obama chose to award them with the Presidential Medal of Freedom, the nation's highest civilian honor. Some calls President Obama made himself, the one to President George H. W. Bush, for example. Mostly, though, he delegated the honor to one of us on the review committee.

The process of choosing the medal winners began months before they were ever announced. President Obama would give us a list of people he wanted to consider. We would then check the long list of medal winners selected by prior presidents to avoid duplications. We'd vet his list carefully so there were no unpleasant surprises, and then we'd go back to the president with our proposed additions in an edited list. He often added new names and took some of our recommendations off before approving the final list.

No matter how accomplished the recipients were, the call always came as a shock. Here's how one of them went:

"Michael?" I said.

"Yep."

"Hi, it's Valerie Jarrett."

"Hey, Valerie. What's up?

"President Obama asked me to give you a call to inform you that he is giving you the nation's highest civilian award, the Presidential Medal of Freedom."

Silence.

"You're kidding, right?"

"I hope you know I would never joke about this."

That was my call to Michael Jordan, my favorite basketball player ever. Back in the nineties the Bulls won six championships, and from the time Laura was six until she was twelve we were at each final game played in Chicago.

Michael Jordan is one of the greatest who ever played the game, and even he was left speechless. When I called Meryl Streep from Air Force One, it took a full minute before I could convince the actress this was not a prank call. Then she cried. When I tracked down Tom Hanks in the middle of a street in Europe, he let out a scream that no doubt caused stares.

The ceremonies were each special. I never missed one. And on the fiftieth anniversary of the creation of the Medal of Freedom by President John F. Kennedy (who had died before the first medals were awarded), the president and First Lady hosted an event for all living recipients. Simply extraordinary to see so many people who had made positive impacts on our country and the world all in one place!

One day Harrison Ford came by the West Wing to lobby us against a tax on private planes. It wasn't my first time meeting the movie star. In 1995, while shooting *The Fugitive* in Chicago's city hall, he knocked on the door of my office. It was the weekend, but I was there working. He said he was tired and asked if he could lie down on my couch and take a nap for about an hour. An odd request.

"Yup, you sure can," I said, delighted to have him nap in my office. "Take as long as you want."

Ford and I took a photo together, which then ended up in a file somewhere. Well, over twenty years later, the day Ford was scheduled to visit the White House, I showed up to work to find, to my great astonishment, that my assistant, Kathy, had fished the photo out and put it in a frame on my desk. (I told you she was good.) When the actor arrived, he saw the photo and said, "My God, we used to be young."

Speak for yourself, I thought.

L ife in the public eye meant that security was never far from my mind, whether I was in the White House, on the road, or even at home. Though men with guns had previously been foreign to me, they quickly became part of my everyday routine.

The reality first began to sink into my psyche the day Barack announced his run for president in Springfield. While we were all swept up in the moment, I looked up and saw the Capitol Police scattered strategically on the tops of the buildings that looked down on the crowd. I found their presence both reassuring and disconcerting. A sign of more to come.

Barack initially resisted, but when he finally relented and requested Secret Service protection after credible threats, earlier in the campaign than any candidate before him, I was relieved. I understood that to succumb meant acknowledging that the threats were real. But his safety was not just about him, but also about the reaction that his harm would cause in our nation.

The infrequent moments, usually aboard planes, when his agents would take off their jackets, exposing the guns, wires, and other equipment, were jarring reminders of how prepared they needed to be in the event of an attack.

Walking through the White House, I frequently encountered clusters of counterassault teams moving into place as their shifts changed. I knew their sole purpose was to keep the first family and White House safe, but the sight of them always made me shudder a bit.

It would have been impossible for me to have only a professional relationship with these extraordinary men and women. They overheard our private conversations, exercising restraint by never commenting, just staring straight ahead. They were always right there but tried to be inconspicuous.

Because the Obama family attended Laura's wedding, the Secret Service advance team practically moved into my mom's home a week in advance. When my dad died, they were there with sad expressions of their own when I emerged from his hospital room.

One day, President Obama and I had just lifted off on Marine One, heading to Camp David, when we received the news that someone had jumped the fence and pushed through the north door of the White House before being wrestled to the ground by an agent. Fortunately Michelle and the girls were already at Camp David, but my vivid imagination could not help but think of what might have happened had the Obamas been at home. It was a sign of how even the best-trained agents in the world are still human.

The presence of agents in the lives of the Obamas, and then later in my own life, gave me an appreciation for the sacrifices they all make, and for their sense of patriotism and duty.

Although they were certainly not the reason we came to work, our surroundings were extraordinary: from the M&Ms bearing the presidential seal given out in the White House mess to the military uniformed guards who stood at attention and opened the door as we entered and exited the West Wing; from the Rose Garden, replanted numerous times a year, to the Truman balcony (our refuge); and the precious works—including the original copy of the Emancipation Proclamation that was loaned to President Obama to hang in the Oval Office, and the famous painting of Ruby Bridges walking to school, as well as the Monets, Cézannes, and modern art selected by the Obamas. There were reminders everywhere that we worked in the most coveted eighteen acres in the world.

It's easy to succumb to awe there, but we were there to work, not gape. I do admit that on some mornings when I was facing a special challenge, I would go sit in one of the reception rooms on the first floor (known as the "State" floor)—the red, green, or blue room, depending on my mood—and have a quiet moment to read or collect my thoughts before my day (and the tours) began. The art on the walls showing our nation's history helped motivate me, much as the family photos in Pudden's home had always done.

Chapter 11

The Fight of Our Lives

Irrational, costly, discriminatory, cruel, and, yes, even deadly—these are a few of the characteristics that described our nation's health care system before the implementation of the Affordable Care Act. The law is not perfect, but there is no doubt that Americans are far better off with it than without it. So why all of the controversy, fear tactics, and turmoil? Politics.

From his time in both the Illinois and U.S. senates, President Obama knew that the ballooning cost of health care to both the public and private sectors was unsustainable.

And the issue was deeply personal to the president. He had watched helplessly when his own mother was stricken with an aggressive cancer and worried, as so many others do, about whether her insurance would cover her care.

As a candidate during the 2008 presidential campaign, Barack heard nightmarish stories from Americans who had been denied insurance based on "preexisting conditions"—asthma, diabetes, cancer, heart disease, arthritis, pregnancy, and many more. He heard stories from parents who could not afford to buy health insurance and were forced to choose between paying rent and caring for a sick child, and from far too many uninsured people who were forced to declare bankruptcy trying to keep up with health care debt. There were those who hit annual and lifetime caps on their insurance just when they became really sick and needed it most. And he heard from women in their childbearing years who were paying higher premiums than men and from senior citizens who cut their dosage in half to make their medications stretch further.

Before coming to Washington, I had chaired the board of trustees at the University of Chicago Medical Center, a source of great pride to my father, who delighted in calling me his boss. There, I learned the intricacies and weaknesses of our nation's health care system. We had expensive, but flawed, technology that slowed down the efficient transfer of data; we spent huge sums treating uninsured patients, including those who would arrive at our emergency room in acute pain. Some were destined to die because they had been unable to afford treatment when their symptoms were milder and easily treatable. Michelle, through her role as a vice president for community and external affairs, saw all this, too, as well as people who used the medical center's emergency room for primary care any time they were sick. It's a double problem, since these people rarely received necessary follow-up care after being discharged from the emergency room.

The problems were clear, but solving them was overwhelming and the odds of meaningful success were long. Seven presidents before President Obama had tried and failed to reform our nation's health insurance system. There were so many different pieces of the puzzle that had to fit into place—the biggest of which was money. If we spent money to expand coverage, protect people with preexisting conditions, and invest in technology to improve health outcomes, that would reduce costs in the long run, but how would we pay for the costs until savings materialized? What would we cut to make up for it? For every dollar we spent, Congress required that we save a dollar. If, as we promised, we gave the states the resources to expand Medicaid to include the working poor, how were we going to pay for it in the middle of the biggest economic crisis since the Great Depression? And whatever we proposed, we needed to also convince a skeptical Congress to pass it. All of that had to be figured out, and by the time we were done, electing a black man president of the United States would look easy in comparison.

D uring the campaign, President Obama assembled a team of health care policy experts to explore viable options. The team expanded during the transition, so that by the time he was sworn in his team was able to hit the ground running. Once we reached the White House, we added personnel from the economic team, budget office, and legislative affairs team (responsible for working with Congress), as well as staff from my offices of Intergovernmental Affairs and Public Engagement, who were responsible for ensuring that we consulted with state and local governments, the wide range of stakeholders who were adversely impacted by the existing health insurance system, and partners whose cooperation we needed, such as the insurance companies and other businesses, large and small.

The quarterback of the team was Nancy-Ann DeParle, a brilliant, soft-spoken, self-deprecating expert on health insurance. She assembled the team to think more creatively about ways to maximize access to insurance, and she negotiated with insurance companies over the terms within which they would agree to expand coverage by removing restrictions—such as annual and lifetime caps—and no longer denying coverage or charging more to people with preexisting conditions. This required insurance companies to cooperate with one another, which is not what competitors normally do. Nancy-Ann went head to head with seasoned economists, budget analysts, and political operatives without ever losing sight of her mandate from President Obama. Without complaint, she stayed true to the core mission of achieving health care reform for all, despite all the sharp elbows that came her way. There wasn't a health care decision the president made without consulting her first. Because she shied away from the spotlight, demurring from taking any credit, she's not a household name. But without her, millions of Americans would not have the improved health insurance they have today.

Nancy-Ann is modest in every way, including her dress, with the exception of her gorgeous high-heel shoes, which were rivaled in quality and style only by those of the White House counsel, Kathryn Ruemmler. Kathy was also a superstar in her field, having prosecuted Enron when she was a young assistant U.S. attorney. She'd held a senior position at the Department of Justice before moving to the White House. Their shoes were a sign that they could be both the best at their jobs and also be comfortable showing their appreciation for a touch of fashion flare—progress from my early days when I tried to conform my attire as a young associate.

My contributions on health care reform spanned all three of my responsibilities in the White House—as senior advisor, as head of the Office of Intergovernmental Affairs, and as head of the Office of Public Engagement. For every president, the role of senior advisor is dictated by what the president wants. Though others would follow, at the start of the first term, President Obama selected three of us with different backgrounds and experiences and portfolios: David Axelrod, expert on communications and messaging; Pete Rouse, guru of all things related to the legislative process and an expert in policy; and me. The senior advisors report directly to the president; everyone else reports to the chief of staff. Our role as a group and individually was to give him advice and counsel on every decision that he made, based on subject matter and our expertise. If President Obama was making a decision about a regulation that the Department of Labor was making on equal pay, I would weigh in. If he was deciding on messaging for the State of the Union, he would go to Axelrod. Pete Rouse weighed in on every decision that had to do with policy or Congress. We all reviewed all of the documents before they went to the president. We would debate the content among ourselves and the other senior staff, with the goal of giving a consensus recommendation to the president. If we weren't able to all agree, we would attach cover memos with our differing views. We each had our different roles, but we all came together as a group to weigh in on every major decision made by the president.

Given that health care reform encompassed virtually every aspect of our respective portfolios, we all worked together reviewing every issue that percolated up through Nancy-Ann and her team.

For the health care battle, many of the advocacy organizations put us in touch with people who were being hurt by the existing health care system. And letters flowed in to the White House by the thousands.

We tried to distill our goals into the essential and attainable. Many of the president's supporters wanted a single-payer system, but there was no way we could garner the votes for it. The next best thing was to re-fashion the private insurer system to combat the most inequitable aspects—ensuring that no one would be denied coverage because of a preexisting condition; that children could stay on their parents' insurance plan until turning twenty-six; that there would be no annual or lifetime benefit caps; that affordable insurance would be available to everyone, regardless of employment, and we would offer to subsidize an expansion of Medicaid in the states for those who could not afford private insurance.

It was based on the health care reforms that Republican governor Mitt Romney had passed in Massachusetts in 2006. Our goal in building off that plan was to craft a bipartisan piece of legislation. Exhaustive and protracted consultation with various committees in Congress led to the formation of the national health care exchange, which would allow states to design their own systems. If they opted not to do so, a federal exchange would be available. The Affordable Care Act also offered states a subsidy for 100 percent of the costs for three years to broaden Medicaid benefits to low-income individuals. In order to induce insurance companies to absorb the cost of covering everyone, including those with preexisting conditions, we needed to offset that cost by increasing the size of the pool. We accomplished this by mandating that everyone—including young, healthy people—purchase insurance.

Have I lost you? I know. Health care, alas, is a subject so complicated and convoluted that most people don't have the time or patience to try to understand it, even though their lives literally depend on it. To sell the program to Congress and to the American people, we needed a campaign that would make ordinary Americans want to understand the policy details to grasp why it was so important for each of them and their families, and for generations to come. I knew the best way to do that was to show them the impact our plan would have on normal folks like them, because thinking of those stories was how I made it through all those interminable policy deliberations myself. While we debated the various theoretical policy options for health care reform, no matter how complicated, I always tried to put a human face on whatever we were talking about. I thought about the impact our decisions would have on the folks I had met at the University of Chicago Medical Center. While economists were talking about "bending the cost curve," I was thinking about the stories of the many patients in the University of Chicago's emergency room and the people I, too, had met on the campaign trail. They touched me profoundly, so as we prepared to go public with our proposals. I knew that if we were going to get the bill passed, we needed to tell a good story. And we had a good story to tell—but we lost control of it early on, and it took us years to win it back.

President Obama decided to have a press conference to frame the debate before we went into our first summer recess. We knew that members of Congress would be meeting with their constituents in their districts, and if the president spoke directly to the American people about his plan, they could ask their own questions about the Affordable Care Act when their members of Congress came home.

The press conference was held in the East Room on the State Floor on July 22, 2009. Standing off to the side with other senior members of the team, I watched the president respond to questions about what the proposed legislation did and didn't do and explain what we were trying to achieve. As he started to wind the proceedings up, I thought the press conference had gone very well. Then came the last question, from

Lynn Sweet, the DC bureau chief of our hometown paper, the *Chicago Sun-Times*. "Recently," she said, "Professor Henry Louis Gates Jr. was arrested at his home in Cambridge. What does that incident say to you, and what does it say about race relations in America?"

Six days earlier, Gates, a black professor at Harvard, had forgotten his house keys. So he'd jimmied the lock to his house to get back in, and someone reported a possible burglary to 9-1-1. When the police arrived, Gates was already inside, and, although he showed the officers identification with his address on it, he was arrested for disorderly conduct. When one of the country's most prominent scholars of African American studies was thrown in jail for trying to get inside his own house, it made national news. The president knew "Skip" Gates, as the professor was called by his friends, from his days at Harvard and had seen the press coverage of the incident in the days before.

"Well, I should say at the outset that Skip Gates is a friend, so I may be a little biased here," President Obama said, pivoting smoothly away from health care. "I don't know, not having been there and not seeing all the facts, what role race played in that, but I think it's fair to say that any of us would be pretty angry. Number two, the Cambridge police acted stupidly in arresting someone when there was already proof that someone was in their own home. And number three, what I think we know, separate and apart from this incident, is that there is a long history in this country of African Americans and Latinos being stopped by law enforcement disproportionately. That's just a fact. . . . Race remains a factor in society."

In the time it took me to go from the East Room to my office, the president's comments had gone viral—and totally wiped out the coverage of the content of the Affordable Care Act. Although it had certainly not been his intention to insult the men and women in blue around the country, his observation about the absurdity of a man being arrested and handcuffed inside his own home was received by some as an attack on the police. The seemingly innocuous statement taught us how quickly we could lose the narrative if we said *anything* off message. And also it taught us that on the third rail of race, every word mattered. "Stupidly." That one word drove the negative reaction. But the president had to answer Lynn Sweet's question, and he gave his honest opinion, not some PR spin.

A week later, when the hubbub still hadn't subsided, President Obama decided that rather than go through another round of speeches and clarifications, he'd invite Gates and the responding officer, Sergeant James Crowley, to the White House for a meeting, aka the Beer Summit. The professor and the officer met with the president and Vice President Biden near the White House Rose Garden. My team even gave the officer's family a tour around while he was in the summit. As they walked through the White House, the members of the Secret Service were extra kind to the cop's little boy, giving him keepsakes. My team and I fielded immediate blowback from those in the black community with their own painful experiences of being harassed by police who didn't want the president to apologize for his original statement (not that he did), who didn't even think the meeting should be happening. The point of the Beer Summit wasn't to instantly solve the very real issues between the police and black Americans. The point was to show that the two men could sit down and have a calm and civil conversation over a beer, modeling behavior others might be inspired to follow. But also the president wanted the press to move on so we could return the focus to the immediate concern: passing health care reform legislation.

Barack Obama is famously even-tempered. His highs are not high, his lows are not low, and he's the master of internalizing stress or drama, appearing calm and collected even to someone who knows him as well as I do. Throughout the drama of the Skip Gates arrest fiasco, and as we worried that the economy wouldn't improve or debated whether the multibillion-dollar auto bailouts would work, I never saw the president sweat. He also had a poker face. The first Friday of every month, the Labor Department would release the numbers of jobs created, or lost, for the prior month. Early on, we all dreaded that announcement, and even as the economy bounced back, we awaited the figures anxiously. It was an important barometer of whether our policies were working. The president was always briefed on the results the evening before, but because the data could move the markets, it was a very close hold. On those evenings, if I saw President Obama, I began the fruitless habit of trying to read the president's expressions and body language to try to figure out how bad the next day would be. I never could. He was absolutely inscrutable.

The best known example of his ability to mask his emotions was on the night of the 2011 White House Correspondents' Dinner when, as Seal Team 6 was closing in on Osama bin Laden, President Obama delivered a deliciously witty speech making fun of himself and many others, including Donald Trump. The camera kept cutting to Trump's face as he watched in stony silence. *Why can't he just smile and go along with the joke?* On a side note, later that night, during a break in the program, Trump spotted me from a few tables away. He started making a beeline toward me, and I panicked. Making chitchat with the man who fueled the birther lie, a blatant attempt to delegitimize President Obama's presidency, was out of the question. The manufactured conspiracy theory was not only cloaked in racism, but also ginned up anger and hatred that put the entire first family in harm's way. I looked around, but there was nowhere to hide. In the end, all he did was walk up to me and say, "Such a pleasure to meet you. I've heard wonderful things about you." Later that day, Susan Rice and I compared stories. Turns out Trump had said exactly the same to Susan. But my real point is that you'd never have known from President Obama's demeanor that a historic, seminally important mission was in progress while he was speaking.

Particularly in those first few months, as much as I worried constantly about our economy and the general welfare of the nation, I was also concerned over the toll all of the pressure was taking on the president. During our daily senior staff meetings with him in the Oval

Office, I would usually sit on the end of the couch closest to his chair so I could watch him closely. I was searching for a sign in his expression or voice that would let me know if he was really as calm as he appeared. I was so preoccupied with trying to read him that I forgot how well he reads me. One day, midsentence, he stopped talking, looked at me, and said in a whisper I hoped only I could hear, "What?"

Startled to have him pause in front of my colleagues, I mumbled quietly, "I'm trying to figure out if you're OK."

"Stop staring," he said softly. "I'm fine."

I was embarrassed in the moment, but later I appreciated that he was trying to keep his game face on, and our friendship (and my concern) were getting in the way. I kept worrying, but from then on I tried not to stare, at least when he could see me.

Reflecting back now, I believe our friendship was strengthened by my time as President Obama's senior advisor, through sharing so many extraordinary experiences during his moment in the history of our nation. And I was also a better senior advisor because of our friendship. I had a keen appreciation for what inspired and motivated him, his true north. Whenever he seemed distracted, he knew that I knew what was likely weighing on his mind.

We all dealt with the pressure of being in the White House in different ways. In general, President Obama was very disciplined about his diet, and he was also a creature of habit—perhaps because he had a slightly chubby period in his youth, or maybe because he just doesn't care about food very much. An exception were the delicious pies created by the White House pastry chef. On the campaign trail, he almost always ate the exact same meals: salmon, broccoli, and brown rice or chopped salad with chicken. He made an exception when we visited local restaurants with specialties. Then he would indulge, to show appreciation to his host. He continued to eat his same usual meals for lunch well into his time in the White House, despite the fact that Michelle told him, "You know, you can have a different menu." One day in the first term while I was traveling with the president, he looked at his salad and said, "This makes me sad." Finally! There was a huge sigh of relief from the other staff present and me, because we ate whatever he ate. From then on, luckily, he decided to change up the menu a bit, but not much.

The president's pragmatic handling of the Gates affair worked, and thanks to his steadfast focus on the long game, we were able to bring the nation's attention back to health care. Unfortunately, just as we began to tell our story, the Republican opposition was waiting with one of their own, only theirs was based in fiction.

Following the president's press conference, in July, just before recess, House Speaker Nancy Pelosi introduced HR 3962, the legislation that was, at that point, known as the Affordable Health Care for America Act. In response, at town halls they held over the summer throughout the country, Republicans started floating the idea that the bill called for "death panels." They made up the diabolical phrase just to scare people into thinking "the government" was going to convene committees to decide who received medical care and who didn't, and it was effective. Stoking fear to gain leverage is an age-old tactic. Nobody knew what a death panel was; they just knew they didn't want one. Confused people responded to polls with comments such as "Keep the government out of my Medicare!" But of course, Medicare *is* the government, and what we were trying to do was *expand* coverage.

Republicans weren't just spinning words; they were also using every possible legislative maneuver to try to stop the bill in its tracks. We were all so frustrated that Republicans weren't remotely interested in a plan to deliver affordable health care to millions of people, many who had never had it before, but what was even more stunning was that they would choose instead to distort the proposal's benefits for blatant political purposes. My experience in local government in Chicago was that although there was plenty of political theater, most of the elected officials on all sides would eventually try to do the right thing for their constituents— and then they'd fight over who received credit for it. This was different.

I knew from the University of Chicago that we could not only achieve better medical outcomes but also save a lot of money in the long term by ending the epidemic of the emergency room as a replacement for primary care. But you didn't need to be chairman of a medical board, only human, to recognize the scope of the benefit our law would provide. I couldn't imagine how members of Congress calling the Affordable Care Act a threat to America's freedom explained to their own constituents why they should be uninsurable because of a preexisting condition. Health care should never have been a partisan issue, but I was very naive as to the lengths to which the Republicans were willing to go in trying to make President Obama a "one-term president," in the words of Senate Republican leader Mitch McConnell. Using health care as a weapon, and being willing to deny it to people to win a political victory, was unconscionable. And, as we would soon learn, they were very good at it.

While the disastrous town halls in summer recess were taking place, the president and his senior advisors regrouped one morning in the Oval Office to assess the damage from the GOP scare tactics. We all felt beat up by the death-panels ploy, and President Obama asked each of us to weigh in on next steps. Every day spent trying to pass health care was delaying the rest of our legislative agenda from moving forward, including comprehensive immigration reform and clean energy.

Phil Schiliro, head of the White House legislative affairs department, was first. Phil was an unusual combination of optimism and creativity, with a healthy dose of the reality that with Congress you must expect the worst. Phil knew better than almost anyone else that our goal was a long shot given the strong opposition in Congress. But his mantra was always, "If one way doesn't work, try a second way. If they both don't work, there must be a third way, and that will work." Because of that, the president nicknamed him Third-Way Phil.

"What say you, Third-Way Phil?" President Obama began.

Phil made a strong case for a narrow path forward. Then the president asked the rest of the senior team for their views. Some cautioned that we should cut our losses and just protect children. Others said that even that was a long shot. My view was that we should go big or go home. Nancy-Ann agreed. After hearing everyone out, the president returned to Phil, who said, "Well, Mr. President, if you're feeling lucky, there may still be a third way."

Some of the advisors looked down. Others just shook their heads in disbelief. Third-Way Phil was resting the success of his third way on luck!

President Obama nodded to himself, stood up from his chair, and, leaving us sitting on the couches by the fireplace, walked over to the Resolute desk, a gift from Queen Victoria to President Hayes, and used by many of Hayes's successors. With his back to us, he looked out of the windows facing the South Lawn and asked, "Phil, where are we?"

Phil looked around at all the other advisors, hoping one of us might know what the president was talking about, but we just shrugged.

"We're in the Oval Office," he said tentatively.

"Yes, and what's my name?" the president said.

"President Obama?"

"No, Phil, it's President Barack *Hussein* Obama, and we're in the Oval Office, and you're asking *me* if I'm lucky? Of course I'm lucky. Now, everyone, back to work and figure out how to accomplish the third way."

After working on this issue nonstop for months, we were all totally beaten down. But in that moment, the president pierced the heavy mood in the room, and we all started laughing. Even Phil. In reminding us how he had already beat the long odds just to be there, this was no time to quit trying, for the impossible is only impossible until we make it become inevitable.

We were making slow progress even with the Democratic majorities because Senator Max Baucus, who was chairman of the committee responsible for the bill, wielded much power, and he was determined to try to strike a deal with Senator Chuck Grassley (his longtime Republican colleague), who was the ranking member of the committee. Then tragedy struck. On August 25, when the Obamas, Pete Rouse, and I were all on Martha's Vineyard for vacation, Senator Ted Kennedy died of a brain tumor. His death was a huge blow to both the president and the First Lady, who had become close friends with him and his wife, Vicki. Pete had worked with Kennedy for decades, and he flew with us on Marine One to the funeral, sharing stories of their adventures together. But the tragedy of the senator's passing was not just a personal one. He'd been a staunch supporter of the president's efforts on health care reform, and his seniority and moral authority was vital to any chance of bringing both parties in the Senate together. We often wondered if, had he lived, his Republican colleagues would have behaved any better.

His death also dealt another terrible strategic blow to the campaign. Democrats controlled both houses of Congress, having swept in on a big wave on the president's coattails. We had a 257-vote majority in the House, but more important, we had a 60-vote supermajority in the Senate, meaning we had just enough votes to overcome a Republican filibuster. Because Massachusetts had a Democratic governor, Deval Patrick, we could be assured that he would appoint a Democrat to fill Kennedy's seat temporarily, but a special election would soon follow, putting our supermajority at risk. Plus, health care reform was bottlenecking the rest of our legislative agenda, and we knew the closer we came to the midterm elections, the harder it would become to pass anything. We had to move fast, and we set the end of the year as an ambitious goal to finish it up.

And so, all through the fall, we never let up. My team planned events with people who would benefit from our proposed reforms, such as moms with sick children and people who might go into bankruptcy trying to pay health care bills. Speaker Pelosi whipped the votes in the House while Leader Reid fought to hold the Democratic Caucus together in the Senate. We could afford to lose a few Democratic votes in the House, but in the Senate we'd need every last one.

And we mustered the votes. In November, the House passed its version of the health care bill, HR 3962, with 219 Democratic votes and 1 Republican vote, with 39 Democrats and 176 Republicans voting against. Six weeks later, on Christmas Eve, the Senate passed its version of the bill, called America's Healthy Future Act, with all 60 Democrats in favor, 39 Republicans against, and 1 Republican abstaining. We were so close!

In any normal legislative process, the next step would have been for leaders in both houses to create a joint conference committee to iron out the differences between the two bills, formulating a compromise bill acceptable to majorities in both chambers. But before that could happen, in January Republican Scott Brown won the special election to fill Ted Kennedy's seat, having made it explicitly clear during his campaign that he was opposed to the president's health care plan. Our supermajority was lost. Now, even if Congress produced a unified health care bill, there was no way for it to get past the Republican filibuster. And if no new legislation could pass the Senate, that meant the House was stuck with the Senate version of the bill, which many House Democrats found unacceptable. (The more liberal Democrats wanted the public option, and the conservative Democrats thought it was too liberal. Welcome to Washington.)

We were stuck. What could possibly be "the third way" now?

With Republican support completely off the table, our only hope for passing the bill lay in cajoling and convincing the hesitant House Democrats to come down off the fence and vote for the Senate version of the bill. This battle had to proceed on two fronts. First, Speaker Pelosi and the White House had to do some serious political horse-trading with undecided members to bring them on board.

Second, we had to keep up the engagement of members' constituents. Contrary to popular belief, representative democracy actually can work, and a broad network of supporters sent a flood of letters and phone calls demanding action. And since Republicans were keeping the phone lines jammed with bogus claims of "death panels" and "government take-over," thankfully our supporters were out there calling and writing their members of Congress as well.

Our fortunes began to change when we were given a gift from the political gods. In early February, the health insurance company Anthem Blue Cross announced to its customers that they were going to see rate increases of 30 to 39 percent that year. It couldn't have been a timelier or a more perfect reminder of what was wrong with the health care system and why we were fighting to reform it. President Obama was able to drive home the Anthem story during a pre–Super Bowl interview with Katie Couric, one of the biggest media platforms of the year.

Then, in late February, the president hosted a bipartisan meeting with Republicans and Democrats to discuss how to move health care forward. Many Democrats felt it was a huge waste of time, since Republicans had refused to come to the table, but in the end it was a brilliant bit of political theater on the president's part. It showed him as reasonable by reaching out to the other side after Scott Brown's victory. It also allowed us to force Republicans to put their health care ideas out on the table, at which point it became clear that they didn't have any. They weren't obstructing our solution so that they could implement their solution. They were just blocking our reforms that would help the American people. We were finally back in control of the story, and then we found the perfect voice to help bring victory home.

One way President Obama enjoyed staying connected with everyday people—who we called "real people"—was to read ten of their letters every evening, a representative sample of that day's mail. The letters were from people from all fifty states, all walks of life, and all political parties. The Correspondence Department, tasked with reading all the thousands of letters that pour into the White House each day, had a staff of readers, and part of each reader's job was to recommend a letter from his or her batch to be one of the ten that were sent up to the president; the highlight of a reader's day was if the head of the unit chose his or her letter. The president often responded to the sender with a note, sometimes handwritten.

The letters, circulated to senior staff as well, were an important source of feedback directly from the American people. They often reminded me of the stories I heard in the mayor's office in Chicago when I was deputy chief of staff. From time to time, I would contact senders to let them know that their letter had moved me, and also to add a human voice to any formal response they might receive. I always asked them, "What time of day did you write the letter?" And their answer was almost always "late at night," when the kids were asleep, work was done, and the house was quiet. I told them their stories were important and thanked them for taking the time to write.

During the health care debate, a moving letter found its way to the president's desk. It was from Natoma Canfield, a wonderfully warm and humble woman who wrote about how her insurance costs were skyrocketing due to a divorce, self-employment, and her preexisting condition which was a sixteen-year-old cancer diagnosis that had been in remission for over a decade. She could no longer afford to keep up with her premiums. "I live in the house my mother and father built in 1958 and I am so afraid of the possibility I might lose this family heirloom as a result of my being forced to drop my health insurance," she wrote. "Please stay focused in your reform attempts as I and many others are in desperate need of your help."

After one of my staffers, Ann Widger from the Office of Public Engagement, tracked down the Medina, Ohio, letter writer, the president chose her story to help tell the bigger story of why America needed the Affordable Care Act. He knew her gut-wrenching experience could help people understand the importance of the legislation, because everyone could imagine themselves, or someone they loved, in Natoma's predicament. The president read Natoma's letter out loud in a meeting with insurance executives to personalize the devastating impact of our current system, and we then released the letter to the press. He even framed her letter and hung it in the Oval Office as a daily reminder of why he was fighting so hard. It was a closing argument for which the other side had no rebuttal.

The president then invited Natoma to introduce him at a rally in Ohio to make the final push for Congress to pass health care reform legislation. But Natoma couldn't make it. What we didn't know was that she'd collapsed a week before the event and had been diagnosed with leukemia. Her sister, Connie Anderson, appeared in her place, telling the crowd that Natoma, who had dropped her insurance earlier that year because of the unaffordable rate hikes, was now lying in a hospital bed with cancer, terrified about how she would pay the bill. "So you want to know why I'm here, Ohio?" President Obama said. "I'm here because of Natoma."

Natoma used her soft voice to tell the most powerful man in the world her story. President Obama amplified Natoma's voice and the Affordable Care Act received a shot in the arm. Just an ordinary person who made an extraordinary difference.

With less than a week to go before the vote, dozens of Democratic lawmakers were still wavering. But by then we had found our third way: budget reconciliation, a parliamentary procedure that allowed certain budget-related laws to pass with only 51 percent of the votes. The House would vote to approve the Senate version of the bill, and then the differences would be ironed out in reconciliation. It wasn't an elegant solution, but it would work. Speaker Pelosi had the votes.

On March 21, 2010, the night Congress was set for the final vote on the Affordable Care Act, Susan Sher and I decided to go home to watch it on television. I had everything set up—big TV, couch, popcorn, wine. But just as we plopped down on the couch in our pajamas, the phone rang. It was the president's assistant, Katie Johnson.

"Valerie, the president would like you to come back to the White House to watch the vote," she said. "Susan, too."

"Katie, we're in our PJs with a bowl of popcorn on our laps. We're good."

"Valerie, *President Obama* would like everyone who worked on the Affordable Care Act to come to the White House."

So back to the White House we trudged—dressed—just in time to catch the tail end of the vote from the Roosevelt Room, where everyone was gathered. The president, beaming when the Affordable Care Act passed, impulsively said, "Come on upstairs, everyone. Let's celebrate!" And the crowd all cheered.

Because most of the White House was like a museum, with its occupants often on display for the public, the Obamas kept the Executive Residence very private. Few of the staff had been upstairs. So everyone was excited by the spontaneous invitation.

Champagne and appetizers appeared out of nowhere; I could only imagine the scurrying around that went on in the kitchen when news that nearly a hundred people were on their way upstairs hit the household staff. But for the guests it was a terrific party. And that night our famously calm and cool president was positively bubbly. He was so grateful to his team, and he showed it. When I introduced him to Ann Widger, the staffer who'd found Natoma Canfield and nurtured the relationship, giving Natoma and her sister the courage to use their voices, the president put both hands on her shoulders and said, "Thank you so much. It's because of your hard work that Natoma became our symbol and we got this done." Ann had never spoken to the president before, and now he was beaming at her and giving her credit for the country's first successful health care reform bill. She was mesmerized.

We stayed outside on the Truman Balcony into the wee hours of the morning. After the crowd started to thin out, I walked over to the president as he was expressing his gratitude to Nancy-Ann. More than anyone else, he knew she was the unsung hero responsible for the bill's passage. The president was so effusive with Nancy-Ann that she began to look a little uncomfortable. When Nancy-Ann extricated herself from our emotional commander in chief, I sidled over to him.

The Truman Balcony, with its view spanning the South Lawn, is by far my favorite place in the White House. In the spring of our first year, the Obamas discovered what became their favorite spot, too. The majestic view of the South Lawn, with the monuments in the distance, brought me the same sense of peace that Lake Michigan did back home in Chicago. The Obamas hung out there as often as possible when the weather permitted. There we all felt we could smell the fresh air, catch our breath, and exhale. As we leaned over the edge of the balcony that first night of spring, on an unseasonably warm evening, it reminded me of election night in Chicago. I looked up at the president. "You seem so happy," I said. "How do you feel tonight compared to election night?"

"There is no comparison," he said, looking out at the Washington Monument and Jefferson Memorial. "Election night was just the means necessary to make this night possible."

Chapter 12 ·

Where's My Boom?

"Turn on the television, Valerie. There's been an explosion in the Gulf!" Straut nearly shouted as he ran into my office out of breath. He must have climbed the two flights from the entrance to the West Wing adjacent to his office next door in the Eisenhower Executive Office Building. I could always tell when he didn't wait for the elevator. And that's when I learned that on April 20, 2010, the Deepwater Horizon oil rig exploded in the Gulf of Mexico, killing eleven workers and creating the largest oil spill in our nation's history. It quickly spread through the gulf waters of five neighboring states: Louisiana, Alabama, Florida, Mississippi, and Texas. Through my work in the Office of Intergovernmental Affairs, my team and I knew all of the nation's governors. We were their gateway to the administration; if they had a problem and the federal government could help (and often when we couldn't), they came to us. The day after the explosion, when it was clear there were no easy solutions, President Obama called me into the Oval Office and said, "Your job is to talk to those governors whose states are affected every single day until the oil spill is behind us. Not their staff. The governors and you. I want them to know any concerns they have are being communicated by you directly to me." *OK*, I thought. *No big deal. How long could this last? A few days, a week max.*

Every day, seven days a week, for three months straight, I had a 9 a.m. phone call with the five governors: Louisiana's Bobby Jindal,

Mississippi's Haley Barbour, Alabama's Bob Riley, Florida's Charlie Crist, and Texas's Rick Perry. It just so happened that the governors of the five affected states were all Republicans, but to us their political party was always irrelevant. Solving the massive environmental disaster with minimum damage to their states was our sole objective. Every morning I'd start the call by saying, "How are we doing today? What can we do?" I always used the word "we" so they would understand I viewed us as being on the same team, working through the mounting challenges on the ground together. Many of the conversations revolved around boom, the floating physical barriers that corralled and contained oil on the water's surface. Because Louisiana had the biggest part of the spill, Jindal received the lion's share of boom, and the other governors always wanted to know, "Well, where's our boom?"

I wish I had a transcript of some of those conversations, because they reveal a fundamental truth about politics and governing. Behind all the posturing on cable news, when people of different ideological backgrounds are faced with a crisis, they can—and often do—actually work, and solve problems, together. Their constituents were our constituents. Sometimes our commitment to goodwill across the aisle meant spending hours in line taking photos at state dinners, or holiday parties with people who had publicly slammed the president that very same day, or smiling at Republicans who came to the White House for the Congressional Ball but refused to walk through the receiving line to greet the Obamas, their host and hostess. Governor Jindal once hung up the phone after asking for some assistance and went directly to a press conference within sixty seconds, criticizing us for not completing what he had asked. I was annoyed by his duplicity, but that's politics. The next day I was back on the phone asking how we could help.

In my twenty-four years of public service, it has always been my practice to have an open door. If someone who disagrees with me or has a beef or a problem is willing to come in and talk, I go into the conversation confident that we can find common ground. In part it may have stemmed from those early days in Iran learning to play happily with children of all backgrounds. Certainly when I worked for the city of Chicago, I interacted with a range of constituents from all over the city. Just because they were openly critical did not give me an excuse to ignore them. And when I gave their tempers the space and respect to subside, more often than not we made progress. Public service does not mean you pick or choose to work only with your friends. Anyone could walk in at any time for any reason, and I would hear them out and try to help. As commissioner of the Department of Planning and Development, I had to work with stakeholders from a wide array of groups, groups that were very often working in strident opposition to one another or to us. Indeed, one of the most satisfying parts of public service, to me, was bringing those disparate groups together and discovering common ground.

I brought that same attitude with me to Washington, DC. I also recognized that, especially in Washington, without broad-based support nothing can be accomplished. As President Obama has said, appealing only to your own base might be a worthwhile strategy for winning elections, but it doesn't allow you to govern. To govern, you need buy-in from as many people as possible, so that everyone has a stake in the success of your policies and programs. Which is why, in my West Wing roles, I had a responsibility to work with everyone and couldn't afford to close my door to anyone.

Possibly the strangest of my strange-bedfellow relationships was with Mark Holden, general counsel to Koch Industries. No single entity worked harder to make sure Barack Obama and every other Democrat at every level of government were not elected than the one led by the Koch brothers, whose names are synonymous with the libertarian conservative agenda. For decades, billionaires Charles and David Koch have funded federal, state, and local candidates who promote their views—as well as soft-money political organizations that have spent a fortune campaigning against every candidate they oppose.

In early 2015, I heard Mark Holden had scheduled a meeting with Cecilia Muñoz, by then promoted to be the head of the Domestic Policy Council, because he was interested in working with us on criminal justice reform. President Obama had given me responsibility for overseeing our criminal justice reform efforts in his second term in office, so when Cecilia told me about the scheduled meeting, I dropped by, mostly out of curiosity. Who was this guy who stepped voluntarily into what I assumed he viewed as enemy territory? Right at the start of the meeting, I asked Mark, "What are *you* doing in the *Obama* White House?"

He smiled, and then, much to my surprise, he gave a really good answer. He said for one of his first jobs, when he was eighteen years old, he'd worked for a year in the Worcester House of Corrections in West Boylston, Massachusetts, and he'd seen firsthand the problems with incarceration in America. "There were probably fifteen people I knew growing up who were locked up in there," he said. "I was arrested once for underage drinking, but the case was dropped, and I was really lucky I didn't get arrested for anything else, and lucky I had parents who rode me hard. My former classmates weren't as lucky. They didn't have any real support systems or resources and ended up incarcerated. It was a there-but-for-the-grace-of-God-go-I experience, and it sticks with me to this day."

One person who also moved me deeply who I called was a federal judge. He had written President Obama a letter that told the story of a young man he had sentenced to life in prison twenty years earlier under mandatory sentencing guidelines. While the judge believed the man should have received a reduced sentence and a second chance, his hands were tied by the mandatory sentencing law. The injustice of it had haunted the judge for twenty years. Frustrated by Congress's inaction, President Obama had stepped up his efforts to commute the sentences of nonviolent drug offenders, who were often the victims of these harsh and inhumane mandatory sentencing laws. By the fall of 2016, he had commuted more sentences than the prior eleven presidents combined.

Because I was responsible for criminal justice reform, a staffer in the correspondence office sent me the letter from the judge. Every time we published the list of the people whose sentences President Obama had commuted, the judge wrote, he combed the list hoping to find this man's name. Finally it appeared on the list, and the judge felt inspired to write to President Obama, expressing his gratitude for the peace of mind he now had that would allow him to enjoy a good night's sleep.

Over the eighteen months that Mark and I worked closely on criminal justice reform together, we often joked that our conversations were very limited in scope. We were aware there were plenty of topics where we weren't likely to agree, but we never let that get in the way of making progress where we could. Once, after yet another mass shooting, I asked Mark if he thought we should pass a law to help keep guns out of the wrong hands. "I don't own a gun," he responded. After a short pause, we realized that was as far down that path as we were going to be able to go, and we went back to criminal justice reform. We eventually garnered about eighty votes in the Senate in support of a bipartisan bill to reduce mandatory sentences for nonviolent drug offenders. Although thanks to Leader McConnell, who refused to have the bill called up for a vote in the judiciary committee, it did not pass before President Obama left office, the progress we did make would not have been possible without Mark. And since the end of the Obama administration, Mark and I continue to collaborate on criminal justice reform. We coincidentally bumped into each other on the street near where we both live in DC on the eve of the passage of the First Step Act in December of 2018. We both acknowledged that it should have passed sooner, but were grateful that Congress finally decided to act.

My team and I were also regularly in touch with members of the evangelical community, who, by and large, didn't support President Obama, but who were firmly committed to criminal justice reform and immigration reform because of their belief in forgiveness and family unification.

In addition to keeping channels open to work with anyone who was willing, we also brought those with divergent views together in hopes of using our good offices to help them find common ground. When President Obama was deciding whether to sign an executive order banning workplace discrimination against LGBTQ employees of the federal government and federal contractors after Congress failed to pass legislation covering all employers, advocates for the LGBTQ and faith communities had strong opinions, not just about the issue but also about each other. Before making a recommendation to the president, my team and I heard out all the groups for and against it—from organizations, such as Focus on the Family, and religious leaders, to the Human Rights Campaign and the Center for American Progress.

When they were alone with me, the faith community leaders were often uncompromising and even strident in their attitudes. Finally, after my team had had dozens of separate meetings with no progress, I thought, *Why am I playing shuttle diplomacy here?* So I invited leaders whom I trusted from both sides of the issue—the ones I knew would be both candid and respectful—to sit across the table and talk to each other directly. The tenor of the conversation was completely different when they had to face each other, as opposed to speaking behind each other's backs. By the time the president decided to move forward with the executive order, I like to think that the reason we didn't get a lot of pushback on it from the faith community was because they'd had a chance both to listen and to speak to their LGBTQ brothers and sisters in a safe place.

In the course of bringing all these groups together across a variety of issues, my team and I absorbed a great deal of pain. But it was usually worth it. My outreach to Mark Holden, Rupert Murdoch, Jim Daly, and evangelicals and other conservative groups was founded in the belief that where there is common ground there doesn't need to be unanimity. There were those in the progressive community who questioned why we reached out to the "enemy." But we fundamentally didn't see it that way. Just because we disagreed with someone on ninety-nine issues never prevented us from working together on the hundredth one.

And my willingness to join forces with partners of all stripes was not unique at the White House. This approach started at the top. The president mandated that his team have open lines of dialogue with everyone who wanted to engage. He invited members of Congress, the same ones who said horrendous things about him, to meetings, state dinners, private dinners, and holiday parties in the hopes of breaking down the barriers in the way of finding common ground. He also had countless meetings, large and small, with business leaders who disagreed with him on a range of policy issues—as well as with our supporters who disagreed with us, including progressives who were concerned that he was not forward leaning enough on closing Guantanamo Bay and torture, with the immigration advocates who were demanding faster action on reforms, and with the LGBTQ advocates unhappy about our progress on repealing "Don't ask, don't tell." Before making a significant decision, he would want to hear how it would directly impact those affected.

I n terms of bringing disparate groups together to create meaningful change, one of our greatest successes was the repeal of "Don't ask, don't tell," the ban on gay people serving openly in the military. Together with Democratic leadership in Congress, the White House started working on the repeal of the law from day one. Another campaign promise and a top priority. While we had the votes to repeal "Don't ask, don't tell" in the House, we had to overcome a Republican filibuster in the Senate being led by John McCain. President Obama knew that the key to repeal was to get the military to buy in.

To head up my office's LGBTQ efforts, I'd recruited Brian Bond, a deeply committed LGBTQ advocate who grew up in the conservative fifty-thousand-person city of Joplin, Missouri. Brian was both gay and, since 2001, HIV positive. Passionate about his work, he was highly respected by his colleagues. Brian had deep roots and relationships in the LGBTQ community, and he caught a lot of heat for what many advocates thought was foot-dragging by the Obama administration. They wanted President Obama to unilaterally direct the military not to discharge service members who were openly gay. We agreed that the law was morally wrong, but it was the law. We also had a strong preference whenever feasible to seek congressional action, since executive orders can be repealed at the will of any future president (as we have seen President Obama's successor do). Bringing the military to the table to solicit their support was going to take time, but the advocates burning up Brian's phone lines wanted action *now*, and understandably so.

When "Don't ask, don't tell" was originally passed into law in 1993, I didn't know any gay service members personally. I remember thinking it was bizarrely hypocritical, to say the least, for a law to require service members who take an oath to uphold the Constitution to lie, but it wasn't until Brian brought several service members into the White House to meet me in early 2010 that the full impact of the law's injustice hit home. Fearing being "outed," they had come to the meeting out of uniform. These were men and women who'd dedicated their lives to serving this country, yet they couldn't even come to the White House openly and honestly. One of the service members was a woman named Major Casey Moes who oversaw ethics training at West Point, and she talked about the ethics of teaching ethics while living a lie. She said, "I shouldn't have to trade my values for my service." She told me about her partner, who had been diagnosed with terminal cancer, and not being able to share her grief with her colleagues at work. How she felt "disrespectful as well as dishonest" to never be able to acknowledge her relationship. Another described how she was deprived of simple acts such as displaying her partner's photo on her desk or bringing her to work functions. It was painful for the service members to open up and share their stories, but they touched me profoundly and gave me a new sense of urgency to get the law repealed.

Although LGBTQ advocates put a lot of pressure on us, President Obama refused to move the bill forward until we'd tried to go through the process recommended by the military's leadership. If the secretary of defense, joint chiefs, and rank-and-file were not on board, we knew a favorable vote by Congress would be impossible. Through the summer and fall of 2010, the military was taking months to survey its members and analyze how lifting the ban would be implemented. Meanwhile, tempers in the advocacy community were hitting a flash point, and poor Brian was the tip of the spear.

Before he scheduled yet another meeting to ask them to keep waiting, he pleaded with me, "I need your help. I can't go back to these groups one more time. Can *you* assure them we are committed?" Periodically my staff would bring advocates in to meet with me to improve my understanding of the issues and demonstrate to the advocates that their issue was a priority—particularly when we had no actual progress to show them.

On the day the meeting was scheduled, it happened that I was in the Roosevelt Room with President Obama on another matter just beforehand. As I started to leave, the president asked what I was doing next. "I'm on my way to get beat up by our LGBTQ friends because we haven't repealed 'Don't ask, don't tell' yet," I said.

"They're giving you a hard time, huh?"

"They're giving Brian a hard time. I'm trying to absorb some of his pain."

"Bring them over here, and I'll talk to them."

Yes! Quickly, before some other crisis absorbed him, I brought the group over to the Roosevelt Room. They didn't shy away from voicing their frustrations. "Mr. President," they said, "it's taking too long. Every day, good people are being discharged."

"Hear me," he said, measuring his words carefully. "I know the way to do this, and we will get there." We could all feel the president's sincerity and conviction. They took a deep breath and although they kept the pressure on us, they also directed their frustration toward Congress.

And it worked. In late November, the Department of Defense issued the results of its exhaustive survey, which concluded that repealing the law would have little or no impact on combat readiness, and that

70 percent of service members believed that the impact would be positive. Defense Secretary Robert Gates and Joint Chiefs Chairman Admiral Michael Mullen both testified before the Senate, calling for a swift repeal. Admiral Mullen's heartfelt testimony sent shock waves through the Republican members of Congress. He said, "No matter how I look at the issue, I cannot escape being troubled by the fact that we have in place a policy which forces young men and women to lie about who they are in order to defend their fellow citizens. For me, personally, it comes down to integrity—theirs as individuals and ours as an institution." Within the next three weeks, repeal passed in the House in a vote of 250–175 and passed in the Senate in a vote of 65–31—even picking up a few Republican votes in both houses, in large part because we'd brought the military on board. It was the only time I went up to the Senate to watch a vote. I knew it would be historic.

On December 22, 2010, President Obama signed the repeal into law, seventeen years after "Don't ask, don't tell" was enacted. All the activists who had been yelling at us behind closed doors and criticizing us in the press showed up like dear old friends to hug us and cry tears of joy. At the signing ceremony, Brian sat me (with a touch of irony) next to a man I'd seen just days before the bill passed lambasting President Obama on TV. But all was forgiven, because I knew he had just been doing his job. The pressure, and the pain, led to a better end result. President Obama had been willing to take the heat, holding out to achieve sustainable change. Bringing the military into the process slowed it down but ultimately led to the passage of the bill, and, even more important, broad-based acceptance of openly gay men and women in the military.

The repeal of "Don't ask, don't tell" was a triumph and an example of how governing should work. It was a validation of my core beliefs stemming from the lessons I'd learned in my early days in city government in Chicago about how to build public, bipartisan support from the ground up—especially in a cause as clear and right as we knew this one to be—those lessons held true.

Until they didn't.

President Obama has a gesture he uses from time to time, and when he does, he's close to a breakthrough. He holds his hand up and twists his fingers, like he's opening a combination lock or a safe. "We just need to figure out how to unlock this," he'll say, twirling the invisible dial in front of him. It's the metaphor he uses whenever he's trying to figure out a problem. Every safe has a combination; you just have to be patient enough to figure it out.

A devout believer in reason and the power of communication, Barack Obama believes that there's a rational solution to be found to just about any challenge. And why wouldn't he? From editor of the *Harvard Law Review* to winner of the Iowa caucuses to the presidency, his entire rise had been based on his ability to reach people, find what motivates them, touch their hearts as well as their minds, and bring them together on common ground. But then he encountered a safe that had no combination, that couldn't be opened by any amount of patience, cajoling, logic, or reason—or by sledgehammers and blowtorches, for that matter.

From the day he entered office, congressional Republicans refused to work with us, period. Nonetheless, we continued to treat elected officials from both sides of the political aisle with respect. For the two years we enjoyed Democratic majorities in both houses in Congress, we did our best to still bring the other side to the table. We managed to wrangle a few Republican votes here and there, such as the handful who voted to repeal "Don't ask, don't tell." But for all of our efforts we made very little progress persuading the Republicans in Congress to work with us. We spent precious months deferring to Senator Baucus while he tried hopelessly to secure Republican support for the Affordable Care Act. Over two hundred amendments were made in the hope that at least Senator Olympia Snowe would break rank with her Republican colleagues.

We kept hoping the Republicans were reachable. Their strategy— outrageous, I think—was just to say no.

The Republican leaders in Congress made no secret of their imperviousness to logic and compromise. For two years, then Senate Minority Leader Mitch McConnell used his encyclopedic knowledge of Senate procedure to turn obstructionism into an art. McConnell famously said the night of the 2009 inauguration, "The single most important thing we want to achieve is for President Obama to be a one-term president." It interfered with the business of governing and was a great disservice to the American people, but we had enough votes to keep moving forward.

"Why?" you might ask. Race, power, control? Possibly all of the above.

After the 2010 midterm election, House Minority Leader John Boehner went even further, vowing not just to stop President Obama's actions in the future but to go back and undo the past. On a conservative radio show he vowed to dismantle all the reforms the Affordable Care Act had set in motion: "We're going to do everything—and I mean everything we can do—to kill it, stop it, slow it down, whatever we can." And he wasn't talking only about the Affordable Care Act. He was talking about how they wanted to run the country.

Having successfully wound up the Tea Party and even some less extreme conservative citizens through inflated fears of "death panels" and "socialist government takeover," the Republican Party gained sixty-three seats, recapturing the majority, taking the speakership away from Nancy Pelosi, and giving it to John Boehner. In the Senate, Republicans gained six seats, leaving us with a slim fifty-one-seat majority. "We got shellacked," President Obama said.

Still, ever the optimist, he proclaimed that now "the fever will break." By "fever" he meant the Republicans' fevered efforts to oppose him and everything his administration was trying to do—even the kinds of proposals that traditionally enjoyed bipartisan support, such as for infrastructure investment. Now that the Republicans were responsible for leadership of the House, the president thought they would be motivated to work with him. They couldn't just block our agenda. They had to create one.

That did not happen.

We tried every possible approach. Private dinners at the White House, public dinners at restaurants (President Obama's treat). Invitations to play golf with the president and attend state dinners. Private phone calls. Televised meetings, including one where President Obama engaged in a spirited back-and-forth with just the Republican Caucus. Nothing worked. They said no to "cap and trade" to reform our national energy policy. No to infrastructure investments and other ways to create jobs and strengthen our economy. By the time President Obama left office, the Republicans in the House had voted over fifty times to repeal the Affordable Care Act, knowing their bill would fail in the Senate—what an incredible waste of time. Just imagine what good we could have accomplished during all those hours wasted on their symbolic bill going nowhere.

After the 2010 midterms, life in Washington was a lot like the final, dismal months of my marriage: the legislative branch sitting alone in its man cave, drinking wine with headphones on, and the executive branch leaning in the doorway in sexy lingerie, waiting for them to come upstairs and govern the country with us. And they never would. They simply weren't interested. Barack Obama had fundamental assumptions about how the federal government should work, assumptions that in retrospect seem no longer true. We believed that the viability of our democracy depends upon government functioning, which requires listening to one another and, yes, compromise. Because if we believe in democracy, then there is no exit from this union. We are in this together, and either we find a way to work together or the system breaks down and people, *millions* of people, are seriously hurt.

In the first term we hit rock bottom with the debt-ceiling debacle in the summer of 2011, when some members of the Tea Party Caucus argued publicly that it would be good for the country if we defaulted on the full faith and credit of the U.S. government for the first time in its history. The government had until August 2 to vote to raise the debt ceiling in order to allow the treasury to pay its bills, expenditures already approved by Congress, which was typically done with minimal debate. Now the Tea Party Caucus believed that we, the Democrats, were spending too much money, and they wanted to teach us a lesson by forcing us to not pay our bills, including debt on treasury bonds, despite the fact that U.S. Treasury bonds are what stabilizes the world economy. To default on them would send shock waves through international financial markets. The Tea Partiers' obliviousness to the very real and potentially irreparable damage they would do to the world economy was simply astounding.

While at Camp David that July, several friends and I were sitting out by the pool when the president disappeared. I went looking for him and overheard him on the phone, talking with Speaker Boehner. "John," the president said, "if we stand together and you raise taxes on the wealthy, and I support entitlement reform—'the grand bargain'—the country will follow our lead." It was an audacious compromise for the greater good. But Speaker Boehner could not be cajoled or convinced; he knew if he went along with raising taxes he would lose his speakership. As the August 2 deadline neared, the president's financial, political, and legislative advisors worked around the clock to try to come up with a budget proposal that would be acceptable to the Republicans. But all we heard back was "no."

Eric Whitaker, Marty Nesbitt, and I had made a pact during one of our many discussions in Marty's man cave in Chicago before I left for Washington. If I ever really needed them, they would drop whatever they were doing and come to Washington. It was the Friday before the vote, and I decided it was one of those times. The weekend could trigger a historic catastrophe, and, with Michelle out of town, I thought we needed moral support, particularly from someone who wasn't knee deep in this mess. Since Marty's youngest daughter was still a baby, I decided to spare him—and stay on his wife Anita's good side—and so I called only Eric. Eric had a presence I found soothing. I thought he could lighten the mood, just as he and Marty had done in Indiana during the dark days of the presidential campaign, when they made us laugh by doing their version of Reverend Wright's chicken dance. I rang him up and said in no uncertain terms, "You need to come to town. I need you here." And, good friend that he is, he came right away.

The president, Eric, and I spent the long summer evening on the Truman Balcony, punctuated by the trips President Obama kept making down to the West Wing to check on the negotiations' progress. Or lack thereof. Finally, late in the night, after his umpteenth trip downstairs, the president, uncharacteristically agitated, said, "I better find out what happens to me if I direct my treasury to pay the bills without congressional authority, because it doesn't look like they're the least bit interested in working this out." We called his personal lawyer, Bob Bauer, who had previously been White House counsel, to talk it through.

Bob didn't need long to lay it out for us. "The answer is simple," he said. "He'll be impeached, and he will have to hire his own lawyer and pay some part of his legal fees for acting outside the scope of authority."

Oh my.

Two days later, just hours before the August 2 deadline, Speaker Boehner blinked. An agreement was reached to avoid default, but it wasn't the historic deal that it could have been. It had all been political theater, with a final encore by the Speaker, who called the president at the eleventh hour trying to tack on one last stipulation: the defunding of Planned Parenthood. "No, John," the president said. "We're not doing that."

Boehner was so worried about holding on to his speakership that he ceded the authority of his position to a rogue minority faction. But what is the purpose of occupying a leadership position if you refuse to lead? If Boehner had made the grand bargain that President Obama implored him to do, yes, he might have lost his speakership. But he would have gone down in history as having successfully tackled a long-term fiscal challenge, in much the same way President George H. W. Bush did when he increased taxes to reduce the deficit in the 1990 budget. Bush lost reelection but is remembered as a principled leader, because he did what he thought best served the country regardless of the personal consequences to him. The irony, of course, is that Speaker Boehner resigned and lost his speakership anyway, and who even remembers why?

From day one, the Republicans were determined to thwart all of our attempts to work constructively across the aisle and address the very real challenges that our country faced. In the spirit of our program, for two and a half years, whenever I spoke publicly, and even in our private meetings, I always dug deep to project optimism, even though I thought their behavior was reckless and irresponsible. But by that summer, I was incapable of containing my rage.

A couple of days after the deadline, we were back at Camp David to celebrate the president's birthday. A group of about twenty friends were hanging out late into the night in the Hickory Lodge game room. I had been gloomy all day, the president noticed, and he walked over and joined me at a corner table for a private moment.

"You OK?" he asked.

"No," I said. "I'm not OK." Unable to hold back my tears of fury and exhaustion, I said, "They are obstructionists not because they actually disagree with you. They simply and irresponsibly will stop at nothing to try to hurt you." He knew who I meant.

With a very worried look on his face, the president assured me that, yes, what had happened was messy and totally irresponsible of the Republicans, but we had averted an economic meltdown and survived to fight another day. He was right, but my anger did not fade.

"It's going to be OK." The president tried to soothe me as our friends, shooting pool and playing shuffleboard around us, pretended not to notice that the normally even-tempered Valerie had cracked.

"No, I don't think they will ever change," I murmured.

"Yes, they will," he said. "If I can just get reelected, *then* the fever will break."

• *Chapter 13* •

We Can't Wait

I attended the 2009 inauguration with Laura. A man of medicine who dedicated his life to improving the health of others, my father had been battling a serious illness himself for six months. My dad spent his whole childhood in DC peering through the gates of the White House, never once having the opportunity to venture inside. So it was especially poignant that he was not well enough to attend the inauguration. He watched back in Chicago with my mother at his side.

His health first failed in 1973, when I was just seventeen and away at boarding school. I'd flown home for Thanksgiving break and was so eager to hear my parents' voices that I called them from a pay phone at the Chicago airport the moment I landed. My mother, never one to mince words, picked up the phone, and the first words out of her mouth were "Your father has had a heart attack." The irony was that he'd quit smoking and lost twenty pounds the year before, which just didn't seem fair.

He had a type-A personality. Whatever he had to do he just did. After he recovered from his heart attack, his doctor told him he had to start exercising, so over the next six months he worked up to jogging six miles a day. Forced to take a leave from work, in addition to the exercise, he started watching afternoon soap operas like Pudden, a task he took up with equal dedication. I'd grown up watching them with her, too, and we all agreed that *All My Children* was our favorite. For the rest of his recuperation, Dad and I spent most of our Sunday calls catching up on our "stories," which my mother barely tolerated.

My dad stayed healthy for the next couple decades until, in 1998, he had to have an uneventful surgery to remove one of his kidneys, diagnosed with cancer—luckily early. He came through the other side with flying colors, resilient as always and wholly undiminished in spirit. Then, in the summer of 2008, he was diagnosed with cancer again, this time of the larynx. When I joined my father for a consultation with his oncologist, I was so scared I could scarcely process what the doctor was telling us. So I went back again, this time bringing Eric Whitaker with me to help absorb what the doctor said. The outcomes for this type of cancer were bleak, and there were few options when it came to treatment. Without an aggressive course of chemo and radiation—which was life-threatening in itself—my dad would have an excruciatingly painful death. Recovery, particularly for a man in his eighties, was a long shot. Still, true to his character, he was determined to fight it.

That summer, my dad began a fourteen-week treatment of both chemotherapy and radiation that dovetailed with the crush of the 2008 presidential campaign's final stretch. The first couple of weeks were a breeze for him, but the cumulative effect of the treatments grew more painful with each passing week. My mom was exhausted but kept her traditional stiff upper lip and made his hospital room their home. Even though he was receiving the best care possible, in a hospital where he had worked for over forty years and where I was chairman of the board, my mom believed that there was no substitute for a present and engaged spouse to make sure nothing went wrong. At the end of each week of treatment we were relieved to count down one less session to face.

I came home as often as I could during that brutal period. By the end of his treatment, he was terribly weak and barely able to eat, having resisted the feeding tube that the doctors had recommended. But the tumors shrank, and he survived. The nurses all clapped as we wheeled him down the hospital hallway when he was discharged for what we thought was the last time. Then, less than a week later, a minor cough quickly grew worse and his congestion led to trouble breathing. My mom, always preparing for the worst, rushed him to the emergency room, where he was diagnosed with aspiration pneumonia.

By the time I arrived, he had been admitted and a big group of doctors was assembled in his room. Dr. Louis Cohen, my father's cardiologist for decades, had cured every one of his illnesses since his heart attack in 1973. He pulled me aside to say, "Your dad needs to go on a ventilator. He's not getting enough oxygen. Without it, he is not going to make it."

As the reality of what that would mean sunk in I said, "He won't do that. He and my mother made a pact years ago. 'No extraordinary measures.'" And they had both reminded me of their decision on a regular basis.

"Why don't I talk to him?" Dr. Cohen said.

He did, and to my complete surprise my dad agreed to the ventilator. My relief was short-lived. We soon entered a nightmare of around-the-clock intensive care, worry, and waiting. On day three of the ventilator, my dad required an electric shock to correct an abnormal heart rhythm. By that point I was almost as worried about my mom as I was about my dad. I begged her to go home for a nap, which she finally did.

Once she was gone, I sat there in my dad's room, alone, my mind flooded with memories of all the times he'd wake me up at 6 a.m. to play tennis before he went to work, the twinkle in his eye when I finally beat him at chess, his calming influence when he walked me down the aisle, reminding me of the love in the room so I would relax. My heart also ached with questions. Had I told my dad often enough how much I loved him? Did I express directly how I treasured him for stepping in and helping me take care of Laura?

As I sat there, the potential election of America's first black president was less than two weeks away. Other than dialing in for the campaign senior staff calls twice a day, I'd put all of that as far out of my mind as possible. While lost in my own thoughts, I was jarred by the sudden ringing of my phone. It was Barack, who'd just landed in California to refuel his plane on the way to Hawaii. He was on his own sad family mission. His grandmother, Madelyn Dunham, or "Toot" as he called her, the woman who helped raise him, was dying, and he'd left the campaign trail so he could fly out and see her for the last time. He asked about my dad, and I asked about his grandmother. Both of us were facing such excruciating personal loss just on the verge of what seemed like his historic victory. What horrendous timing, we remarked.

Amazingly, the following day my dad was strong enough to come off the ventilator. He moved out of intensive care a few days before my mom's eightieth birthday on October 30. Since none of us were in the mood to celebrate, the three of us spent a peaceful evening together in his hospital room, grateful that once again he had survived.

With assurances from Dr. Cohen that my dad was on the mend, I reluctantly left the next day for the final stretch of the campaign. Thanks to the incredible medical staff at the University of Chicago, my indefatigable mom, and my dad's stubborn will to live, he pulled through. Tragically, Toot wasn't as lucky. She died on November 3, the day before Barack won the election.

Though my father wasn't well enough to attend the inauguration, going on that ventilator gave him the chance to recover enough to make his first-ever visit to the White House. He marveled that I was a senior advisor to our friend, the first black president, and that my office was in the West Wing. He also lived to attend Laura's graduation from Harvard Law School in 2010. Though frail and unsteady by that point, he was determined to walk to the ceremony without the help of anyone or a wheelchair, and he did. There we spent time with Laura's boyfriend, Tony Balkissoon, and Tony's family from Canada. Laura was in love and about to begin the first chapter of adulthood. No doubt it was one of the happiest days of my dad's life.

But in the summer of 2011, while the president and I were at Camp David fretting over John Boehner's threats to torpedo America's credit rating, my father's health started failing. We'd installed a lift in my parents' home to take him from the first floor to the second, because he was having trouble walking and stairs were becoming harder and harder. He was also weak because he hadn't been eating enough to keep up his strength, and he was losing too much weight. The cancer in his larynx had destroyed his taste buds and made it difficult to swallow, so he'd lost interest in food. My mother kept trying to get him to drink Boost because he was losing so much weight. She tried Boost with ice cream, Boost with chocolate sauce. Nothing worked.

In early September we were worried enough that my mom took him in for a checkup and I boarded a plane to come home and help. His doctors decided to check him into the hospital, did more tests, and found that the cancer had metastasized to his liver.

At that point my father asked the obvious question. "How long?"

"A few months," the doctor told him. "But you'll need a feeding tube."

My dad shrugged, almost imperceptibly, and shook his head. "No." He could barely talk, but the doctor and I both understood what he was saying.

A couple days later he took a real turn down. He couldn't speak at all, and he was having trouble writing, too. For ten minutes or so, he kept trying to write me a note. He was struggling to scratch it out and I couldn't read it, and then finally I realized what he was writing: "Pain." How could I have missed that? They started giving him morphine, and he just kept slipping and slipping until he was unconscious. The doctor thought we should start to arrange for hospice so that we could move him home later that week.

Meanwhile, I was still working in the White House, Congress was back in session, and there was a crisis brewing with concerns that China was manipulating its currency. I remember thinking, bizarrely, *Well, better return to DC.* So I said good-bye to my dad, not knowing if he would be alive when I returned, wondering if this was how Barack felt when he left his grandmother for the last time. I booked a ticket back to DC and left Laura and my mother to handle the hospice arrangements. In retrospect, I cannot believe I left. It's as though I was on autopilot returning to work.

On the plane ride back I felt miserable. The next morning, I called my mom and she sounded terrible. He had regained consciousness long enough to have asked the nurses for her in the middle of the night. I went into the office and started to prepare for a meeting with the president about the China currency issue. I was sitting in my office thinking, *Am I really essential to the China currency meeting? No. Should I be home with my family? Yes.*

Arranging for the Secret Service to reverse gears so quickly isn't easy, but I alerted them and they made all the necessary accommodations, and thanks to them I was back in my dad's hospital room by 1 p.m. I tried to eat lunch with Laura and my mom in the hospital restaurant, but nobody had an appetite. Then, around 3 p.m., it was clear he was failing, and word had gotten quickly around. My cousin Jeff, a physician, kept encouraging nurses to make sure he had enough morphine so he was not in any pain. Anita Blanchard, Marty Nesbitt, and Eric Whitaker had joined me and Laura and Laura's soon-to-be fiancé, Tony, at my father's bedside. My mother, too distraught to go in the room, sat outside in a chair by the door. Anita said to me, "Do you mind if I hold his hand?" I told her of course not, so she took one hand and I took the other and my dad gradually and quietly let go, and died.

I can't imagine not having been there. It was a classic example of being so caught up in my work that I forgot for a moment what was truly important.

We didn't stay at the hospital long after he died. My father had donated his body to science, so we didn't have to arrange for much. Laura, being her ever-efficient self, took care of all the paperwork in about ten minutes. Then, as I was walking out of the hospital, the phone rang. It was Barack. He was right there, as always, making sure I was OK. And during the memorial service, Michelle Obama sat next to me, holding my hand throughout.

B ack when Laura was just ten years old, my parents took her on a tour one day, showing her some of the Chicago landmarks that had been a part of their lives before she was born. One stop on the tour was St. Luke's Hospital, where my father had completed his residency in pathology. They showed her the facility and explained to her how he wasn't allowed to live with the other residents. They were a bit taken aback when she bluntly asked her grandfather why he'd swallowed his pride. As Laura had grown up in a world of relative privilege and advantage, the indignities of Jim Crow were an abstraction for her, and her young mind couldn't fully fathom why this proud and dignified man had put up with being treated as a second-class citizen.

The fact is that black Americans have always been very pragmatic revolutionaries. We fight as hard as we can to change the system, showing up to vote, marching in the streets, and pushing relentlessly in the courts. But there are times when the status quo refuses to change, when you simply don't have the leverage to make it change. And those are the times when you stop and do a reality check, when you learn how to pick your battles. If you can't fight the system, you figure out a way to maneuver within the system as it exists in order to make progress. You find the cracks and the loopholes and you slip through them to get where you need to go. If the only way to be a resident at an all-white hospital is to live five miles away and commute, then you live five miles away and commute. If the quickest route to joining the faculty at the University of Chicago is to spend six years at a hospital seven thousand miles away in Iran, then you spend six years at the hospital seven thousand miles away in Iran. You do what you have to do. And in the fall of 2011, once John Boehner made it clear to us that the Republican Party was willing to default on the full faith and credit of the United States of America simply to prevent Barack Obama from engaging in the act of serving as the duly elected president of the American people, it was clear that we'd reached a point where the system was refusing to change anymore.

At that point, in just a few short years, we'd elected a black president; we'd passed the Recovery Act that helped jump-start the economy, the Dodd-Frank bill to reform Wall Street, and universal health care legislation; and we'd repealed "Don't ask, don't tell." In the face of our accomplishments, the very entrenched powers-that-be were now making it clear that they would hold on to every ounce of power they had, even if it meant ceasing to govern the country. So, faced with impossible circumstances, President Obama decided that if the system wouldn't change, we would change what we could within the system.

That October, after the Republicans' debt-ceiling fiasco, President Obama launched what became known as "We Can't Wait," a series of executive actions—from spurring job creation to helping the environment to student loan relief. He was hesitant do to it in part because he knew the changes would be vulnerable to the whims of his successor—and also because he'd wanted so much to find meaningful compromise and collaboration with the opposition. But he felt he had no choice given Congress's refusal to show up for work.

I realized that for my own mental health I needed to do the same. I needed to develop an art-of-the-possible agenda and focus my efforts on places where I could actually move the needle. I called my entire team in and said, "We have to figure out what we can do that's within our control. What are our priorities to which Congress has said 'no' where we could convince governors and mayors to say 'yes'? Let's switch our focus and stop wasting time on Congress when our time could be better spent making a difference in our portfolio." My only regret was that I hadn't come to that conclusion sooner.

A prime example was my push for policies to help working families, including equal pay for women, raising the minimum wage, affordable child care, paid sick days, and flexibility in scheduling for hourly wage workers. Having been a single working mother, it was an issue close to my heart. Soon after I was promoted to commissioner of the Department of Planning and Development, I was in a meeting with Susan Sher, then the city's corporation counsel, and Mayor Daley. Her son Evan and my daughter, Laura, were in the second grade at the Lab Schools. That morning was the school's annual Halloween parade, and the longer this meeting dragged on the closer we were to missing it. But Mayor Daley was very intimidating. Like all employees, we didn't want to upset the boss by leaving early. But we kept looking at our watches during this meeting. Finally he realized we weren't paying any attention at all and he said, "Obviously you two are not interested in this meeting. What's going on?"

"Well," I said, summoning every ounce of my courage, "the Lab Schools' Halloween parade starts in twenty minutes, and the school is twenty-five minutes away." Silence. I'm sure I was holding my breath. No doubt Susan was, too.

He looked at us for a split second, and then said, "Well then, what are you two still doing here?"

We felt an enormous sense of relief, we ran out the door and practically flew down Lakeshore Drive. We pulled up in front of the school just as our kids spilled out the front door in their costumes, scanning the crowd for their moms. And we were there thanks to Mayor Daley, a fact that made me eternally grateful to him, and loyal as well. I have often wondered if I would have had the courage to say anything if Susan had not been there. There's safety in numbers. It certainly would have been harder if I was alone. Too often, working moms do not feel empowered to speak up for our needs for fear of the repercussions.

Years later, once I was in the White House, I wanted to make sure both public- and private-sector employers understood that the needs and priorities of the twenty-first century worker are changing. Women are half of the workforce now, and working fathers have more responsibilities at home, too. (Or, at least they should.) Forty percent of working moms are the sole or primary breadwinner, so a woman's contribution to the family income is more important than ever. We consulted with academics and advocates and had the White House Council of Economic

Advisers compile all the available evidence to support the fact that when employers invest in policies that allow working families to thrive, it results in more productive, more efficient, and happier workforces, and greater profits. Treating workers with dignity is simply good business.

Tina Tchen and I traveled the country, bringing businesses, local governments, and ordinary working people together to sit at the same table and figure out how they address these important needs together. One of our first forums was in Philadelphia, which had adopted paid leave policies after a laborious six-year process led by Mayor Michael Nutter. He accomplished at the city level what we were trying to do at the federal level. He brought all the relevant stakeholders to the table—the business community, people who had no paid leave, advocacy groups, experts, budget analysts—and crafted a plan that provided for paid leave. At that summit I met a man, probably about forty-five years old, who'd never had a single paid sick day in his entire adult life—a stark reminder of the fact that forty-three million Americans go unpaid, or risk being fired, if they are sick.

I started calling other mayors, asking them if they would follow Philadelphia's example, and then planned trips around the responses I received. I called Kasim Reed, the mayor of Atlanta, and told him I would like to visit his city to discuss better paid leave, and then within a month, he'd already passed the measure through his city council because he wanted it done before I arrived. That showed the power of the bully pulpit and the positive impact of using my voice. For the rest of my time in the White House I continued to work directly with mayors and governors, and corporate CEOs and small business owners alike, to show that good policies for working families isn't just a nice thing to do for women. Greater diversity allows businesses to be more globally competitive, so investing in support for working families is a business imperative. While I would have preferred to work with Congress on comprehensive legislation, the Republicans made that impossible, so we moved the needle where we could.

My office took a similar approach to the issue of sexual assault on college campuses, an issue that was deeply personal to me, having a daughter who'd just graduated from college. When I dropped Laura off at Amherst College in the fall of 2003, I worried about it a lot. Would she regret her choice? Would she get along with her roommates? Would she maintain her study habits without any nagging from me? I didn't worry about whether or not she would be safe. I assumed that everything would be OK. Before Laura left for college, I made sure that she had a prescription for a morning-after pill in case she needed it. We were both aware, as many women are, that the danger of sexual violence is always present. But I wasn't aware that it was happening in such epidemic proportions. It wasn't until years later, when Secretary of Education Arne Duncan briefed me on the statistics that one in five women are sexually assaulted on college campuses, that I understood the scope of the problem. I scolded myself: *How could I have not known it was that bad?*

Arne took on the issue by beefing up the dormant Civil Rights Division of the Department of Education, and in 2011 he sent a letter to all the presidents of colleges and universities that receive federal funding, saying that the issue had been swept under the rug for far too long and that the federal government expected them to fulfill their responsibilities to create a safe college environment. He then published a list of colleges and universities that had open civil rights claims against them, claims filed by people who felt that the schools hadn't dealt with their allegations of assault seriously. There were over seventy schools on the original list, and that was a wake-up call. No school wanted to be on that list.

When President Obama was briefed on the statistics, he created a task force to end college sexual assault chaired by the White House point person on violence against women, who reported directly to Vice President Biden, and me. After a couple of months of engaging with the full range of stakeholders—from survivors to school administrators, from academics to campus police, from rape crisis center operators to student body presidents, sports coaches, and even fraternity and alumni organizations—we concluded that there was no silver bullet. Enforcement of laws was important, but if we really wanted to prevent assault from happening in the first place, we needed to change the culture. To change that mind-set, we needed everyone's support. An outside advertising association offered us pro bono help and came up with the name "It's On Us" to describe how we would put our grassroots organizing strategy to a new purpose. President Obama and Vice President Biden were featured in a PSA that we distributed widely. We encouraged the media and entertainment industry to pitch in and help. We worked with experts to create new training models that were engaging and not mocked by the students.

When we announced the findings of the task force, we had a sexual assault survivor come and speak. Research shows that most sexual assault happens the first or second week of school, during freshman or sophomore year, and this survivor had been through precisely that. "I was raped my freshman year," she said, "my first week of school, and after that my entire first year felt like pantomime. I was just going through the motions." She'd been raped on the same floor of the dorm she lived in, and all year, every time she came out of her room she would look down the hall to see if her rapist was there. The following year, when she learned that the young man had raped someone else, she willed herself to come forward and report the crime.

As I listened to that courageous young woman describe this deeply personal and traumatic experience, I was in awe of her strength and determination, her willingness to be a public face for the campaign to end this scourge of violence. And her words were particularly chilling for me, because this young woman had been a student at Amherst, so of course I couldn't help but think that Laura could have easily been in her shoes.

My hope with "It's On Us" was to set up an initiative that didn't live in the White House, but rather that would live on beyond us, owned by those with a vested interest who would continue the work long after we left. And that's what's happened. All across the country, colleges started supporting their own "It's On Us" initiatives.

As the 2012 election approached, despite a recalcitrant Republican Caucus, we had accomplished a great deal. We'd brought the nation back from the brink of economic collapse, killed the world's most wanted terrorist, and passed several pieces of landmark legislation. But for me, none of those compared to the single greatest event of that year: my daughter's wedding.

For years I'd watched with pride as Laura cleared every bar she set for herself, no matter how high. She'd graduated from the Lab Schools, then Amherst College and Harvard Law School. From there she had gone on to clerk for two federal judges and worked as a litigator in two prestigious Chicago law firms. I'd never doubted that she would excel professionally. But from the day Bobby walked out of our lives, I'd always worried about what effects my divorce would have on Laura's ability to have a healthy, long-lasting, and loving relationship with a true partner—an elusive goal of my own. So when Laura met Tony and fell in love, I finally exhaled.

Even though Laura would wind up practicing law for only six years (exactly the amount of time I spent in private practice), law school was well worth it. Not only did she acquire a skill set and credentials that would serve her well throughout her career, but that's where, in a second-year seminar on Title IX and combating sexual assault on campuses, she met Tony Balkissoon. Born and raised in Toronto, Canada, Tony is the son of Bas and Tahay Balkissoon, immigrants of Indian descent who moved to Canada from Trinidad in the early seventies.

I knew that Laura understood what it meant to be well loved. It truly does take a village to raise a child, and ours was mighty. She grew up surrounded by my devoted parents, our extended family and friends, and her caregiver, Mrs. Brown, who missed no more than two days of work in fourteen years. But my father had a unique place in our little village. He drove Laura to and from school every day, from preschool through her senior year of high school, two years after she had a driver's license. The time they spent alone in the car together was special to both of them. A friend of mine who picked up her daughter every day said that in that first hour when everything is so fresh, you capture the "gush" of the day. My dad relished the gush and shared it with me; and it was invaluable, because by the time I arrived home and asked how her day was, her usual response was "Fine." Laura wrote her college essay about those drives back and forth to school with her papa, as she called him. How they negotiated over the radio station, alternating between Laura's hip-hop and my dad's classical stations. How when her own dad died, her papa was the only one who knew what to say to her, and that was to say nothing, and so they drove in the relief of silence. She gave him a copy of her essay on a parchment paper scroll tied with a bow as a present. When he read it, tears quietly streamed down his face.

Tony reminded me of my dad in all the important ways: his unselfish love and devotion to Laura; his desire to always be in her company; the tender way he cared for my dad when he was ill and the most vulnerable. Before I met Tony, it never occurred to me that anyone could be worthy of Laura. He's not just worthy; they are both lucky to have found each other.

Their wedding date was set for June 16, 2012, and the fact that my fiercely independent, feminist daughter was marrying in a remotely traditional ceremony was already a major departure from my expectation of her. A few years earlier, when she was a bridesmaid, she had sworn to never put herself or her friends through such a stressful ordeal. In fact, she had said, why marry at all? Then came Tony.

Thanks to Tony, Laura went from not wanting to get married at all, to wanting to elope, to planning every detail of her idea of a perfect wedding: cocktails served before the ceremony in my mom's backyard; no bridal party other than her best friend, Maude, there to hand her Tony's ring; and my mom and I walking her down the aisle and Tony walking with his parents. All the guests agreed that it was one of the best weddings of all time—not that I had much to do with it. It was all Laura's doing, from the guest list to food and flowers and DJ Mary, who has become a regular presence at family gatherings. The only people Laura and Tony let me add to the guest list were those friends of mine who were close to them both. Even my mother was allowed to invite only her best friend.

Everybody loved most of Laura's modifications to the traditional cere-mony, except for one big one. Laura was adamant that there not be cake. She likes pie, and so she rebelled against the traditional wedding cake, opt-ing for pie instead. I pushed back gently. I hadn't been happy with my own wedding cake, so I thought she could have the one I'd missed out on. But I didn't really care. However, when Laura was asked about her wedding plans at a small friends-and-family holiday party hosted by the Obamas in the White House in December of 2011, she announced she would not be having a wedding cake—and all hell broke loose. Both the president and Attorney General Eric Holder told her she had to have a cake. At first they thought she was joking. When it became clear she was serious, they turned serious, too, and lectured her about the importance of cake.

"No cake?" Eric said. "What kind of wedding doesn't have cake?"

"Mine," she responded. "No cake."

The president piled on; this was not up for discussion. "There must be cake," he proclaimed, as if it were a presidential order. At which point my daughter proceeded to get into a heated argument with the leader of the free world and his attorney general . . . over cake. Laura, insisting on pie, held firm.

Laura has no problem saying no. She was one of the few people I knew who wasn't swept up by the mystique of the White House. Laura is nobody's groupie and the Obamas were her friends, so why would she be starstruck? In fact, she didn't spend that much time in the White House during our eight years in the administration. She was in law school in Cambridge, then in Chicago, where she had a career of her own and was in love. She said her "head was not there." She turned down invitations to all but the last state dinner, and even casual holiday gatherings, because she had her studies and then parties with her friends. She had her own life and separate identity, which was how I raised her. Whenever Laura said she was too busy to attend an event at the White House, I thought to myself, *Good for her.*

As the date drew near, I proposed a compromise on Cakegate. The wedding fell on the birthday of Susan Sher's husband, Neil Cohen, a Cook County circuit court judge who Laura and Tony had asked to officiate the ceremony. I casually floated the idea of at least having a birthday cake for Neil. And so, for Neil and only for Neil, Laura acquiesced. The only cake served that night was Neil's birthday cake, which Laura refused to cut. Instead, I climbed atop the backyard ledge and sang "Happy Birthday" to Neil in some sort of mash-up of Marilyn Monroe's famous version in honor of JFK and Stevie Wonder's. I hardly remember it, no doubt due to the free-flowing champagne, but to my embarrassment most everyone who was there refreshes my memory every time the wedding comes up. I'm just relieved that the videographer had stopped filming by that point. But in all of the commotion Laura did make sure both the president and Eric were served a piece of cake.

Despite my high profile in the White House, and the press's knowledge that the first family planned to attend, none of us were prepared for Laura and Tony's nuptials to turn into a celebrity wedding, complete with front-page news stories about who was and who was *not* on the guest list. There were television cameras filming Laura, Tony, my mom, and me as we walked down the block to the rehearsal dinner, which was really a backyard barbecue, at the home of our dear friends Allison Davis and Susan O'Connor. The morning of the wedding, Laura called me at 5:30 a.m. to tell me that the news was broadcasting the wedding venue live, with footage coming from a helicopter above my mom's backyard. Then there was the issue of Secret Service, which required the guests to come early—not a skill set most of my family possesses—to be wanded at a security kiosk set up a couple hundred feet from the house. But Laura's special touch of serving cocktails *before* the ceremony made everyone forget the inconvenience of arriving early. The Obamas walked from their home a block away, in time to take a photo with our immediate family and slip into their seats just as the last guests were seated.

I loved Laura and Tony's wedding, not a given for the mother of the bride. But being there, surrounded by our newly merged families and closest friends, a crowd spanning three generations, filled my heart with the same joy I had felt the day Laura was born.

The only person missing that day was my dad, but we all felt that he was there in spirit. My father's favorite watch was a Rolex that he'd been given by the head of the United Arab Emirates army while he was there on a consulting trip twenty-five years earlier. My dad cherished that watch, and he wore it every single day until I took it off his wrist the last time he was hospitalized, just days before he died. As I undid the clasp and slipped it off, he grabbed my hand weakly and said, "Take good care of it." I passed the watch on to my mother for safekeeping, and a few days before the wedding, my mom gave it to Tony.

My marriage was the best mistake I ever made, because it gave me Laura, and I did my best to raise her not to make the same mistakes I did, to find her own happiness and not simply live to meet the expectations of others. After a few more years of practicing law, she, too, decided it wasn't for her. She left and found her own calling as a journalist, working for CNN—which would have made my father so proud; CNN was his favorite network. She's found her voice and she knows how to use it—and nothing has ever made me prouder.

Other than the president's shaky performance at his first debate with Governor Mitt Romney, Cakegate would prove to be the most stressful moment of the 2012 election. The American people endorsed the work we were doing, and our Republican opponents, as evidenced by their performance in Congress, had no affirmative vision of their own to offer the country. In retrospect, particularly after Romney's comment that 47 percent of voters who are dependent on government, who believe they are victims, would vote for President Obama no matter what, the president's reelection was never seriously in doubt.

However, as the campaign entered its home stretch in late summer and fall, my mother started volunteering down at campaign headquarters in Chicago. She told me that the president losing in 2012 would be far worse than in 2008, so she wanted to pitch in and help. She said the first campaign was all about hope and change, and had been aspirational and she had never thought he could win. After all, Barack Obama had asked the nation to take a leap of faith and believe in a skinny black guy with a funny name from the South Side of Chicago who hadn't even finished his first term as a U.S. senator. The second win, however, was an affirmation, a vote of confidence that, through the darkest economic recession since the Great Depression, he had led our country forward. Hence the 2012 campaign slogan: "Forward."

Election night was also different. Unlike in 2008—when Laura, Maude, and I collapsed with exhaustion in our hotel room by 1 a.m., skipping the late-night festivities—in 2012 I literally danced until dawn. When I arrived home at 6 a.m., I sat down in my mom's breakfast room, put my head on her cold marble table, and fell sound asleep. About two hours later, she woke me up with a booming "Lally, why aren't you in bed?" I popped up and went over to the Obamas' house, where we had breakfast with close friends and laughed at hilarious *Key & Peele* videos spoofing the election.

With so much accomplished in the first term, we felt like we had the wind at our backs. Unfortunately, the president's prediction that "the fever would break" once he won reelection would prove to be far too optimistic; the fever didn't break then, and it hasn't broken yet. In fact, to extend the metaphor, the patient appears to have contracted a terminal illness, curable only by the engagement and voting of ordinary people. But back then we knew we had to continue to move the ball forward whenever and however we could.

Later that morning I went with President Obama down to his campaign headquarters, where he thanked his team for their hard work, emphasizing how much smarter and more talented he thought they were than he. Before he could finish, overcome with emotion, he had to pause in a futile effort to hold back his tears. It reminded me of caucus night in Iowa in 2008, when his tears were not about a victory for him, but rather about the folks who had worked so hard to make the impossible inevitable.

A few days after the election, Karen Tumulty, a reporter with *The Washington Post*, called me to say that she remembered the story I had told her four years earlier about the man from Austin who had given then Senator Obama his military patch. She said she'd never forgotten the story and wanted to track him down for a feature profile on Inauguration Day. My immediate reaction was panic. Every day for four years, I'd thought of that man as I passed through the gates of the White House on my way to work. He'd given me purpose and inspiration, but I knew absolutely nothing about him except for that one act of unselfish kindness, and I'd held strongly onto my fantasy of him being a wonderfully kind and decent man. What if Tumulty discovered something dreadful—that he was a deadbeat dad, or even an ax murderer?

I told Tumulty that I didn't know his name and couldn't help her, but she pushed me to remember whatever I could, so I told her that I'd met him in a Hyatt Hotel in Austin. She then tracked him down while I was vacationing in Hawaii with the Obamas during the holidays after the election. She sent me an email saying his name was Earl Smith, and he was head of security for the hotel. She also sent me his email in case I wanted to reach out to him directly. Karen's message arrived as I was checking work email on my phone while running on a treadmill (note: don't do this). I stopped, stepped off the treadmill, and stared at his email address for a few minutes, pondering what to do. Then I decided to write to him. What I remember is this:

> Dear Mr. Smith: My name is Valerie Jarrett. You probably don't remember me. I was the woman in the elevator who burst into tears when you gave Senator Obama your military patch. I've thought about you every day for four years. You inspired me to persevere and stay focused on the toughest of days. Of the many unselfish acts of kindness I had the privilege of witnessing, yours was the one that touched me the deepest.

He wrote back immediately.

> Dear Ms. Jarrett: Of course I remember you. I've thought of you
> often, as well. It was my honor to make that small sacrifice.

Later that morning I asked President Obama if he remembered the
man who had given him the military patch. "Of course I do," he said,
since he still kept the treasure close. When I told him about *The Washington Post* tracking Mr. Smith down and my corresponding with him,
the president asked me to invite him to the inauguration and then in for
a visit to the White House the day after.

Having missed the first inauguration due to my dad's illness, my
mother sat with me on the platform as the president took his second
oath of office on January 20, 2013. It felt like a symbolic bookend. My
mom, who'd been too afraid to hope in the first election, had evolved
from fearing his failure to feeling ownership in his success. Laura, on
the other hand, had always assumed, even more confidently than I, that
he could win. Generational differences in perspective based on our own
life experience.

The day after the inauguration, I greeted Mr. Smith outside the
Oval Office and gave him an inappropriately long hug. He was just as
I remembered him: very tall, in his seventies, with graying hair and a
huge smile. Like my father and every other black man of that generation, Mr. Smith had done what he could to overcome the challenges
and hardships that most people today can't even imagine. And yet here
he was, waiting outside the Oval Office to meet the first black president
of the country he had served. Mr. Smith joked around with me for a few
moments, chuckling about how thrilled he was to be there. Then President Obama opened the door to the Oval and came out with a huge
smile, too, and greeted his visitor as though they were old friends. Mr.
Smith's face lit up. Then, before shaking the president's hand, the old
veteran drew up to his full height and saluted his commander in chief.
President Obama returned the salute. And I, of course, burst into tears.

Chapter 14

True North

June 26, 2015, started out like most days at the White House: dramatic events, hard decisions, and a ton of work. On the foreign affairs side, the press was giving the administration a hard time about the president falling short of his stated goal of admitting ten thousand Syrian refugees fleeing Assad's violent regime before the end of the year, while the Republicans—in particular then Alabama senator Jeff Sessions, who was the chairman of the Immigration Subcommittee of the House Judiciary Committee—were using every maneuver to keep the Syrians out. At home the day before, the Boston Marathon bomber Dzhokhar Tsarnaev had appeared in a Boston courtroom and was sentenced to death by lethal injection for killing three people and injuring several hundred more.

In other words: just a regular day at the office.

To add even more pressure, we were also in the final weeks of the annual Supreme Court term, which is always a fraught time because the justices traditionally leave their most controversial decisions to the end. We were never any good at predicting which day decisions would be announced. Even our lawyers, who had clerked for Supreme Court Justices, had no particular insight. So just like everybody else, we had to visit SCOTUSblog.com beginning at 10 a.m. sharp and hit "refresh" every fifteen seconds until the opinions were announced.

That term, we were primarily concerned with two potentially land-mark cases. One was *King v. Burwell*, the Republicans' second legal challenge to the Affordable Care Act. They'd already tried to take one leg out of the act by claiming the individual mandate was unconstitu-tional. Having lost that argument, they were now challenging the legal-ity of the insurance subsidies in about three dozen states that didn't have state exchanges but relied on the federal government to run theirs. If they won, the law would be gutted. Luckily, they didn't win. On June 25, the decision was announced, 6–3 in our favor, with Justice Anthony Kennedy joining Justices John Roberts, Ruth Bader Ginsburg, Stephen Breyer, and Sonia Sotomayor in ensuring that affordable health care was still the law of the land.

Once *King v. Burwell* was decided, that left *Obergefell v. Hodges*, the case litigating the constitutionality of same-sex marriage, perhaps the only issue more contentious than health care. We had already won the decision not to enforce the Defense of Marriage Act on the grounds that it was un-constitutional. The act denied benefits to same-sex couples who were le-gally married under state law. In that case, *United States v. Windsor*, Edith Windsor had sued the government after the IRS forced her to pay $363,053 in estate taxes because it didn't recognize her marriage to Thea Spyer, who had left her entire estate to her wife after her death in 2009. A woman in-heriting the same estate from her husband would have gotten a spousal deduction and paid far less in taxes. The Court ruled in favor of Windsor, stating that same-sex couples married in states that allowed same-sex mar-riage were entitled to the same federal benefits and protections as hetero-sexual married couples.

I was on Air Force One with the president when we received the news. He called Windsor from the plane. "Hello, Edie," he said. "This is President Obama."

"I know who you are," she answered.

Windsor was a win for marriage equality, but it was a narrow ruling that left the issue of a federal constitutional right to marry undecided. Meanwhile, the nation's attitudes on the issue were shifting rapidly, and the law was increasingly seen as a relic of a less-enlightened era. A second landmark test case, *Obergefell v. Hodges*, had been filed in the hope of making same-sex marriage the law of the land.

Because the *King v. Burwell* decision on health care was so important, we presumed that the Court would wait until the last week of the term to rule on marriage equality, thus avoiding back-to-back controversial decisions. We were wrong. The very next day after *King*, on June 26, 2015, while I was sitting in Chief of Staff Denis McDonough's office for an extended senior staff meeting, trying to juggle the various crises of the day, Denis's assistant walked in at 10:10 a.m. and handed me a note from my assistant, Huma Shah. It said the Supreme Court had announced its decision and that, by a vote of 5–4, the Supreme Court had ruled in favor of the constitutionality of same-sex marriage, with Justice Anthony Kennedy providing the deciding vote. Later I read Justice Kennedy's moving opinion in support of the decision. I didn't agree with all of his opinions, but I sure miss him now.

I announced the result and the room erupted with cheers and applause. Because my team had been working on expanding LGBTQ rights since day one, Denis suggested I go and tell the president the historic news. I rushed down the hall to the Oval Office, but when I arrived, the president's assistant, Ferial Govashiri, said he hadn't come down from the residence yet. So, deflated, I returned to Denis's office.

"What did he say?" Denis asked.

"He wasn't there," I said.

"Well, what are you waiting for? Call him!"

Denis's response was so loud that his assistant, Jenny Wang, took it upon herself to dial the White House operator without our even having to ask. I picked up Denis's phone and waited for the president to come on the line.

"*What?*" was all President Obama said. His abrupt tone, so different from his normal affable one, threw me off, so I blurted out, "Sir, the Supreme Court ruled on marriage equality this morning. Five to four."

There was a pause, and then even more tersely he said, "Who won?"

Good Lord, I thought, *how could I have buried the lede?*

"We did," I added quickly. "Sorry about that."

He chuckled and turned back into the president I knew. "This has been a pretty good week," he said. And as far as the Supreme Court went, he was right. But then he reminded me why he'd sequestered himself up in the residence instead of in his office, and it brought me back down to earth. "I was writing the eulogy for Reverend Clementa Pinckney," he said, "but I'll be right down."

Just nine days earlier, a white man in his early twenties had walked into a Bible study class at the Emanuel African Methodist Episcopal Church in Charleston, South Carolina. A complete stranger to the black congregation, he'd asked those gathered if he could join them and was welcomed in. The black churches in our country have a history of racist attacks, but they kept their doors wide open. After spending an hour with the parishioners, he stood up and opened fire, killing nine people, including the church pastor who was a prominent state senator. The shooter spared the life of one woman, telling her that he wanted her to live to tell the story.

B y the time those nine churchgoers were murdered in Charleston, I had already attended far too many memorials for victims of gun violence with President and Mrs. Obama. The first major shooting during President Obama's administration came at Fort Hood near Killeen, Texas, in November of 2009. A U.S. Army major and psychiatrist shot and killed thirteen people and injured more than thirty others. That the most powerful military in the world was vulnerable on its own property was both tragic and unsettling.

More mass shootings followed: Congresswoman Gabby Giffords shot in the head and six others—including a nine-year-old—killed in the parking lot of a Tucson, Arizona, supermarket on January 8, 2011. Twelve people killed in a movie theater in Aurora, Colorado, on July 20, 2012. Six people killed at a Sikh temple in Oak Creek, Wisconsin, on

August 5, 2012. In fact, in 2012 not a single month went by without a mass shooting. In June alone there were six of them. The number for the year is thirty-two thousand if you include all who died from gun violence—two thirds of whom took their own lives. And of course, there are the countless more who are wounded and the devastated friends and family members who are left behind.

Coping with the aftermath of the violence never became any easier, but no day was worse than December 14, 2012, when the press reported that shots were fired at Sandy Hook Elementary School. I was in a meeting in the Oval Office when the president's assistant, Anita Decker Breckenridge, walked in and silently handed President Obama a hand-written note. He read it, folded it, and closed his eyes for a few moments. Then he told us that according to John Brennan, his then assistant for homeland security and counterterrorism, twenty children and six adults had been murdered in a school in Connecticut.

"How old were the kids?" I asked.

"They were first graders," he said.

I felt weak. I could barely even process the information. Who could possibly be so full of hate to carry out such an evil act in an elementary school?

Over the course of the day more facts came to light. The murderer was twenty years old. Before arriving at Sandy Hook, he'd shot and killed his mother, using her own Bushmaster XM-15 rifle. Police arrived on the scene about four minutes after he started shooting at the elementary school, and upon their arrival the shooter shot and killed himself.

I called Connecticut governor Dannel Malloy that evening to check in and offer our condolences. His description of the day's events was gut-wrenching. He told me the Sandy Hook parents had been directed to a nearby fire station where they could be reunited with their children. Once all of the children who survived had been picked up, the parents who remained waited anxiously for more children to arrive. The governor realized he would have to be the one to inform the remaining parents that their children had not survived. The governor said he'd struggled to find the right words, and there weren't any. Attorney General Eric Holder, who'd traveled immediately to Newtown, called me the following day, his voice breaking, to say the photos of the crime scene were the worst he had ever seen in all of his years in law enforcement.

The small Newtown community, devastated by this unfathomable mass murder, quickly organized an interfaith vigil on Sunday, December 16, and invited President Obama to attend. Moving the president around is not easy, and a public event with only two days' notice is nearly impossible. But our extraordinary advance team and Secret Service kicked into high gear and did it.

While traveling on Air Force One to Connecticut, we learned that due to bad weather we couldn't fly by Marine One from the airport to a landing site close to the service. We would have to drive by motorcade for an hour and ten minutes instead. Just the thought of that drive felt like a painful delay of the inevitable. An advance staff member grabbed me to ride with President Obama in his SUV. My guess is the staffer hoped I would know what to say during the long ride as President Obama prepared for what we all knew would be an excruciating afternoon. I had no idea what to say, so I said nothing.

In the car, President Obama read over his prepared remarks. When he finished, I don't know if he was talking to me or to himself, but he put them aside and said, "This won't work." Then, as I'd seen him do many times before, he pulled a yellow pad and pen out of his briefcase and began to write. I wondered how he could possibly craft a message that would console the families before their loved ones who had died had even been buried. I considered reaching out and touching his arm to give him some comfort, since words had failed me, but didn't want to distract him. In fact, I was staying so quiet that I even became acutely conscious of my breathing. We rode in silence with just the gentle roar of the limo's engine and the two Secret Service agents in the front, also staring straight ahead in silence. The president used the entire ride to compose his remarks, and as we exited the SUV, he gave the yellow pad to one of his staff members and said, "Please have this typed up."

The advance team had assembled the families of the victims in multiple rooms in a building in downtown Newtown. As we approached the first room, I was relieved to see Joshua DuBois, who had traveled to Newtown early with the advance team. Although Joshua was only in his early thirties, he was an old soul with plenty of experience in grief counseling. But the concerned expression on his young face caught me off guard. He pulled me close and whispered that the families were in awful shape. I'd expected as much, of course, but Joshua's caution told me I wasn't at all prepared for what we were about to encounter. I took a deep breath as we entered the first room.

Inside, there were four or five family groups, each sitting clustered together in circles, several family members crying and others trying to comfort them. Each cluster was accompanied by a first responder, who I learned had remained with his or her assigned family since the day of the shooting.

President Obama went around the room, talking with each family member individually, listening to their grief and offering quiet words of condolence. Several showed him photos of their deceased loved ones. One photo, which I can still close my eyes and see vividly, was a large close-up of the faces of a young boy and girl—twins. The image had been handed to the president by the surviving twin, a little girl named Arielle whose brother Noah had been murdered that day.

As we moved from family to family and then from room to room, I walked behind President Obama and visited with each family after the president had moved to the next. Some people, who'd held their composure when speaking with the president, collapsed as I approached. Still at a loss for words, I mostly just hugged them, knowing that nothing I said would be remembered or help with their pain.

After an agonizing two hours with the families, President Obama visited with the state troopers and other first responders, many of whom had witnessed the horrific crime scene firsthand. He understood they, too, had experienced profound trauma and deserved words of comfort and appreciation for their service.

The president took just a few minutes to read over his typed remarks, not wanting to keep the families waiting, and then we moved into an auditorium where everyone was already seated for the service. I slipped into an open seat in the front row next to a man sitting alone, thinking nobody should sit alone at a time like that. The room was perfectly quiet. Governor Malloy spoke, and then President Obama began.

"I can only hope it helps for you to know that you're not alone in your grief, that our world, too, has been torn apart, that all across this land of ours, we have wept with you. We've pulled our children tight." Reminding everyone that there is no charge more important than protecting our children from harm, he told stories of the courage and heroism of the surviving children, staff, and first responders. He also shared an emotion that he often used when talking about Malia and Sasha: "Someone once described the joy and anxiety of parenthood as the equivalent of having your heart outside of your body all the time."

The president mentioned each person who had been murdered by name—each one cutting through the air like a sharp knife, bringing home the reality of what had happened. The man next to me could barely catch his breath he was crying so hard. I didn't know what to do. Impulsively I reached out to hold his hand but, unsure of whether such closeness with a stranger would help, pulled back after only touching him lightly. He didn't notice, consumed with his own grief.

How President Obama found those perfect words during the car ride I will never know. I do know that when he finished, I saw one of his Secret Service agents brush tears from her face—I had never seen that before or since.

Sandy Hook was the president's fourth appearance at a memorial after a mass shooting. They never became any easier, and with each one we felt increasingly frustrated by our inability to prevent them. We mourned the victims and consoled their families but felt there must be more we could and should do to stop the epidemic of gun violence. Soon after the memorial in Connecticut, the president made a push to persuade Congress to pass legislation closing background-check loopholes. "Are we really prepared to say that we're powerless in the face of such carnage, that the politics are too hard?" he asked. "Are we prepared to say that such violence visited on our children year after year after year is somehow the price of our freedom?" As they always did after every mass shooting, Republicans and the National Rifle Association exclaimed, "It's too soon!" and accused us of "politicizing" the tragedy. And even though polls demonstrated 90 percent of the American people supported such legislation, Congress refused to act.

The day we realized that we didn't have enough votes to get such simple, obvious legislation passed was one of my most depressing moments. For me the issue was personal. My father's father died from gun violence when I was only fifteen years old. An avid hunter, he owned rifles and handguns, including one he kept in his DC dental office, knowing he could be a target because of the opiates he kept stocked there. On the very last day before he retired, he was closing up shop when two young men broke into his office and pulled a gun on him. Instead of handing over the drugs they wanted, my grandfather pulled out his gun, which they wrestled away from him and then used to murder him. And here's the devastating twist: the men who'd broken in to rob him had only a toy gun. So to all those who say having a gun makes you safer, well, it didn't help my grandfather. There is a reason our military and police go through rigorous, ongoing training on how to use guns. It isn't human nature or normal to take another life.

As President Obama prepared to give a speech announcing the Republicans' latest defeat of reasonable gun-control legislation, a member of my staff came into my office and let me know that a few of the Sandy Hook parents we'd invited to the announcement were gathered in the Roosevelt Room. I knew that I needed to go downstairs and talk with them while they waited for the president. I walked slowly from my office, down one flight to the first floor and through the West Wing lobby to the Roosevelt Room, trying to rehearse what I could possibly say in the face of this defeat. They had lobbied legislators so hard, reliving their personal tragedy over and over, and still we couldn't get anything through Congress. Once again there was nothing I could say that would be comforting. Instead all I said was "Please don't give up." One of the moms who lost her six-year-old son in the shooting said, "I have no choice. I can't give up." And they didn't. Several of the Sandy Hook parents founded Sandy Hook Promise, a grassroots organization advocating for ways to protect children against gun violence. I kept in close contact with two of the parents, Nicole Hockley and Mark Barden, throughout the rest of the second term as we continued to work on executive orders to address this epidemic. When Congress failed to act, executive orders were our only option, and we joined forces with advocates, researchers, and state and local elected officials across the country to push for safer gun laws.

The first round of twenty-three executive actions were signed by President Obama on January 16, 2013. On January 29, Hadiya Pendleton, a fifteen-year-old girl who had marched in the inauguration parade eight days earlier was shot while hanging out with a group of friends in a park in North Kenwood, the community we had worked so hard to improve, less than a mile from my home in Chicago. I attended her funeral with Michelle Obama. Before it began Michelle met with Hadiya's devastated classmates, including Hadiya's best friend, who had been sitting right next to her when the gunshot was fired. The First Lady told them to honor Hadiya by living out the best life Hadiya certainly would have had.

President Obama's final announcement of executive orders to keep guns out of the wrong hands was made in January of his last year in office. By that point any hope of working with Congress had completely faded. The president was introduced at the event in the East

Room by Mark Barden, still raw and grieving from the loss of his son Daniel. Listening to Mark's remarks off camera in the green room no doubt touched President Obama deeply, because in a rare display of emotion he cried openly soon after he began to speak. I was sitting in the front row next to Gabby Giffords, who thankfully held my hand for the entire twenty-minute program.

My last week in the White House, Nicole and Mark came by my office to say good-bye. Seeing them one last time there was emotional for us all. We'd developed a friendship out of tragedy, but what we left unspoken that day was our lack of progress in Congress. For eight years we'd watched Republicans put their short-term political agenda ahead of what the majority of Americans wanted. As I sat with Nicole and Mark on my couch, they talked about how the pain of losing a child doesn't get any easier. For this grief, time does not heal. My emotions were many. There was sorrow. There was impotence. How was it that we are the only developed country in the world with anywhere near this level of gun violence? How could we call ourselves the most powerful nation on earth when we couldn't even keep our citizens safe within our own borders?

But what I felt, more than any other emotion, was anger toward the Republicans in Congress and the NRA, probably the most vile example I know of where the will of a special interest subverts the good of society. While masking itself as a pro–gun rights group, the NRA in reality is a lobbying organization for gun manufacturers. Its strategy, which relies on raising fears that the government is trying to take away all guns, is really about increasing gun sales. The playbook is always the same. After every mass shooting, the NRA bullies anyone who calls for the most sensible and obvious measures to keep guns out of the hands of people who are a threat to others or themselves. It shames anyone who speaks up. It calls for wider use of guns, for arming teachers. The state and federal elected officials in its pocket offer prayers instead of legislative solutions after each mass shooting. How we buy and sell guns in this country is necessarily a matter of public policy—and when it's easier to get an AR-15 or a handgun than it is to register to vote, then it's a *failure* of public policy and political will. When domestic abusers, criminals, and even people on terrorist watch lists can easily avoid background checks and buy guns, that's exactly the kind of crisis our political system is supposed to solve.

Special interests, beyond the gun lobby, are by nature invested in preserving the status quo (or rolling back adverse legislation or regulation), and to take them on, you have to appreciate how fiercely those who stand to benefit will fight to keep the status quo. The coal industry, which didn't want us to control pollution, claimed we were antibusiness when we imposed clean-air regulations. They wanted to be left alone even if it meant creating an unhealthy climate. The banking industry's top institutions, which took risks that required a taxpayer bailout, spent millions of dollars in lobbying to resist Dodd-Frank, because they didn't want the federal government to limit their ability to take risks. But look what happens when any industry sets its own parameters. The lesson here isn't just that industry without regulation will run amok but also that the *only* force that can counter this truth is the will of the American people.

Just as I'd reached out to Governor Malloy of Connecticut after Sandy Hook, in the nine days since the shooting at Emanuel AME I'd been in close contact with Charleston mayor Joe Riley, one of the nation's longest-serving and most respected mayors, about the burial plans. Since President Obama knew Reverend Pinckney, he'd asked me to call the reverend's widow and let her know he would be willing to speak at the service if she would like him to do so. Mayor Riley connected us, and she graciously accepted.

A few days later, I was flying with President Obama on Marine One when he asked his staff to compile data on the number of Americans killed by foreign terrorists on our own soil compared with the number of Americans killed by gun violence. He wanted to demonstrate to the public where the real epidemic lay. Just as the president was making this point to us, Eric Schultz, the deputy White House press secretary, read us a news report. Family members of those murdered at Mother Emanuel were overheard at the assassin's arraignment saying that they had forgiven him. How could they forgive so quickly after such a devastatingly random act of violent hatred? President Obama slowly shook his head, and we were all stunned that they could find that forgiveness in their hearts so soon after their loss. "Such grace," he said.

Having given far too many eulogies already, the president was searching for fresh words to console, and to motivate America to take action. That's why he'd tried to carve out some extra time alone that morning, upstairs. But once the *Obergefell* decision came down, that plan went out the window. The next hour was chaos. The president had to finalize a difficult eulogy while simultaneously writing a speech about a landmark decision guaranteeing that love means love.

I had my own work to do as well. Equality for the LGBTQ community was a victory for all historically marginalized groups, from women to black people to Latinos to those with disabilities. The broader progressive movement understood that we were all linked together. So not only was I responsible for outreach to all the LGBTQ advocacy groups and the legal scholars we'd encouraged to write amicus briefs in support of marriage equality, but I also had to quarterback outreach to a whole range of civil rights groups. I also had to track down James Obergefell, the plaintiff in the case, so that President Obama could congratulate him personally. After my team found him in the middle of his own press conference, Obergefell placed the president's call on speakerphone so that everyone could hear what the president had to say.

Meanwhile, the staff at the White House was furiously assembling the stage in the Rose Garden, where President Obama would deliver his remarks on the Supreme Court ruling, before departing on time for Charleston. Even early in his career, when punctuality was not his strong suit, President Obama was never late to a funeral, for he thought it would be disrespectful to those who were grieving.

For Rose Garden speeches, there's an unwritten rule that staffers, even senior staffers, should all be too busy to hang out and gawk, so anyone not directly involved in the topic of the speech usually watches in the seclusion of their own offices. But on that day the iconic colonnade that runs along the north border of the Rose Garden, connecting the West Wing to the residence, was packed to the brim with staff from all departments crying tears of joy and hugging one another. Everyone wanted to be present for the historic announcement.

The energy in the crowd grew still when the press aide announced the two-minute warning before President Obama emerged from the Oval Office, just west of the Rose Garden, walked out to his podium, and, despite the time crunch and competing emotions of the day, took the time to reflect on the larger context of how all historic change happens in our democracy. "Progress on this journey often comes in small increments," he said, "sometimes two steps forward, one step back, propelled by the persistent effort of dedicated citizens. And then sometimes there are days like this, when that slow, steady effort is rewarded with justice that arrives like a thunderbolt."

In his remarks, President Obama echoed the idea, originally attributed to the nineteenth-century abolitionist Theodore Parker but refined in a quote made famous by Martin Luther King Jr., that "the arc of the moral universe is long, but it bends towards justice." That quote was so meaningful to the president that he had it, together with his other favorite historical quotes, woven into the border of his rug specially designed for the Oval Office.

As soon as the president finished his remarks, he and I walked straight from the Rose Garden to Marine One, where we were joined by Mrs. Obama for the quick hop out to Andrews Air Force Base and then the ninety-minute flight down to Charleston. A sense of dread slowly crept into our euphoria over the marriage equality case as we talked about the day that lay ahead. To ease the mood, President Obama casually mentioned, with a twinkle in his eye, that he wanted to give us a heads-up that he might sing in his eulogy. He would see how he felt in the moment.

I'd learned my lesson a few years back, when I told him not to sing "Let's Stay Together" by Al Green at a fund-raiser in New York. As we waited backstage for the famous soul singer to finish, President Obama joked with the stage engineers that he might sing, too. I strongly discouraged him, but he did it anyway. The video of him singing went viral. It was a huge hit. Clearly, bad advice on my part.

This time I simply said, "Great." More out of curiosity than in disapproval, Michelle asked where exactly he envisioned an appropriate moment in the eulogy for singing. He replied that the eulogy was going to be about grace, amazing grace. She shrugged and said, "You be you."

The Emmanuel AME shooting wasn't just the latest depraved incident in a crescendo of mass shootings and gun violence; it had also come in the midst of what seemed like a constant barrage of violent murders of unarmed, peaceful, and law-abiding black Americans, often at the hands of the police. As a candidate, Barack Obama's remarks on the issue of race had galvanized and united people. But as president, starting with the Skip Gates incident in 2009, each time he spoke about race it often seemed to inflame and agitate some. So he had learned to choose words carefully, as he had on the fiftieth anniversary of both the March on Washington, on the Mall in front of the Lincoln Memorial, and the Voting Rights Act, where we re-created a peaceful walk across the Edmund Pettus Bridge.

The violence endured by black people has been an ever-present issue for America, but it returned to the forefront of the national consciousness during the Obama administration with the killing of Trayvon Martin, a black seventeen-year-old who was attacked, shot, and killed for nothing more than walking down the street eating Skittles in a gated Florida neighborhood—his own neighborhood. In the wake of the killing of Trayvon Martin, I was in the Oval Office with David Plouffe, then a senior advisor, who was prepping the president for a planned announcement about a different subject. President Obama paced in front of his desk, visibly upset about Martin's death. David tried to turn the subject to the purpose of the press conference, but in an uncharacteristically loud, emotional voice, President Obama said to David, "You know, if I had a son, he would look like Trayvon." After a rather awkward silence, he added, "I want to speak about this at the press conference. Ask one of the reporters to ask me a question about it." And so there in the Rose Garden, in front of the press, a slightly calmer President Obama repeated what he had said earlier: "If I had a son, he would look like Trayvon."

Eighteen months later, Martin's killer was acquitted on spurious claims of self-defense. I wasn't surprised by the verdict. Talking to one of my white colleagues, who *was* shocked by the jury's decision, I explained that most black people, including me, have low expectations of justice from the criminal justice system. President Obama summed up this sentiment in an impromptu press briefing after the 2013 not-guilty verdict was handed down. "It's important to recognize that the African American community is looking at this issue through a set of experiences and a history that doesn't go away," he said, choosing his words as carefully as ever.

"How do we learn some lessons from this and move in a positive direction," President Obama asked, "beyond protests or vigils?" He called on the American people to think about how "we bolster and reinforce our African American boys." He gathered his senior team and directed us to develop a plan to break down the barriers that prevent black boys and young men from getting a fair shot—not just yet another government program that depended on the political whims of Congress or the president but rather a sustainable partnership with business and the philanthropic community.

A short time later, I accompanied President Obama home to Chicago, where he was scheduled to give remarks at Hyde Park High School. Before the speech, he sat down at a roundtable meeting with about fifteen black male high school students who were all enrolled in "Becoming a Man," a program that, according to analysis by the University of Chicago Crime Lab, cut violent crime arrests in half and boosted the high school graduation rates of its participants by nearly 20 percent. To the surprise of the boys, the president came down off the pedestal the teenagers put him on, so they could understand that the only difference between them was that he had grown up in a more forgiving atmosphere with a far greater margin for error. President Obama even kept in touch with the young men long after the visit; it meant as much to him as it did to them. Later that year he invited them to the White House around Father's Day, and they decided to sign a Father's Day card for him. One young man admitted, "I've never signed a Father's Day card before," to which President Obama responded, "Me neither."

When we returned to DC, President Obama used Becoming a Man as the guiding example for a program he hoped to launch nationwide. Because of his strong commitment to mentoring young black men and boys, Cabinet Secretary Broderick Johnson was chosen by the president to head up the effort that became My Brother's Keeper. Launched in March 2015, My Brother's Keeper began as a public-private partnership between the federal government, local elected officials, not-for-profits such as Emerson Collective, and businesses such as the NBA, designed to intervene with evidence-based strategies that improve the trajectory of the lives of boys and young men of color. After President Obama left office, he housed the program in the Obama Foundation and it continues to work in over two hundred cities and make a huge impact, one young person at a time.

Obviously, the president identified with the experiences of young black men forced to endure both subtle and not-so-subtle racism directed at them—from watching white women clutch their handbags closer to not being able to flag down a cab, to being mistaken for a server or valet in a restaurant, to being stopped and frisked and harassed, and sometimes shot, by police. I'd had an early lesson on the dangers for black teenage boys when I was about twelve years old. My mom and I were driving near our home when we saw the police had stopped two of our neighbors, black teenagers a few years older than me. The police officers had already gotten out of their police car to question them. My mother immediately stopped our car and started to get out.

"Where are you going?" I asked her.

"I need to go make sure they'll be OK," she said.

I didn't want her to get involved. But she refused my pleas. "No," she said. "I can't leave them here."

Although the boys lived about a block away, the police wanted to know what they were doing in such a "nice" neighborhood. My mother wasn't having it. "I can vouch for them," she said to the police. "I know them both. Please let them go."

Whether it was because they thought she was white or because she intimidated them just as she does everyone else, the officers let them go. At first, I was just selfishly worried about my mom, but reflecting on the incident as I grew older, I always wondered what would have happened to them if she hadn't shown up. I was proud of my mom for intervening. The moment also left a lasting impression on the way race can trump affluence.

More incidents of young, unarmed black men being killed began to surface. In Ferguson, Missouri, where that long-simmering anger erupted into months of protests after Michael Brown, just two days shy of starting college, was shot dead by the police, his body left in the streets for hours. There was Eric Garner in New York City, choked to death by police for suspicion of selling loose cigarettes on the street. There was Laquan McDonald in Chicago, shot sixteen times in the back while walking down the street. There was twelve-year-old Tamir Rice in Cleveland, shot while playing with a toy gun in the park. And on and on and on.

When the Ferguson demonstrations started, the Obamas and I were on vacation together, watching them on TV. Tensions boiled over the night of August 18, when armed police fired tear gas and rubber bullets at crowds of protesters. There were several reported injuries, and a series of businesses were vandalized and looted. I called Missouri's governor, Jay Nixon, to see what his perspective was and he told me he determined it necessary to call in the National Guard. The situation was spiraling out of control. While police in the suburb of St. Louis established a nightly curfew, President Obama, Attorney General Eric Holder, and I evaluated what we could do to calm this community growing more volatile by the day. Some had called for President Obama to go to Ferguson, thinking his physical presence was a necessary sign of support, but the police had their hands full containing the situation and the president's presence would strain local law enforcement. Plus, knowing a federal investigation would surely follow, he was careful about putting his foot on the scale. The person with oversight over the investigation, Eric Holder, went instead. The community knew of the attorney general's lifelong commitment to creating a fair criminal justice system, and his team was on the ground working with local law enforcement to restore the peace. It also helped that he was known to have a very close personal relationship with President Obama.

President Obama was determined to turn this inflection point into an opportunity to improve the bond of trust between communities of color and the police. That December, President Obama issued an executive order creating the President's Task Force on 21st Century Policing, an eleven-member committee charged with recommending ways police can do their jobs while earning the public's trust. One of the members was Brittany Packnett, an executive director of Teach for America in St. Louis and also an activist instrumental in organizing the demonstrations in Ferguson and other protests around the country that became the movement known as Black Lives Matter. The president had met Brittany when he invited her and a few other young activists to the Oval Office earlier that month. My team organized the meeting, and I sat with my back to the Resolute desk, with the group sitting on the couches closest to his chair. The president and I listened as they told us their stories. What I heard were young people who were both strident and exhausted, in awe of where they were but still willing to be confrontational. The president knowingly smiled and reminded them of his early days as a community organizer. "I still remember what it was like knocking on doors in the cold," he said. "I know your frustration." Then, after letting them vent, he offered some good advice. "Don't try to solve world peace," he said. "Just try to move the needle a little bit. And then a bit more."

Brittany—who also cofounded Campaign Zero, a policy platform to end police violence—was so impressive that the president ultimately asked me to invite her to join the President's Task Force on 21st Century Policing. Unsure if her views would be taken seriously and worried about losing her credibility among her fellow activists, she initially turned down the appointment. I called her a couple of times to persuade her, and my staff called many times more. Eventually Brittany agreed to join us, taking a leap of faith that she would be able to accomplish more inside the tent than outside. So Brittany found herself working with Laurie Robinson, one of the nation's foremost experts on criminal justice policy, and former Philadelphia police commissioner Charles Ramsey, as well as other leaders several years her senior—and she took to heart the president's advice to focus on the concrete change you believe will actually make a difference. What the young activist felt most strongly about was that police misconduct should be investigated by special prosecutors, given that prosecutors work so closely with the police. No one else on the task force initially supported her recommendation. But over time she persuaded every other member and they unanimously included her recommendation in the task force's final report.

When we arrived at the College of Charleston for Reverend Pinckney's memorial, nearly six thousand mourners filled the arena. The Obamas paid their respects to Mrs. Pinckney and her two darling daughters, dressed in white. I stood off to the side, fighting back tears and dreading the service. But when we walked into the huge venue, the energy was strong; this was not just a time to mourn but also a celebration of life.

"What a good man," President Obama said of the pastor he had met on the campaign trail in 2008. "Sometimes I think that's the best thing to hope for when you're eulogized—after all the words and recitations and résumés are read, to just say someone was a good man." But the president was not finished. For those of us old enough to remember, the Pinckney service triggered painful memories of the four little black girls who died in the Sunday-morning bombing of the 16th Street Baptist Church in Birmingham in 1963. President Obama schooled all who listened that day on the history of the black church. He spoke of "hush harbors" and "our beating hearts, the place where our dignity as a people is inviolate." Within this narrative, he argued that it was consistent with the tradition of the black church to welcome any stranger, such as a young white man new to an evening Bible study, and for the families of the victims to respond to brutal hatred and violence with amazing grace.

It is a delicate task to go beyond the celebration of life at a moment like that. But I could feel the open hearts of the richly diverse congregation. In the front row with President and Mrs. Obama were Governor Nikki Haley, who just days earlier had announced that she supported taking down the Confederate flag, a gutsy position that could have been political suicide in South Carolina but won her accolades in a national spotlight; Mayor Joseph Riley, sporting his trademark bow tie just like my dad's; and Hillary Clinton, who had peeled off the presidential campaign trail to attend. Every national and local civil rights leader was there, and the congregation was electric in defiant celebration of the lives that had been lost.

Near the end of his remarks, President Obama built to a crescendo. Then he paused, closed his eyes, and—yes—began to sing.

"Amazing grace, how sweet the sound . . ."

He then spoke of the amazing grace of each victim by name. For a moment I wondered how the congregation was going to react. It didn't take more than five seconds, though, for everyone to rise and burst into song together. We were one.

President Obama's challenge to the congregation that day was not to betray the short life of Reverend Pinckney by slipping into "a comfortable silence" but to raise our voices to address poverty, dilapidated schools, hatred of all kinds, and gun violence.

After Reverend Pinckney's memorial, we boarded Air Force One for the flight back to Washington, DC, nearing the end of an unbelievable day, filled with the euphoria of the Supreme Court verdict and the commemoration of a good man's life. Fortunately, I knew a special secret that was in store for that night. A few weeks earlier, Aditi Hardikar, my LGBTQ liaison, had brought me an idea cooked up by Jeff Tiller from our press office. "I know this is probably a crazy idea and can't be done," she said. "We have never done it before, and I'm not sure anyone will think it's a good idea. But if the Supreme Court rules in favor of marriage equality, or rules against it, what if we light the White House in a rainbow to reflect the colors of pride?"

"Excellent idea," I said, imagining an iconic photo that would forever symbolize the extraordinary progress made for LGBTQ equality on our watch. "Now let's figure out if we can do it." The next step was to "run the traps," which meant making sure everyone was on board, including the president and First Lady. This one was a slam dunk. Everyone loved the idea, so Tina Tchen, by then the First Lady's chief of staff, figured out how to do it.

I sent out a tweet shortly after we returned, opaquely mentioning to pay attention to the White House. At dusk, passersby began to notice the colors, the entire northern facade of the White House lit up like a rainbow. The crowd grew. They started posting photos on social media. Long after the sun had gone down, after the colors turned from pale to vibrant, thousands of people were still gathered outside the gates of the White House celebrating, while those of us on the North Lawn who worked on marriage equality shared stories of how impossible this victory had seemed six years earlier.

In that moment, celebrating with many of my colleagues with whom I had worked so hard to help make that day possible, I appreciated how lucky we were that the pendulum of progress had swung so far on our watch. When President Obama took office, same-sex marriage was legal in only two states. Right before that June day, as the result of grassroots organizing by advocates all across the country, it was legal in thirty-seven states and the District of Columbia—each victory, I believe, making it easier for the Supreme Court to reach the right conclusion. But, as is always the case for major leaps forward, the groundwork had been laid by decades of hard work.

In 2010, for my birthday present, President Obama gave me a copy of two documents, side by side in a frame. On one side is the Petition for Universal Suffrage, dated January 29, 1866, signed by a group of suffragists including Susan B. Anthony and Elizabeth Cady Stanton, women who called on Congress to amend the Constitution to grant women the right to vote. Next to it is the Joint Resolution of Congress proposing a constitutional amendment extending the right of suffrage to women, dated May 19, 1919. The two are over fifty years apart! Many of the women who protested with hunger strikes and were arrested and jailed in the movement didn't live to see the fruits of their efforts in 1919. But they carried the baton and then passed it on to others. Change takes time, sacrifice, resilience, and hard work over a sustained period of time. But then, eventually, seemingly like a thunderbolt, it happens.

The many same-sex couples who'd been forced to wait way too long for the constitutional right of marriage to materialize were a tangible reminder that change never happens as quickly as it should. This kind of change often seems impossible until it is inevitable.

That night was not just a victory for, and with, America's same-sex couples—it was a victory for America. And my eight years in the Obama White House only reaffirmed my belief that the movement to fight for equality should be every American's cause. I saw firsthand the impact of women's rights advocates who used their voices to fight for the LGBTQ community, the LGBTQ community who did the same for

Black Lives Matter, and Black Lives Matter activists who spoke out for immigrants' rights. As Dr. Martin Luther King Jr. famously said, "We are caught up in an inescapable network of mutuality, tied in a single garment of destiny. Whatever affects one directly, affects all indirectly." This defines our humanity and what we owe to one another. It should be our true north.

· *Chapter 15* ·

The Changing of the Guard

In the final weeks leading up to Election Day 2016, I began thinking about what I was going to do that night. During the last two presidential elections, we'd obviously planned large celebrations in Chicago, but now what? The president had mentioned to a few of us that he and the First Lady didn't intend to make any plans, but I had no intention of fretting by myself, so I more or less invited myself over. "You know I can't sit home alone," I said to the president. "So if it's OK with you and Michelle, I'll come over and spend the evening with you guys."

He chuckled. "Fine."

In the meantime, we all did our best to keep focused on the business of running the White House. Earlier that year, a few staffers had left to work on the Clinton campaign, but those of us who remained knew the president expected us to "run through the tape, full speed ahead," to complete as many of the items on his handwritten priority list as we could before leaving. Of course, we were all paying very close attention to the presidential race, but during our long workday, we were expected to focus. During Denis's morning meetings, we never talked about the presidential campaign, ever. Even Election Day morning, Denis reminded us, "We still have a transition ahead after tonight, regardless of outcome."

Those of us who stayed in the Obama administration until the end also didn't meddle in the Clinton campaign. We could have called her campaign manager and said, "Tell us everything you are doing." We could have asked John Podesta, President Obama's former senior advisor, to brief us regularly. But it was Clinton's campaign, not ours. We had run President Obama's two campaigns just the way he wanted, and we remembered what it was like to have people from the outside causing us angst by telling us what they thought we should do. So we intentionally did not butt in to hers.

The night before the election, I traveled with the Obamas to Philadelphia for Hillary Clinton's last rally. Our two teams, once rivals, shared hugs and excitement backstage, each in our own way absorbing what we thought would be a historic moment. The outcome seemed so inevitable. I had never really allowed the thought that she could lose to penetrate my conscious thought. In retrospect, there were signs. I did wonder how strange the anticipation must be for the president. On the sidelines, prepared to leave office, but very, very invested in the outcome. As usual, whatever he was feeling, the even-keeled president betrayed nothing but confidence and hope.

The evening of November 8, after finishing up for the day, I popped upstairs to the residence, and the three of us ate dinner at their large, round dining room table. I have no idea what we discussed, but it felt right to be together that night, after having our lives so deeply intertwined since years before Barack started his political journey twenty years earlier. After dinner, to kill time, the president suggested, "How about a movie?"

The movie theaters at the White House and at Camp David both have large and very comfortable chairs upholstered in a soft fabric, each with a blanket, a pillow, and, in the front row, a foot rest. Camp David's even recline. It's well-known among my friends and family that for the eight years we were in the White House, perpetually exhausted from lack of sleep, the second the lights went down and my popcorn was finished, I would immediately pass out. Thinking any movie would put me to sleep and ease my anxiety, I said it sounded like a great idea to me that night.

President Obama and I have very different taste in movies. I enjoy romantic comedies such as *Love Actually*, or classics such as *The Philadelphia Story*. The president's idea of a good movie is one with a complicated plot that involves a great deal of suffering and that ends with everybody dying. That night he selected the new Marvel superhero movie *Doctor Strange*, and Michelle and I went along with his choice. So while voters continued to go to the polls to decide between Donald Trump and Hillary Clinton, we were distracted by a cartoonish action movie, hoping that when it ended, the waiting would be over and we could look forward to a Clinton presidency. But as the lights came up in the theater, Barack pulled out his phone and said, "Hmm."

By now the polls had closed in all time zones except the Pacific, and soon the exit-poll data started to come in. We went back up to the residence and sat in their living room long enough to hear about a few more returns that made the outlook not nearly as good for Clinton as we had expected. It was at that point the First Lady stood up and said, "Good night."

"Where are you going?" I asked, still trying to absorb the news reports.

She looked at me as if to say, "To bed, where people usually go after they say good night."

"Are you really going to sleep?" I asked.

"Yup."

And that was it. Off she went.

I didn't know what to do. Should I sit there and keep the president company, or did he want to be alone? The White House political director, David Simas, had been sending the president status emails, so soon after Michelle went to bed, I stood up and said I was going down to David's office. The president didn't object, so I took that as a sign that he'd rather be alone.

In David's office I found a few staffers, including my chief of staff, Yohannes Abraham, looking extremely worried. Yohannes had gone from field director in Iowa in the 2008 campaign to deputy national political director in 2012. He had kept his ear to the ground during the campaign. He had even returned to Iowa the previous week and become concerned when he visited a few of the neighborhoods that had supported Obama and were now supporting Trump.

"She can still do this," said David, the eternal optimist. "There are still enough votes."

Even in our lowest moments in the White House, David always entered any room with a big smile and a warm greeting. But as time went by and he continued to report the results, he began to run low on contingency plans that would make the end result OK. By midnight, his face had turned grave; all expression of hope had faded.

I stayed for another couple of hours, as the situation only became worse and worse, until the outcome seemed both inevitable and impossible to absorb. I then followed Mrs. Obama's example by going home and trying to sleep. Laura, who was living with me at the time, came home from her job at CNN around 3 a.m., and I woke up and asked her if the outcome had changed. She said, "Nope, Trump is the next president."

The next morning, when reality hit again, I couldn't fathom how our country, which had elected Barack Obama twice, could have possibly elected Donald Trump. The election outcome was soul crushing.

Although most of us had been up late, everyone showed up on time, though we were all clearly shattered. But right after the senior staff meeting I knew my team, many of whom had been a part of the family for a decade, and all too young to have had enough experience to put this nightmare in context, needed to hear from me. I gathered them to try to buck them up. Their distraught look of shock and pain, and yes, tears, said it all, but they hoped I could help them understand what had happened. I told them that democracies always have setbacks and twists and turns, and that it was important to be resilient in the face of this defeat. I could tell by their expressions that they were hungry for words of wisdom; I just tried to mask my own emotions and reassure them that I was so proud of what they had all done.

During our meeting, we received word that President Obama intended to give remarks in the Rose Garden, so we abruptly adjourned. When my colleagues and I walked out onto the colonnade, I knew the press would have cameras out to capture our reactions, so I put my game face on. Or so I thought. The photo of several of us clustered together as President Obama addressed the public showed unmistakable evidence of our soul-crushing pain. President Obama tried to reassure the country by publicly committing to a smooth and successful transition, just as Bush had done for us, because "the peaceful transition of power is one of the hallmarks of our democracy." He went on to emphasize that we are Americans and patriots first and that our country needed "a sense of unity; a sense of inclusion; a respect for our institutions, our way of life, rule of law; and respect for each other." And he said that he hoped Trump "maintains that spirit." And he, too, congratulated his team for all they had done, "without fanfare or a lot of attention," to make our government function better for all. And as though reading the thoughts of my team, he said, "But to the young people who got into politics for the first time, and may be disappointed by the results, I want you to know, you have to stay encouraged. Don't get cynical. Don't ever think you can't make a difference." President Obama concluded his remarks, and then it was back to work, continuing the job of running the government, as well as preparing for its transition to another leader.

I'd been dreading January 20, 2017, since January 20, 2009, and I woke up that morning thinking back on a conversation the president and I had shared on a balmy night the previous September. The Obamas had invited me over for dinner, and afterward Michelle left for a commitment with her mother and Sasha. The president and I had decided to share an after-dinner drink and unwind in our favorite spot, the Truman Balcony.

Staring out at the majestic view, I started to wax nostalgic about the last eight years and how extraordinary the experience had been, even on the hardest days, of which there had been many. The first four years had been so challenging, bringing together this team of people, none of whom had worked together in the White House. Before long we were all navigating new roles, trying to keep the world economy from collapsing, transform our health insurance system, and grapple with two wars. It seemed like every single day we were choosing between bad and worse options. Although it was messy, when we had control of Congress, we had accomplished so much. But by the second term, many of us had worked together all four years. We knew our strengths and weaknesses and trusted one another completely—not that every day didn't have its challenges, for it certainly did, but the White House was running smoothly. We understood that Congress was dysfunctional, most recently by the Republicans' refusal to grant Judge Merrick Garland, President Obama's nominee to the Supreme Court, even a hearing. And so we had moved beyond them, utilizing executive orders, the bully pulpit, and partnerships with state and local government, civil society, and the business community to make progress where we could.

The pinnacle for me in our final year was the United State of Women Summit in June. We wanted to protect the progress we had made through the White House Council on Women and Girls by extending the ownership to those on the ground who'd carry on the work and scale it upward. At the summit, we showcased leaders of all backgrounds who were successfully tackling issues that included economic empowerment and entrepreneurship, equal pay and paid leave, women's education and health care, violence against women, and civic engagement. Our over two hundred speakers ranged from Billie Jean King and Warren Buffett to Ayanna Pressley and Brittany Packnett. We also chose Marley Dias, the eleven-year-old founder of the campaign #1000Black GirlsBook, to speak. While in sixth grade, Marley launched an effort to put the spotlight on the paucity of books with black girls as the main characters. Her goal was to collect a thousand books to donate to black girls. Within just a few months she had collected *nine* thousand! Poised and extraordinarily confident, she blew the audience away with her compelling remarks. She sold the message that, at a young age, it's hard to be what we cannot see.

I, too, had made progress. Not only was all of my youthful shyness replaced by a voice I trusted that was full of passion and conviction, but after the privilege of eight years of using it to push for equality and justice on a national scale, I was returning to the vital office of citizen. I had learned to take criticisms and absorb any pain in stride. I was now convinced that extraordinarily positive change happens where there is hope, hard work, perseverance, and luck. All this has helped me have the patience and strength to never give up.

Now, three months from the end, just as we were humming, I didn't want to let it go. As the president's assistant, Ferial Govashiri, observed to me, "Anywhere else, when you leave a job, you can go back and visit. When we leave this one, it disappears."

I'm old enough to appreciate the brevity of eight years and the finite opportunities it offered us, yet there were so many times in that last year when I desperately wished we could have extended his term. With the monuments twinkling in front of us, and as I moved on to my second martini—I wasn't keeping track of his—I started pushing the president to indulge my fantasy of a third term. "I am so going to miss this place," I said. "Don't you wish we could just stay for four more years? Just imagine how much more we could get done."

I had become a bit wistful, so he moved to the seat on the couch next to me and, with one arm draped over my shoulder, said gently, "Valerie, we cut the unemployment rate in half; twenty million people have health care, many for the first time; any couple can marry; we brought Osama bin Laden to justice and a hundred fifty thousand troops home from two wars. We have an agreement to keep Iran from developing nuclear weapons. There hasn't been a major terrorist attack on our shores. We restored diplomatic relations with Cuba and we led the effort for the historic Paris climate accord signed by two hundred countries around the world. There are two additional extraordinary women serving on the Supreme Court. Our country is not perfect, but it is more just and fair for those who have historically been left behind. I'm alive. My family is alive. You're alive. Yes, there's more work to do, but there always is. We did our best." He then paused and lowered his voice even further and said, "It's time for us to go."

As his words sank in, seeming rehearsed, probably from repeating them often to himself, the reality of all we had accomplished seemed more real. We were given the most time our laws allow, and we had done our best in extraordinarily challenging times. It was time to wrap up whatever we could and prepare emotionally to face the end. Seeing my expression, he added lightheartedly, "And besides, I hear 'former president' is actually the better job."

Maybe so, but I awakened on January 20, 2017, with a very heavy heart. When I arrived at the White House that morning, I paused a bit longer for my morning ritual of thinking of Earl Smith on my way in. I thanked him in an inaudible whisper for both inspiring me and helping me stay focused and grounded every day for eight years. I wondered if I would continue to think of him, and I have.

To avoid the crush of too many people's paperwork being processed at the same time, my staff had been leaving one by one since the new year. My assistant, Kathy Branch, with whom I had worked for twenty-five years, and my trusted chief of staff, Yohannes Abraham, were two of the last to go. I even had to give up my lead Secret Service agent, Collin Johnson, a week before the inauguration. It had been his plan to stay with me until I left on Inauguration Day, but he had been requested by name to join the security detail for the secretary of homeland security, which was a huge honor. I had mixed emotions. I was so proud he was chosen from all the agents in the country for the assignment, but I couldn't imagine spending those last few days without him.

Tina Tchen and I had started together on January 20, 2009, and we always planned to turn out the lights together as well. With nearly everyone gone, we were left wandering the empty, lonely halls by ourselves. No more senior staff meetings with the chief of staff. No more morning huddle with my team. Just an empty office full of eight years of extraordinary memories.

Soon after Tina and I arrived on the State Floor, the Obamas came down from the residence, and we gathered in the State Dining Room for a traditional ceremony where the head usher presented the Obamas with two folded flags: one that had flown over the White House on the first day of his term and a second that had flown earlier that morning. Shortly afterward the Bidens arrived, and as the two couples shared an emotional moment with hugs and expressions of appreciation, Tina and I tried to fade into the woodwork.

The Obamas returned upstairs to say a final good-bye to their home and await the Trumps' arrival. Tina and I were making our way through the Great Hallway toward the East Room for one last peek at the place where we had overseen so many events. After taking some final photos of ourselves together, Vice President–elect Pence walked out of the Blue Room reception with the leadership from Congress. He caught my eye, and although I tried to demur, not trusting my emotions, he came over to say hello. He thanked me for my service, letting me know that he appreciated how I had always been available to him when he was governor of Indiana. I mumbled, "Thank you. Good luck," and scurried away, unsure of what else to say.

Just then Anita Blanchard and Marty Nesbitt arrived and we all hung out in the usher's office that looked onto the North Portico that was packed with camera crews awaiting the arrival of the Trumps. When the Trump advance team called ours to say they were on their way, the Obamas came back downstairs and were greeted by several of the butlers, who had come to say good-bye. These men, some of whom had been in the White House decades before we arrived, had always been especially kind to me. In the beginning, when I was lost, literally, they would gently point out the right way. When I was nervous at events, they made small talk with me or gave me a reassuring nod from across the room. They always asked about my family. After our holiday parties, they made sure I was fed in the dining room that they closed off for the residence staff after the guests left. Tina, Susan Sher, and I spent many a late night exhausted, with our shoes off, eating with them and rehashing funny stories from the event. Those small acts of kindness, knowing they were rooting for me, always helped me relax and exhale, if only for a moment.

I watched Michelle close her eyes, which had been brimming with tears, as she hugged the butlers one by one for that last good-bye. While the Obamas went outside to greet the Trumps, we peeked out of the window in the usher's office and watched Mrs. Trump unexpectedly hand Mrs. Obama a blue Tiffany box. (It had been previously agreed by the staff that there would be no exchange of gifts—the first indication that the new administration had no intention of complying with traditional norms.) President Trump started to take off his coat. One of the butlers walked over to take it, and President Obama introduced them.

It was excruciating to watch the butlers seamlessly assume their job of taking care of the soon-to-be president, just as they had every president before him. Years earlier, when we invited President George W. Bush and President Clinton to join President Obama at the White House for the announcement of the Haiti Relief Fund, the former presidents hung out in the Cabinet Room in the West Wing waiting for the event to begin, and a few of the butlers who had served in their administrations ventured over to the West Wing to say hello. As I watched them all joking and laughing together, they looked like a reunion of old friends obviously delighted to see one another again. I only hoped our newest president would treat them with the respect they well deserved.

After the Obamas and the Trumps left for the inauguration, Tina and I walked down the colonnade toward the West Wing for the last time, on our way to the Roosevelt Room to turn in our iPhones and access passes. President Obama's office carpet and furniture were already wrapped and stacked neatly outside of the Oval Office. We both paused for just a second, reality hitting us again, and without a word, we kept walking. Then, after leaving the Roosevelt Room, a bit ghoulishly, we peeked into the Oval Office, where the president-elect's curtains were already up and his furniture was being moved in, per custom. We felt in that moment like visitors, no longer welcome in a place we had come to believe we belonged.

I returned to my office for one last good-bye. I paused and looked around slowly at the barren room stripped of the photos and memorabilia I had accumulated over the years. I soaked up my memories and turned off the light. Tina, who had done the same, met me by the basement, the spot where we had met countless times over eight years, and my Secret Service detail drove us to Andrews Air Force Base.

We greeted the cabinet and senior staff, all gathered in a large lounge with a TV on in the background for those who had the stomach to watch the inauguration. One look at the stoic expressions of President and Mrs. Obama captured on camera told me to turn away and treasure the moment with my colleagues, all of whom were saying their good-byes. In an empty airplane hangar, we awaited the Obamas with about a thousand political appointees from the administration. When the Obamas arrived, they said a quick good-bye to the staff, all gathered, many of whom had been a part of our lives for ten years. While they went around shaking hands and giving farewell hugs, I boarded Air Force One with Tina and a few other close friends and staff who were tagging along for the president and First Lady's last flight on the aircraft. Kneeling on the couch that had been my bed for so many trips, I watched through a window as the Obamas walked toward Air Force One, climbed the stairs, and turned to wave to the crowd, one last time.

· *Chapter 16* ·

The Long View

At Barack's very first campaign rally in South Carolina, which took place in the tiny town of Greenwood way out in the middle of nowhere, he showed up late, drenched from the pouring rain, and there were only a few dozen people there. A lot of people were still skeptical about this guy from Chicago with the funny name, and the room wasn't particularly festive. Then, as Barack spoke, from behind him Edith Childs started to shout. "Fired up!" she chanted. "Ready to go!" Soon the whole room was chanting along and everyone, including the candidate, was suddenly fired up and ready to go. Alongside "Yes, we can," that slogan became one of our rallying cries for the next year. Whole stadiums would chant "Fired up! Ready to go!" The hope and enthusiasm the phrase carried was infectious, and that story, repeated at every event, carried us all the way to the White House.

As presidential hopeful Barack Obama said in his final 2008 campaign rally on election eve in Manassas, Virginia, Edith Childs showed that "One voice can change a room. And if a voice can change a room, it can change a city. And if it can change a city, it can change a state. And if it can change a state, it can change a nation. And if it can change a nation, it can change the world."

As I think back now about Barack's perspective on his loss in the 2008 New Hampshire presidential primary, it is clear to me that he was right. It was far better for the campaign over the long term that success did not come too easily. The nearly two years that he spent traveling the country, persuading supporters—sometimes one at a time—fueled the energy required for Barack to not only win the election, but govern successfully for two terms. As I learned early on back in Chicago's city hall, trust must be earned, and it requires time. It also requires the support of people like Edith Childs, who recognize the power of their voices to inspire change.

Since leaving the White House, I have been encouraged by so many ordinary people working to make their communities better by undertaking extraordinary endeavors. Champions of Change, we called the ones we honored with recognition when we were in the White House. I've seen tremendous activism: from the Women's March to the demonstrations opposing the Muslim travel ban and for civil rights. There have been protests against the separation of families at the border and against the confirmation of Supreme Court Justice Brett Kavanaugh.

I've watched in awe as the students of Marjory Stoneman Douglas High School in Parkland, Florida, demanded action after a former student killed seventeen people in their school with a semiautomatic AR-15 rifle on Valentine's Day of 2018. As part of their #NeverAgain movement, they organized a nationwide school walkout and the 2018 March for Our Lives protest in DC and eight hundred other cities and towns around the country. Devastated by tragedy, those young people turned their grief into a movement that has awakened America's efforts to keep us all safe from gun violence.

Those smart, powerful messengers are examples of what a good public education can do. Many of them had just taken a course in civics and debate, which helped them give voice to their advocacy. Others before them had made the same plea and there has been progress at the state and local levels. But these young people—outraged, motivated, fearless, and savvy users of social media—didn't ask for national grief, but instead captured the nation's heart and demanded a legislative response. The only reason there are new laws on the books in Florida is because they got in the faces of their representatives and unapologetically said, "Don't pray for us; do something to keep us safe." Although the NRA is weakened, Congress still has not yet taken any action.

Six thousand people showed up in Los Angeles for our second United State of Women Summit, proving our hope that our fight for gender equity would continue.

I've also marveled at the record number of first-time candidates who won their elections in November 2018, and the many more who ran and lost, but tried hard, and I am sure we will see run again. More women are in Congress than ever before. This is true of state and local offices as well. In 2018, 114 million cast votes in the midterm election, an increase of 31 million votes over the 2014 midterms. Youth voting increased from 21 to 31 percent, also a record.

This new generation is ready to lead, and their stories and passion to do good have filled me with hope. They demonstrate that there are still millions of Americans who feel empowered to participate in the arduous task of making a more perfect union—Americans who know that a government of the people, by the people, and for the people depends on "the people" vigorously engaging.

Civic engagement is hard and often very frustrating work, but who said democracy was easy? Even among those on "the same side" there are inevitably passionate differences. But if we do not commit to each do our part to strengthen our nation, we and our children will live with the consequences. There are those who believe that in this era of information on demand, where we curate our own communities and information through our devices glued to our hands, we are becoming more polarized. But isn't it also true that more and more voices are empowered to speak up, challenging the status quo, where historically they were silenced?

At the same time, however, I've also observed a disturbing trend—that of Americans who have lost confidence in the institutions that have traditionally strengthened the fabric of our democracy, institutions such as government, the press, labor unions, organized religion, and even higher education.

S ince the night Donald Trump became president of the United States, I've been going through the five stages of grief, sometimes all five in the same day. In the beginning, denial and anger were high on the list; I still haven't embraced acceptance. To me, the thousands of what-ifs of that election all come down to one fact: nearly 43 percent of eligible voters did not vote. How could so many people, especially young people with so much to lose, feel so disempowered that they would shun their most basic and fundamental responsibility of citizenship—to vote. That so many would cede their power to those who do show up is simply stunning.

Do many of our institutions need to be disrupted? Yes. Do they need us to hold them accountable? Absolutely. But the answer isn't to abandon the institutions we find lacking. The answer is to use our voices to engage with them and make them better.

So how do we motivate and empower the next generation of leaders to use their talents to be forces for good, just as the young Michelle and Barack were determined to do when we met back in 1991?

In June of 2018, I returned home to Chicago to visit my mother. I'd just been the target of a tweet that used a racist trope comparing me to an ape and accusing me of being a member of the Muslim Brotherhood. I did not think much of the tweet when I first heard about it, having seen so many hateful ones about me over the last eight years. I had grown accustomed to my birth in Iran, my relationship with the Obamas, and my race and gender eliciting negative comments, and, over time, I had learned to ignore them. But since this tweet was from someone with a popular TV show, it—and the reaction to it—went viral.

Before we even sat down, my mom launched right in about how angry that tweet made her. Taken aback by her strong emotion, I said, in a lighthearted way, "I'm just fine," echoing the refrain she had used so many times when I was younger. And then, much more seriously, I assured her that I was far more worried about those who are actually harmed each and every day by racist remarks or discriminatory behavior. She responded, "Of course, I know you're OK, but what annoys me is the fact that even today all of us in the black community, no matter how accomplished, are still subject to public ridicule just because of our race. An attack directed at you is an attack on all of us."

That prompted a long conversation about the current climate. We began with how far too many young people of color still grow up painfully aware that they are not being judged on their merits, but, rather, stigmatized by their race, and what that does to their spirit and ambition. My mother was particularly concerned that, after our country had taken what she had considered an impossible leap forward by twice electing a black man as our president, it felt like we were now quickly regressing. She raised the troubling undercurrent of aggression (conscious and unconscious, blatant and subtle) directed not just at people of color, but also at the LGBTQ, Muslim, and immigrant communities—in fact, at any person labeled as "other."

We both lamented the speed with which the tone of our national discourse had degenerated, and how it seemed harder and harder for people to listen with open minds and hearts to those with whom they disagree. We were both stunned by how rapidly the Trump administration was unraveling many of the Obama-era policies.

Mom and I had talked before about the Muslim travel ban and the white supremacist rally in Charlottesville. We had been reassured by the loud public reaction to both, but in the face of that outcry, the mean-spirited and divisive rhetoric and policies nonetheless continued. My mom also brought up the erosion of advancement of basic rights for women and working families for which I had worked so hard. I countered with the brave survivors who had launched the #MeToo movement and how optimistic I was about their work—and that of so many others—to improve the legal standards and social norms on workplace sexual harassment and abuse. Never one to give an inch, she drilled down on voter suppression laws and our gun violence epidemic, and I mentioned the number of new progressive candidates running for office and the amazing young students from Parkland who had also inspired a national movement to end gun violence. I was especially excited that they were going to spend the summer traveling the country to encourage young people to vote. But, as for the declining reputation of the United States around the world, we both wrung our hands.

I told my mom that despite the many setbacks, I continue to take heart from the countless ordinary people with an indefatigable spirit of activism, who are still accomplishing the extraordinary. My mom, always preparing for the worst—and a witness to the painfully slow dismantling of Jim Crow, and then the long ongoing fight for civil rights—feared that the catastrophic reversals of the last eighteen months could take years to overcome. It depressed her to think that after having seen so much progress over her lifetime, she might not live to see the day when all the damage was corrected.

We sat in silence for a few minutes, each trying to absorb what the other had said, before my mom summed up our differing perspectives quite neatly: "Lally," she said, "you have the optimistic belief that we are almost at the mountaintop . . . but I believe we are dangling over the precipice."

Since our conversation, I have shaken my head time and time again over the hateful words and the emotions beneath them that too often continue to saturate the airwaves. But, at the same time, I still believe in the power of each voice to make the impossible inevitable. I'm heartened by the turnout of people who worked on midterm campaigns and showed up to vote. We are all better represented by the historic number of diverse candidates who won their elections, particularly so many women. I am also enthusiastic about the momentum that is building around several of the talented prospective Democratic presidential candidates who are prepared to jump into the 2020 election arena.

Today, as I reflect back on the conversation with my mom six months ago, I realize that we were both right. Our nation is at a pivotal crossroads. The direction we take depends on you.

Acknowledgments

I never planned to write a book. But when my daughter, Laura, interviewed me for a StoryCorps oral history, the first question she asked me was, *What would you tell a thirty-year-old Valerie Jarrett?* And there it began, for as it turns out I had a lot to say, and not just to a thirty-year-old me, but to women and men of all ages. So thank you, darling Laura, for inspiring each chapter of my life since the day you were born and for all of the happiness and pure joy that you bring to me.

Our childhood memories are often molded by others and embellished with the passage of time and our fantasies, so without my mom's countless hours spent encouraging me to tell my story, helping me separate fact from fiction and filling in the blanks, this story would be neither true nor complete. I would not be the woman I am today without her love and support.

Although my dad did not live to see this work, I think he would approve. "Call it as you see it and let the chips fall where they may" was always his mantra. He has been my compass of true north. And his willingness to always tackle challenges head-on inspired me to spend real time thinking about the truths that I sought to tell.

Michelle and Barack Obama, thank you for welcoming me into your lives and trusting me to share this extraordinary journey. I may be your big sister, but you have both taught me so much about true leadership, the awesome courage of hope, the grace in resilience, and how to inspire people to make the impossible inevitable.

To my family of cousins who are a part of my mom's Sunday dinner crew, especially Becky, who is there day in and day out, thank you for taking such good care of my mom while I have been busy traveling near and far. Your love and presence in our lives gives me such comfort and a place to call home.

To my cousins who live in New York, Washington, DC, and Miami, you know who you are—you're also the siblings I never had and my dearest friends. The time we spend together is precious, especially each summer on Martha's Vineyard. Yes, we all squabble from time to time, as families do, but our love for one another is steadfast and unconditional and you have all given me the gifts of laughter and support.

It is true that it takes a village to raise a child. It also takes a village for us to be grounded and whole. To my rock-solid old friends who have withstood both the vicissitudes of life and the brutal test of time, you are the family that I choose. I look forward to growing old with each of you in my life.

It is the people who believe in me even when I doubt myself that I treasure and never take for granted. Daniel Levin hired me and brought me into both The Habitat Company and his life with his wife, Fay. He taught me the business, and then trusted me to run our company. He gave me the opportunity to help improve the landscape of the city I love and the lives of many of its residents, as well as the space to dedicate so much of my time and energy to my civic and board commitments, and to help a long-shot presidential candidate win.

I have always tried to surround myself with people who are smarter than I and whose strengths complement my weaknesses. So to my teams from the Department of Planning and Development, The Habitat Company, and the White House, my accomplishments would not have been possible without each and every one of you. I love you all dearly and no matter the paths that life takes us on, you will always be my team.

When people ask me what I miss most about the White House, the answer is simple: the colleagues with whom I had the honor to serve. They were all smart, honest, and dedicated true public servants who absorbed a lot of pain, but always did what they thought was in the best interest of our country. You all helped me learn and grow. I will always cherish my memories of our time spent together.

I interviewed over a dozen publishers and Viking was the first. Wendy Wolf, my editor, was the one who I was sure understood the value of my story and cared passionately about helping me tell it. With extraordinary talent, humor, and persistence—coupled with the ability to say no—she has helped me tell the story in a way I hope you enjoyed and found useful in your life; with amazing dedication and patience from Terezia Cicel; as well as the team at Viking: Louise Braverman, Tricia Conley, Sara Leonard, Gabriel Levinson, Brianna Linden, Lindsay Prevette, Jason Ramirez, Andrea Schulz, Kate Stark, Mary Stone, and Brian Tart.

My collaborators, Rebecca Paley and Tanner Colby, embraced my story and helped me ensure my memoir stayed true to my voice.

Thank you to Anita Dunn, Amy Brundage, and the team at SKDKnickerbocker, as well as Bob Bauer and Rio Hart, for helping me share my story with you. And thank you to my whole crew at CAA.

And to all of the ordinary people across America and the world who I have had the privilege to know and watch dedicate themselves to achieve the extraordinary, you inspire me and give me complete confidence that our better days lie ahead.